Fresh Ways with
Picnics and Barbecues

COVER
Skewers of lean pork and fresh pineapple barbecued over hot coals face rows of vividly coloured vegetables waiting to be cooked. To lend succulence and flavour, the pork is first marinated in a blend of yogurt, lime juice and Indian spices (recipe, page 76).

TIME-LIFE BOOKS

EUROPEAN EDITOR: Ellen Phillips
Design Director: Ed Skyner
Director of Editorial Resources: Samantha Hill
Chief Sub-Editor: Ilse Gray

LOST CIVILIZATIONS
HOW THINGS WORK
SYSTEM EARTH
LIBRARY OF CURIOUS AND UNUSUAL FACTS
BUILDING BLOCKS
A CHILD'S FIRST LIBRARY OF LEARNING
VOYAGE THROUGH THE UNIVERSE
THE THIRD REICH
MYSTERIES OF THE UNKNOWN
TIME-LIFE HISTORY OF THE WORLD
FITNESS, HEALTH AND NUTRITION
HEALTHY HOME COOKING
UNDERSTANDING COMPUTERS
THE ENCHANTED WORLD
LIBRARY OF NATIONS
PLANET EARTH
THE GOOD COOK
THE WORLD'S WILD PLACES

HEALTHY HOME COOKING

SERIES DIRECTOR: Jackie Matthews
Studio Stylist: Liz Hodgson

Editorial Staff for *Fresh Ways with Picnics and Barbecues:*
Editor: Frances Dixon
Researchers: Heather Campion, Eva Reynolds
Designer: Paul Reeves
Sub-Editors: Wendy Gibbons, Eugénie Romer

PICTURE DEPARTMENT:
Administrator: Patricia Murray
Picture Co-ordinator: Amanda Hindley

EDITORIAL PRODUCTION:
Chief: Maureen Kelly
Assistant: Samantha Hill
Editorial Department: Theresa John, Debra Lelliott

THE CONTRIBUTORS

SILVIJA DAVIDSON studied at Leith's School of Food and Wine and specializes in the development of recipes from Latvia and other international cuisines.

JOANNA FARROW, a home economist and recipe writer who contributes regularly to food magazines, is especially interested in decorative presentation of food. Her books include *Creative Cake Decorating* and *Novelty Cakes for Children.*

ANTONY KWOK, originally a fashion designer from Hong Kong, has won several awards for his Orient-inspired style of cooking and was the *London Standard* Gastronomic Seafish Cook of 1986.

JANE SUTHERING is a cookery writer and home economist who has concentrated on the development of wholefood and vegetarian dishes. She is consultant to Cranks, a major health-food restaurant chain, and has created the recipes for all eight of their cookery books.

ROSEMARY WADEY is cookery editor of *Home and Country* magazine, and a former head of the Food Advisory Department at the Good Housekeeping Institute. An established cookery writer with 25 titles to date, her books include *Cooking for Two* and *The Pastry Book.*

The following also contributed recipes to this volume:
Pat Alburey, Jane Bird, Maddalena Bonino, Gail Duff, Anne Gains, Yvonne Hamlett, Carole Handslip, Cristine McKie, Norma MacMillan, Sally Major, Roselyne Masselin, Louise Steele, Susie Theodorou.

THE COOKS

The recipes in this book were cooked for photography by Pat Alburey, Allyson Birch, Jane Bird, Antony Kwok, Lesley Sendall, Jane Suthering, Michelle Thompson, Rosemary Wadey, Steven Wheeler. *Studio Assistant:* Rita Walters.

CONSULTANT

PAT ALBUREY is a home economist with a wide experience of preparing foods for photography, teaching cookery and creating recipes. She has written a number of cookery books and she was the studio consultant for the Time-Life series *The Good Cook.* In addition to acting as the general consultant on this volume, she also created a number of the recipes.

NUTRITION CONSULTANT

PATRICIA JUDD trained as a dietician and worked in hospital practice before returning to university to obtain her MSc and PhD degrees. For the last 10 years she has lectured in Nutrition and Dietetics at London University.

Nutritional analyses for *Fresh Ways with Picnics and Barbecues* were derived from McCance and Widdowson's *The Composition of Food* by A.A. Paul and D.A.T. Southgate, and other current data.

This volume is one of a series of illustrated cookery books that emphasize the preparation of healthy dishes for today's weight-conscious, nutrition-minded eaters.

Fresh Ways with Picnics and Barbecues

BY

THE EDITORS OF TIME-LIFE BOOKS

BROCKHAMPTON PRESS

Contents

Fresh Fruits in a Watermelon Bowl

Aromatic Leg of Lamb

Wholemeal Loaf Filled with Smoked Chicken Salad

Barbecued Vegetables

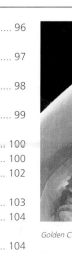

Golden Chicken Salad in a Vegetable Squash

3 Menus to Match the Occasion 107

Caribbean Fish Barbecue

4 An Indoor Aid to Outdoor Meals 129

Food, Friends and Fresh Air

No setting could be more conducive to the enjoyment of fine food than the great outdoors, the natural environment that is itself the source of all that is good to eat. Out in the open, appetites are sharpened, and the flavour of fresh ingredients simply prepared is imbued with a special magic.

As with all meals, the more care that is taken in preparation, the more rewarding will be the results. The choice of dishes, the order in which they will be prepared, then their packing and serving — all these considerations must be thought through well before the countdown begins. But beyond these commonsense procedures, there are no absolute laws governing the delightful alchemy of outdoor eating. Invite four friends or 40. Lay a blanket on the grass and serve sandwiches and lemonade, or else set up tables and chairs, and spread out a princely feast of delicacies on a starched damask cloth. At whatever level you choose to do your entertaining, informality and good humour prevail, and even your most punctilious guest will close his or her book of etiquette under the open sky.

mood of a warm summer night.

Cold foods are by no means second best. For those who think of picnics in terms of hastily assembled sandwiches and stodgy bought pies, a carefully planned picnic array can come as a revelation. Soups, salads, pies, cold meats, terrines, flans, cakes, ice cream — no other social occasion so comfortably encompasses both elegance and informality.

Whatever the menu, there is a sense of celebration about any outdoor meal, a festive atmosphere that tempts even the most health-conscious guest to come back for a second, even a third, helping. Eating outdoors gives many people a feeling of freedom — that their diets and calorie charts no longer apply. While enjoyment of food is always to the good, overeating is never to be encouraged. To prevent backsliding, the most important step you can take is to ensure all dishes are prepared within Healthy Home Cooking's nutritional guidelines. Use fresh ingredients to prepare dishes that are low in sodium, cholesterol and saturated fats, then relax and let the party begin.

Fresh Ways with Picnics and Barbecues explores the world of healthy outdoor eating at all levels — from simple sandwiches to cold stuffed fillet of beef; from grilled home-made sausages to spit roasted leg of lamb. Separate chapters are devoted to picnic food and to barbecued specialities, but this is not to imply that picnics and barbecues are in any way mutually exclusive. Many dishes can be precooked on a barbecue and eaten cold; and a picnic can be enhanced by hot foods prepared on a portable charcoal-fuelled cooker. Chapter 3 offers a selection of menus which show how dishes and techniques can be imaginatively combined to suit different outdoor occasions. A fourth chapter describes ways in which a cook preparing food for a picnic or barbecue can make use of a versatile ally, the microwave oven.

Picnic or barbecue?

To cook or not to cook? is one of the very first questions to be answered by anyone planning to entertain outdoors. Few people can resist the taste of fresh food — meat, poultry, fish or vegetables — grilled over charcoal in the open air. Cooking over a fire, however, involves time preparing the coals and attending the grill, time that might be spent chatting to your guests if all the food had been prepared beforehand. Furthermore, outdoor cooking restricts your choice of location. Most barbecue equipment cannot conveniently be carried for long distances and is unsuitable for many sites that are otherwise ideal for picturesque picnics: the rowing boat and the rocky ledge are out of bounds for the barbecue. When entertaining nearer home, the arguments for outdoor cooking become increasingly persuasive. On the patio or the lawn, with your kitchen and a volunteer close at hand, cooking over coals may seem the only way to match the

Planning and packing for picnics

No one knows exactly how or where the word "picnic" first arose. In its earliest sense, some 200 years ago, it described a meal to which each guest contributed a dish. By the mid-19th century the picnic had moved outdoors and acquired its modern meaning. One vestige of its original sense remains, however: a picnic today is often a multi-coursed affair, as if several cooks still had a hand in its preparation.

The number of courses and the fact that they must all be packed and transported safely to the picnic site make careful planning essential. Fortunately, most picnic dishes can be prepared a day in advance and stored in the refrigerator over-night — some even improve with keeping. Sandwiches, how-ever, are best made with bread bought on the morning of the picnic and assembled just before packing. Salad ingredients and dressings should be packed separately and only combined im-mediately before serving, unless a recipe gives instructions otherwise. Terrines, pies and cold roast meat can often be pre-sliced for convenience before packing. Transfer chilled soups directly from the refrigerator to vacuum flasks; soups intended to be served hot should be reheated and poured into flasks when all the other food and equipment are ready to go.

Rigid plastic containers with tight-fitting lids are the picnic packer's best friend. To save space and prevent food from drying out, choose one that most nearly matches the shape and size of the food you are packing. Biscuit and cake tins, lined with greaseproof paper, serve as useful alternatives. A light wrapping of kitchen foil helps keep sandwiches and pre-sliced food such as roast meat moist and compact; alternatively, seal in the flavour and freshness of meat, terrines or pies with a layer of greaseproof paper wrapped tightly in an outer layer of plastic film. Large or awkwardly shaped dishes for which you can find no container or tin must be wrapped either in kitchen foil or plastic film and packed securely and conspicuously at the top of the picnic basket or box.

If space is at a premium and you are unable to take a salad bowl with you, make sure that one of your salad containers is large enough to accommodate all the assembled ingredients. A screw-top jar is ideal for salad dressing, but check that the lid does not leak and twist-tie it in a plastic bag before committing it to the picnic box. Plastic bags with twist-ties are also useful for crudités and other ingredients that will not crush easily.

Picnic drinks are heavy and awkward to carry for any distance. If you have to walk to reach your picnic site, stick to a simple se-lection of beverages — mineral water, perhaps, to be served with slices of lime or lemon, and vacuum flasks of tea or coffee, with milk in a separate flask. Wrap up wine bottles in several layers of newspaper; this will protect them from damage and serve as insulation for chilled wine. Beer and sparkling wines are explosive immediately after a hot, bumpy journey; allow them to rest in a cool place for a while before opening them — or leave them at home for a garden barbecue.

To keep food and drink cool and secure while in transport, the ideal container is an insulated plastic case known as a cool box. Ice bags containing a pre-frozen chemical cooler block are use-ful for packing around food that must remain chilled, and for picnics that have a long hot journey ahead of them.

If you lack such specialized picnic equipment, a sturdy cardboard box with home-made insulation will serve nearly as well. Wrap and pack your food items directly from the refrigerator, then wrap the individual items in newspaper and pack them into the carrying carton surrounded by more, crumpled, newspaper. This will both keep the food cool and act as a shock absorber. Bubble-wrap plastic packing material and even folded newspapers also serve as effective insulation.

For the concert party or the fashionable sporting event, when cardboard packing boxes would appear unseemly, a picnic hamper provides a distinguished note. Hampers are light, rigid carrying cases, generally made of woven willow. They are avail-able empty or fully equipped with food and drink containers, cutlery and tableware. Knives, forks and plates conveniently strap to the inside of the cover. However, the traditional airy hamper provides no insulation for chilled food, and may not be spacious enough to contain all the paraphernalia required for a special picnic. Be prepared to supplement your elegant picnic with food from a cool box or carton.

Sturdy cardboard or plastic plates and cups are adequate for many picnics, but the tone of the occasion — and some say the taste of the food — is improved by pottery or china tableware. Stack plates securely, interleaved with table napkins or tissue paper to prevent them rattling. Plastic eating utensils are widely available, but not strong enough for all types of picnic food. If weight is not a factor, use stainless steel cutlery instead. Wrap them in paper towels or table napkins.

Before leaving home, make a list of all the equipment you will need and check that everything is packed. As well as plates and cutlery, you will normally require a cutting board and sharp knife, serving utensils, a tablecloth, napkins, paper towels, and a large plastic bag for rubbish. A damp cloth or sponge for wiping hands is also useful. Depending upon your beverages, bring a bottle opener or a corkscrew. Consider whether folding garden chairs and a card table are appropriate for the occasion. Finally, check the weather forecast: umbrellas, suncream or insect repellent may well be in demand.

Cooking over coals

Because so many barbecue parties take place just a few steps away from the kitchen, the problems of packing and transpor-tation generally do not arise. The food itself, however, still re-quires preparation. Cold accompaniments such as salads should

The Key to Better Eating

Healthy Home Cooking addresses the concerns of today's weight-conscious, health-minded cooks with recipes developed within strict nutritional guidelines.

The chart on the right gives dietary guidelines for healthy men, women and children. Recommended figures vary from country to country, but the principles are the same everywhere. Here, the average daily amounts of calories and protein are taken from a report by the U.K. Department of Health and Social Security; the maximum advisable daily intake of fat is based on guidelines given by the National Advisory Committee on Nutrition Education (NACNE); those for cholesterol and sodium are based on upper limits suggested by the World Health Organization.

The volumes in the Healthy Home Cooking series do not purport to be diet books, nor do they focus on health foods. Rather, the books express a commonsense approach to cooking that uses salt, sugar, cream, butter and oil in moderation while including other ingredients that also contribute flavour and satisfaction. The portions themselves are modest in size.

The recipes make few unusual demands. Naturally they call for fresh ingredients, offering substitutes should these be unavailable. (Only the original ingredient is calculated in the nutrient analysis, however.) Most of the ingredients can be found in any well-stocked supermarket; the occasional exceptions can be bought in speciality or ethnic food shops.

About cooking times

To help the cook plan ahead effectively, Healthy Home Cooking takes time into account in all its recipes. While recognizing that everyone cooks at a different speed, and that stoves and ovens may differ somewhat in their temperatures, the series provides approximate "working" and "total" times for every dish. Working time stands for the minutes actively spent on preparation; total time incudes unattended cooking time, as well as any time devoted to marinating, soaking, cooling or chilling. Because the recipes emphasize fresh foods, the dishes may take a bit longer to prepare than those that call for canned or packaged products, but the difference in flavour, and often in added nutritional value, should compensate for the little extra time involved.

Recommended Dietary Guidelines

		Average Daily Intake		Maximum Daily Intake			
		CALORIES	PROTEIN grams	CHOLESTEROL milligrams	TOTAL FAT grams	SATURATED FAT grams	SODIUM milligrams
Females	7-8	1900	47	300	80	32	2000*
	9-11	2050	51	300	77	35	2000
	12-17	2150	53	300	81	36	2000
	18-53	2150	54	300	81	36	2000
	54-74	1900	47	300	72	32	2000
Males	7-8	1980	49	300	80	33	2000
	9-11	2280	57	300	77	38	2000
	12-14	2640	66	300	99	44	2000
	15-17	2880	72	300	108	48	2000
	18-34	2900	72	300	109	48	2000
	35-64	2750	69	300	104	35	2000
	65-74	2400	60	300	91	40	2000

*(or 5g salt)

be made ready in advance. The tenderness and flavour of the lean cuts of meat used for recipes in this volume are often improved by allowing the meat to stand overnight in an acidic marinade. It is important to take the meat out of the refrigerator an hour or two before you are ready to cook it, to allow it to reach room temperature; chilled meat can easily burn on the outside before it is sufficiently cooked.

The preparation of the fire for cooking will depend on the type of fuel and barbecue that you decide to use. The most commonly used fuel for outdoor cooking is charcoal, which can be burnt either in a permanent outdoor fireplace made of brick or stone or else on a portable barbecue. A wide range of the latter is available from garden shops, especially in the spring and summer months; they vary considerably in size, sophistication and expense, but all are similar in principle. The charcoal-fuelled portable barbecue essentially consists of a metal firebox, which is usually mounted on legs in order to stand at a convenient height, and a chromium-plated grill for cooking the food. The firebox often comes equipped with adjustable vents for controlling combustion; many models include a grate to promote circulation of air under the fuel. The height of the rack can in most cases be adjusted to control the cooking temperature.

Make sure you choose a barbecue that will be adequate in size for the number of people you intend to entertain. A circular grill measuring 45 cm (18 inches) in diameter will normally be large enough to cater for eight guests. You can then decide what other features you need — and can afford. A simple wind shield, attached to the firebox rim, is a very welcome aid if you are intending to cook in an exposed location. Collapsible legs make a barbecue convenient for transporting to picnics; alternatively, choose a table-top model such as the popular hibachi. Most barbecues can be fitted with an electrically driven — either battery or mains — rotisserie grill, which brings back all the romance of spit-roasting with little of the work.

With the exception of the cast-iron hibachi, most barbecues are made of sheet steel. Since this must be thick enough to withstand long exposure to extreme heat, choose a model made of 20-gauge steel or heavier. A porcelain enamel finish is more durable than heat-resistant paint, with which cheaper barbecues are sometimes finished.

Two types of charcoal are generally available for outdoor cooking. Briquettes are nuggets of pulverized and compressed hardwood; lumpwood charcoal consists simply of unprocessed charcoal pieces. Briquettes take about 45 minutes to reach the correct temperature — 15 minutes or so longer than lumpwood — but they burn hotter and last nearly twice as long. Use enough charcoal to form a bed of coals about 5 cm (2 inches) deep and at least 2.5 cm (1 inch) wider all round than the area taken up by the food.

A barbecue fire can be lit with paper and dry sticks, but purpose-made solid or liquid barbecue firelighters speed up the operation. Do not use paraffin or petrol, which are dangerously inflammable and can taint the flavour of food.

To start the fire, stack the charcoal into a pyramid and use the firelighter following the directions on the packet. When any flames have subsided and a white film of ash covers the coals, rake them gently into an even bed in preparation for cooking. Check the temperature of the coals by holding your hand at grill level. If the fire is hot enough to sear meat you will be forced to withdraw your hand within 2 to 3 seconds; you will be able to tolerate about 4 seconds over a medium-hot fire.

Control the cooking temperature of a barbecue by raising or lowering the grill. Most of the recipes in this volume are cooked over medium-hot coals. Opening the firebox vents will increase the heat, as will raking the coals together into a compact bed. If it is necessary to replenish the fire, add fresh charcoal around the edges. Towards the end of the cooking time, small branches of rosemary, bay or sage placed on top of the coals will impart a delicious flavour to any grilled food.

The simplest alternative to charcoal as an outdoor cooking fuel is hardwood. Over glowing wood embers, the food may be cooked on a metal grill supported by home-made walls of bricks. Well-seasoned oak, beech and ash are among the best woods for burning; fruit woods such as cherry and apple release a delicately scented smoke that flavours the food. Pine, spruce and other softwoods are not recommended; they burn too quickly and can taint the food with their resinous fumes. The principle disadvantages of wood as a cooking fuel are that it burns at a faster rate than charcoal, and maintaining the fire in the right state — a glowing bed but with no flame — requires both skill and constant attention.

At the other end of the scale — centuries away from the wood fire — are gas and electric barbecues, which require neither wood nor charcoal. Instead, they heat up a layer of volcanic rock until it glows like a bed of coals. This source of heat gives off no aroma of its own, but fat and juices dripping from the meat as it cooks create an aromatic smoke that enhances the flavour of the food. Gas and electric barbecues require only 10 minutes to heat up and are extremely easy to control. For some outdoor cooks, however, they take away half the fun of a traditional barbecue by removing nearly all of the effort.

Whichever type of fuel or fire you use, make sure that you have equipment close at hand before beginning to cook. It is a good idea to use tongs for turning meat; a fork will pierce the surface and allow juices to escape. Use a basting brush made with bristle — not nylon or plastic, which may melt. Douse any flare-ups caused by dripping fat with water.

When the barbecue is over, allow the ashes to cool completely before disposing of them. If you are using a portable cooker, do not extinguish the hot coals with cold water, because this may cause the firebox to warp. The twilight of a barbecue, however, need not be wasted. The dying coals provide an ideal heat source for toasted marshmallows, a delicacy that can be safely prepared — and best appreciated — by children.

1 *Individual quiches, filled with mussels and leeks in a golden saffron custard, make an appealing and colourful picnic lunch (recipe, page 52).*

The Pleasures of Picnics

A picnic, the most moveable of feasts, is defined by its setting, not by what food it consists of. As long as it is eaten outdoors, it may be a snack or a banquet, fruit and cheese or an eight-course meal. The only restrictions are that the food must be convenient to transport and easy both to serve and to eat. The almost infinite range of possibilities is reflected in the 53 recipes in this chapter, which are designed to tempt even the most agoraphobic guest into the open air.

Sandwiches, the ultimate outdoor convenience food, need never be dull. Experiment with fillings and vary the bread — sourdough, black rye or poppy seed rolls, for instance. The sandwich ideas on pages 20 to 21 are imaginative meals in themselves. Several other recipes in this chapter extend the concept of bread and filling: for a change, try the Mediterranean lamb baguettes *(page 23)* — French bread filled with seasoned minced lamb — or sample the mushroom-stuffed fillet of beef enclosed in a hollowed-out loaf of bread *(page 22)*. For guests who prefer to make up their own open sandwiches or salads, there are a number of recipes for cold meats, roulades and terrines that can be sliced at the picnic site.

Any food that is parcelled in pastry lends itself to outdoor eating. Rump steak pasties *(page 49)* are particularly convenient for picnic menus, and international variations on this theme include Indian samosas *(page 48)*, baked rather than deep-fried in order to keep the fat content low. Greek phyllo pastry, available in ready-made sheets, provides a neat, crisp, low-calorie wrapping for dishes such as mushroom strudel *(page 53)* and salmon phyllo parcels *(page 54)*.

Soup may not be a traditional picnic food, but it is easy to transport and to serve. In anticipation of hot summer afternoons, two of the following recipes are for chilled soups; a third is for a warming saffron and pumpkin soup, served with a cheese and herb bread.

Even salads find a place in the picnic basket. Pack green, leafy ingredients separately and toss them with the dressing and other ingredients just before serving. The fresh taste and texture of a newly made salad is well worth any extra effort and brings a welcome change of pace to the conventional picnic menu.

Chilled Mange-Tout Soup

Serves 6
Working time: about 40 minutes
Total time: about 3 hours and 30 minutes (includes chilling)

Calories **70**
Protein **3g**
Cholesterol **0mg**
Total fat **4g**
Saturated fat **1g**
Sodium **70mg**

30 g	polyunsaturated margarine	1 oz
350 g	mange-tout, stems and strings removed	12 oz
8	spring onions, trimmed and chopped	8
90 g	potato, peeled and grated	3 oz
4 tsp	plain flour	4 tsp
60 cl	unsalted chicken stock (recipe, page 139)	1 pint
⅛ tsp	salt	⅛ tsp
	freshly ground black pepper	
30 cl	skimmed milk	½ pint
10	fresh basil leaves	10

Melt the margarine in a heavy-bottomed saucepan over medium heat. Set aside four of the mange-tout; add the remaining mange-tout to the pan, with the spring onions and potato. Stir the vegetables for 1 minute, then add the flour and stir for another minute. Gradually mix in the stock, and bring it to the boil, stirring continuously. Add the salt and some freshly ground black pepper. Cover the pan, reduce the heat, and simmer the mixture for 15 minutes, stirring it occasionally. Remove the pan from the heat.

In a food processor or blender, purée the mixture with the skimmed milk. Press the purée through a sieve. Finely chop four of the basil leaves, and stir them into the soup; reserve the remaining basil leaves for garnish. Allow the soup to cool, then chill it in the refrigerator for at least 2 hours.

Blanch the reserved mange-tout in a saucepan of boiling water. Drain them, refresh them under cold running water, and drain them again thoroughly. Cut the mange-tout into thin, diagonal strips.

Pour the soup into a chilled vacuum flask. Pack the mange-tout strips and reserved basil leaves in a small, air-tight container or polythene bag. Carry the soup and garnish to the picnic in a cool box.

Garnish each serving of soup with a few slivers of mange-tout and a basil leaf.

Saffron and Pumpkin Soup with Parmesan Bread

Serves 8
Working time: about 45 minutes
Total time: about 1 hour and 30 minutes

Calories **210**
Protein **10g**
Cholesterol **5mg**
Total fat **3g**
Saturated fat **1g**
Sodium **280mg**

¼ tsp	saffron threads, or ⅛ tsp powdered saffron	¼ tsp
¼ tsp	salt	¼ tsp
¾ litre	unsalted vegetable stock (recipe, page 139)	1 ¼ pints
750 g	pumpkin, peeled, seeded and cut into 5 cm (2 inch) cubes	1 ½ lb
2	strips of orange rind, each about 2.5 cm (1 inch) long	2
¼ tsp	freshly grated nutmeg	¼ tsp
⅛ tsp	white pepper	⅛ tsp
4 tsp	freshly grated Parmesan cheese, for garnish	4 tsp

Parmesan bread

250 g	plain flour	8 oz
100 g	wholemeal flour	3 ½ oz
1 tsp	bicarbonate of soda	1 tsp
4 tbsp	freshly grated Parmesan cheese	4 tbsp
1 tbsp	finely chopped fresh marjoram	1 tbsp
1 tsp	muscovado sugar	1 tsp
35 cl	buttermilk	12 fl oz

First make the bread. Preheat the oven to 200°C (400°F or Mark 6), and lightly grease and flour a baking sheet and a 20 cm (8 inch) round cake tin. Sift the plain flour, wholemeal flour and bicarbonate of soda into a mixing bowl, and add the bran from the sieve. Stir in the Parmesan cheese and marjoram. In a separate bowl, dissolve the sugar in a little of the buttermilk, then stir in the rest of the buttermilk. Make a well in the centre of the dry ingredients and pour the buttermilk into the well. Stir the mixture quickly but thoroughly with a wooden spoon, to make a moist dough. Sprinkle the dough with a little flour, gather it up with well-floured hands and place it in the centre of the prepared baking sheet. Shape the dough into a flat round, about 18 cm (7 inches) in diameter. Mark the round into eighths with a sharp knife, scoring about half way through the dough.

Invert the cake tin over the dough, and bake it in the oven for 15 minutes. Remove the tin, and continue baking the bread until its base is brown and a skewer inserted into the centre comes out clean — about 10 minutes more. Let the bread cool on a wire rack.

Meanwhile, prepare the soup. Using a pestle and mortar, grind the saffron threads with the salt; if you are using powdered saffron, stir it into the salt. Bring the stock to the boil in a large, heavy-bottomed pan, then add the pumpkin, orange rind, saffron and salt. Cover the pan, reduce the heat and simmer the pumpkin until it is completely tender — 20 to 30 minutes. Remove and discard the orange rind. Lift out the pumpkin cubes with a slotted spoon, and purée them in a food processor with a little of the cooking liquid. Add the remaining liquid, and blend it in. Season the soup with the nutmeg and pepper, and pour it at once into preheated vacuum flasks to take on a picnic.

Transport the Parmesan for the garnish in a small, screw-top jar, and wrap the bread loosely in paper towels or greaseproof paper. Serve each portion of soup sprinkled with ½ teaspoon of the cheese, and break the bread into eight wedges.

EDITOR'S NOTE: *The bread may be made up to 24 hours in advance of the picnic. Wrap it tightly in foil as soon as it is cool, and store it in the refrigerator.*

Carrot and Cardamom Soup

Serves 8
Working time: about 35 minutes
Total time: about 3 hours (includes chilling)

Calories **75**
Protein **3g**
Cholesterol **trace**
Total fat **2g**
Saturated fat **1g**
Sodium **275mg**

8	cardamom pods	8
2 tsp	virgin olive oil	2 tsp
1	onion, roughly chopped	1
2	sticks celery, roughly sliced	2
750 g	carrots, cut into chunks	1½ lb
¾ litre	unsalted chicken or vegetable stock (recipes, pages 139)	1¼ pints
125 g	cucumber, peeled and cut into chunks	4 oz
20 cl	plain low-fat yogurt	7 fl oz
½ tsp	salt	½ tsp
	freshly ground black pepper	
1 tsp	caster sugar	1 tsp
2	slices wholemeal bread, crusts removed	2
	celery leaves, for garnish	
	ice cubes, for garnish (optional)	

Wrap the cardamom pods in a double layer of paper towels and crush them lightly with a rolling pin, to split them. Heat the oil in a large, heavy-bottomed pan over medium heat. Add the onion, celery, carrots and split cardamom pods, and cook the mixture, stirring it occasionally, until the vegetables begin to soften — about 3 minutes. Stir in 45 cl (¾ pint) of the stock, and

bring the liquid to the boil. Reduce the heat, cover the pan, and simmer the vegetables until the carrots are soft — 8 to 10 minutes. Set the pan aside, and let the mixture cool for about 10 minutes.

Purée the cucumber chunks with the cooked vegetable mixture in a food processor or blender. Pour the purée into a bowl and add the remaining stock, then stir in 15 cl (¼ pint) of the yogurt, the salt, some pepper and the sugar. Pass the soup through a coarse sieve to remove the cardamom pods. Put the soup in a lightly covered container, and refrigerate it until it is thoroughly chilled — at least 2 hours, or overnight.

Toast the bread on both sides, then cut it into 5 mm (¼ inch) dice. Place the diced toast, the celery leaves and the remaining yogurt in separate small containers. Pour the soup into a chilled vacuum flask, and place some ice cubes, if you are using them, in a well-insulated ice bucket with a tight-fitting lid. Arrange everything in a cool box to take to the picnic.

To serve, pour the soup into individual bowls and add a few cubes of ice, if you wish. Swirl 1 teaspoon of yogurt on the surface of each portion. Garnish with the celery leaves, and serve with the diced toast.

Mushroom Loaf with Basil Mayonnaise

Makes 12 slices
Working time: about 1 hour
Total time: about 12 hours (includes cooling and chilling)

Per slice:
Calories **160**
Protein **12g**
Cholesterol **40mg**
Total fat **8g**
Saturated fat **2g**
Sodium **130mg**

1.5 kg	button mushrooms with stalks, wiped clean on paper towels	3 lb
2 tbsp	polyunsaturated margarine	2 tbsp
1	large onion, finely chopped	1
2	large garlic cloves, finely chopped	2
90 g	dried ceps, rinsed thoroughly to remove all grit, soaked in ¼ litre (8 fl oz) warm water for 1 hour	3 oz
300 g	skinned and boned chicken breast, diced	10 oz
4	thick slices white bread, crusts removed (about 60 g/2 oz), soaked in 6 tbsp skimmed milk	4
2 tbsp	soured cream or crème fraîche	2 tbsp
2 tbsp	chopped parsley	2 tbsp
¼ tsp	salt	¼ tsp
	freshly ground black pepper	
2	large sweet red peppers, skinned (page 138), trimmed into large rectangles	2
2	large sweet yellow peppers, skinned (page 138), trimmed into large rectangles	2
Basil mayonnaise		
1	egg yolk	1
2 tbsp	safflower oil	2 tbsp
20 g	Parmesan cheese, freshly grated	¾ oz
15 g	fresh basil leaves, chopped	½ oz
1 tbsp	skimmed milk	1 tbsp
1 tbsp	plain low-fat yogurt	1 tbsp

Reserve six whole button mushrooms, and coarsely slice the remainder. Set the button mushrooms aside.

Melt the margarine in a large, heavy-bottomed saucepan over medium heat, and fry the onion and garlic for 3 to 5 minutes, until they are translucent. Increase the heat to high and add the sliced button mushrooms. Fry the mushrooms, turning them constantly, until they start to release their liquid — 2 to 3 minutes. Coarsely chop the ceps and add them to the pan with their soaking liquid. Mix them in and boil hard until almost all the liquid in the pan has reduced and the mushrooms are just moist — 15 to 20 minutes. Set the pan aside and leave the contents to cool.

Put the diced chicken breast in a food processor and process it to a smooth paste. Add the soaked bread and process for 30 seconds, then pour in the soured cream and process the mixture for 10 seconds more. Fold in the cooled fried mushrooms, together with the parsley, salt and some black pepper.

Preheat the oven to 200°C (400°F or Mark 6), and line a 28 by 10 by 7.5 cm (11 by 4 by 3 inch) loaf tin with non-stick parchment paper. Slice the six reserved button mushrooms, and arrange the slices in the bottom of the loaf tin in three parallel lines.

Divide the mushroom and chicken mixture into three equal portions. Spoon the first portion into the loaf tin, being careful not to disturb the mushroom slices below; smooth the surface evenly with the back of the spoon. Place the red pepper rectangles on top, laying them along the length of the tin but keeping them 1 cm (½ inch) in from the sides; trim them further if necessary. Leaving the border free will prevent the loaf from breaking into layers when it is served.

Spoon the second portion of the mushroom mixture over the red peppers, smoothing it evenly, and place the trimmed yellow peppers on top in the same way as the red peppers were arranged. Top the yellow pepper rectangles with the final portion of mushroom mixture, smoothing the surface as before.

Place the tin in a baking pan and pour in sufficient boiling water to come two thirds of the way up the side of the tin. Bake the mushroom loaf for 40 minutes, until it is firm to the touch, then remove the roasting pan from the oven and allow the loaf to cool in the water bath. Refrigerate the loaf overnight in its tin.

To make the mayonnaise, whisk the egg yolk in a small bowl until it is thick and creamy, then gradually add the oil in a thin stream, whisking continuously as you do so. Using a pestle and mortar, mash the cheese into the basil, then add this to the egg mixture, together with the milk and yogurt. Stir the sauce well, and place it in the refrigerator until required.

When you are ready to go to the picnic, transfer the mayonnaise to a container with a tight-fitting lid and pack it, upright, in a cool box. Cover the loaf, still in its tin, with foil, and pack it in the cool box too. To serve the loaf, turn it out on to a flat platter or board and peel off the lining paper. Cut the loaf into slices and serve it with the basil mayonnaise.

about 10 minutes, until only 2 to 3 tablespoons of liquid remain. Strain the marinade and allow it to cool; reserve the bay leaf for garnish.

Put the strips of venison in a bowl, and pour the cooled marinade over them. Cover the bowl, and leave the meat to marinate in the refrigerator for 24 to 72 hours, turning the pieces occasionally.

At the end of the marinating period, lift out the venison pieces from the bowl with a slotted spoon, and pat them dry with paper towels. Reserve the un-absorbed marinade. Select 60 g (2 oz) of irregularly shaped venison strips, and set them aside.

Cut one rasher of bacon in half crosswise, and reserve it for garnish. Combine the rest of the bacon with the 60 g (2 oz) of venison strips, and dice both finely. Put the diced meat in a bowl, and add the reserved marinade, the minced pork, the bread-crumbs, thyme, orange rind, nutmeg, salt and pepper. Stir the ingredients together well.

Preheat the oven to 170°C (325°F or Mark 3). Line the base and sides of an 18 by 9 by 7.5 cm (7 by 3½ by 3 inch) loaf tin with non-stick parchment paper. Using the back of a tablespoon, press one third of the minced pork mixture into the base of the tin. Press four juniper berries into the mixture. Arrange about half of the venison strips over the pork layer, laying them end to end, lengthwise, in the tin. Cover the venison strips with another third of the pork mixture, and add four more juniper berries. Repeat the process with the remaining venison strips and pork mixture, shaping the top layer of pork so that it rises slightly in the centre. Decorate the terrine by pressing the reserved bay leaf and bacon slices, and the remaining four juniper berries, into its surface.

Cover the terrine tightly with a double layer of foil, lightly oiling the section that will come in contact with the terrine. Place the tin in a roasting pan, and pour in sufficient boiling water to come two thirds of the way up the side of the tin. Bake the terrine for 1 to 1½ hours, until clear juices run out when a skewer is inserted into its centre.

Remove the terrine from the water bath, and loosen the foil round the edges of the tin. Arrange weights from a kitchen scale — about 1.75 kg (3½ lb) in total — evenly over the surface of the terrine, to com-press it, and leave it to cool to room temperature. When the terrine is cool, remove the weights. Chill the terrine in the refrigerator for at least 24 hours.

Transport the terrine to a picnic in its tin, wrapped in foil and packed inside a cool box. To serve the terrine, turn it out on to a wooden board and slice it using a sharp, serrated knife.

Game Terrine Scented with Orange Rind

Serves 10
Working time: about 1 hour
Total time: about 2 days (includes marinating and chilling)

Calories **170**
Protein **26g**
Cholesterol **50mg**
Total fat **7g**
Saturated fat **2g**
Sodium **175mg**

500 g	haunch of venison, trimmed of fat and sinew, cut into 4 by 1 cm (1½ by ½ inch) strips	1 lb
60 g	streaky bacon rashers, rind removed	2 oz
350 g	pork tenderloin, trimmed of fat and minced	12 oz
30 g	fresh white breadcrumbs	1 oz
1 tsp	chopped fresh thyme	1 tsp
¼ tsp	finely grated orange rind	¼ tsp
¼ tsp	freshly grated nutmeg	¼ tsp
¼ tsp	salt	¼ tsp
⅛ tsp	white pepper	⅛ tsp
12	juniper berries	12
Spiced port marinade		
12.5 cl	ruby port	4 fl oz
½	orange, rind only, cut off in strips	½
4	black peppercorns	4
1	blade mace	1
2	fresh thyme sprigs	2
1	bay leaf	1

First prepare the marinade. Put the port in a small, non-reactive saucepan and add the strips of orange rind, the peppercorns, mace, thyme and bay leaf. Set the pan over gentle heat, and simmer the contents for

---

SUGGESTED ACCOMPANIMENT: *a salad of oakleaf lettuce leaves and orange wedges; crusty bread; redcurrant jelly.*

EDITOR'S NOTE: *Fresh venison may be obtained during the season, ready trimmed and prepared, from game merchants and most large supermarkets. Frozen venison is available all year round.*

Duck with Blackberries in Port Jelly

Serves 6
Working time: about 50 minutes
Total time: about 6 hours (includes chilling)

Calories **185**
Protein **17g**
Cholesterol **100mg**
Total fat **8g**
Saturated fat **2g**
Sodium **125mg**

250 g	fresh or frozen blackberries	8 oz
15 cl	port	¼ pint
1 tsp	light brown sugar	1 tsp
600 g	duck breast fillets, skinned, all fat removed	1¼ lb
¼ tsp	salt	¼ tsp
½ tbsp	virgin olive oil	½ tbsp
1	large thyme sprig	1
12.5 cl	unsalted chicken stock (recipe, page 139)	4 fl oz
2½ tsp	powdered gelatine	2½ tsp
	oakleaf lettuce leaves, washed and dried, for garnish	
	extra blackberries, for garnish	
6	thyme flowers, for garnish (optional)	6

Put the blackberries in a non-reactive saucepan with the port and sugar. Place the pan over medium heat, and bring the liquid just to the boil. Immediately remove the pan from the heat, and set it aside.

Season the duck fillets with a little of the salt. Heat the oil in a heavy frying pan over medium heat, and add the duck fillets. Fry them quickly for about 1 minute on each side, to seal them, then add the thyme sprig to the pan. Lay a flat plate on top of the duck breasts and place a heavy weight on top of the plate. Reduce the heat to low, and cook the duck fillets for about 12 minutes, turning them over after 6 minutes, until they are cooked through but still slightly pink in the centre. Let the fillets cool for at least 45 minutes.

Place a nylon sieve on top of a measuring jug, pour the blackberries and their juice into the sieve, and allow them to drain; there should be about 17.5 cl (6 fl oz) of port liquid in the jug. Strain the juices from the duck fillets into the jug, then stir in the stock.

Put 2 tablespoons of cold water in a small bowl, and sprinkle the gelatine evenly over the surface. Leave it to stand for about 5 minutes, to allow the gelatine to soften and swell. Stand the bowl in a saucepan of gently simmering water, and stir the mixture until the gelatine has completely dissolved. Stir the gelatine solution into the port liquid in the jug.

Rinse out six 12.5 cl (4 fl oz) ramekin dishes or other small moulds with cold water. Pour a small amount of the port jelly into the base of each ramekin, and place them in the refrigerator until the jelly has set — about 20 minutes. Meanwhile, cut the cooled duck breasts into 3 mm (⅛ inch) thick slices.

Place three blackberries in a row down the centre of each ramekin, and place a small slice of duck on each side of the berries. Continue adding berries and duck slices to the ramekins in layers, dividing them equally among the six. Pour more port jelly into each ramekin until the meat and berries are completely covered. Leave the jellies to set in the refrigerator for at least 4 hours, or overnight.

To transport the jellies to the picnic site, cover each ramekin with a double layer of plastic film and stand them upright in a rigid container; pack the garnishes in separate containers. Put all the containers in a cool box. Take a thermos flask of hot water and a bowl to the picnic with you. To unmould the jellies, pour the hot water into the bowl and dip the bases of the ramekins quickly in the water. Invert the jellies on to serving plates. Garnish each plate with a lettuce leaf and a few blackberries and, if you wish, place a thyme flower on top of each jelly.

Chicken and Pickled Walnut Mousses

Serves 4
Working time: about 35 minutes
Total time: about 3 hours and 15 minutes (includes chilling)

Calories **225**
Protein **37g**
Cholesterol **90mg**
Total fat **7g**
Saturated fat **2g**
Sodium **195mg**

4	chicken breasts, skinned, boned and sliced (about 500 g/1 lb)	4
1	onion, coarsely chopped	1
15 cl	plain low-fat yogurt	¼ pint
1	garlic clove, crushed	1
¼ tsp	ground coriander	¼ tsp
⅛ tsp	salt	⅛ tsp
	freshly ground black pepper	
2	egg whites	2
4	pickled walnuts, two coarsely chopped, two halved for garnish	4

Preheat the oven to 180°C (350°F or Mark 4). Lightly oil four 15 cl (¼ pint) ramekin dishes or other small, heatproof moulds.

Put half of the chicken and half of the onion into a food processor and process them until they are completely smooth — 1 to 2 minutes. Transfer the purée to a bowl, then process the remaining chicken and onion and add it to the bowl. Add the yogurt, garlic, coriander, salt and some freshly ground black pepper, and beat the mixture until it is smooth.

In a separate bowl, whisk the egg whites until they form stiff peaks. Stir 2 tablespoons of the egg whites into the chicken purée to loosen the mixture, then fold in the remainder using a metal tablespoon.

Half-fill each ramekin with the chicken mousse. Divide the chopped walnuts into four equal portions and sprinkle a portion into each ramekin. Fill the ramekins with the remaining mousse.

Stand the ramekins in a baking pan and pour in sufficient boiling water to come two thirds of the way up the sides of the ramekins. Place the baking pan in the oven and bake the mousses for 35 to 40 minutes, or until they are firm to the touch. Remove the ramekins from the pan and allow them to cool to room temperature, then chill them for at least 2 hours.

To take the mousses to the picnic, cover each ramekin with a double layer of plastic film and place them upright in a rigid container. Put the pickled walnut halves into a separate small, sealed container. Pack the containers in a cool box.

To serve, run a knife round the edge of each ramekin, and carefully turn the mousses out on to individual serving plates. Garnish the top of each one with a pickled walnut half.

SUGGESTED ACCOMPANIMENT: *mixed bean salad.*

Cucumber Dip

Serves 6
Working time: about 15 minutes
Total time: about 1 hour and 45 minutes (includes chilling)

Calories **60**		
Protein **1g**		
Cholesterol **15mg**		
Total fat **5g**		
Saturated fat **3g**		
Sodium **25mg**		

½	cucumber, peeled, seeded and grated	½
½ tsp	salt	½ tsp
15 cl	soured cream	¼ pint
90 g	watercress, leaves only, washed, dried and finely chopped	3 oz
2	spring onions, trimmed and finely chopped	2
1	fresh green chili pepper, very finely chopped (caution, page 63)	1
	freshly ground black pepper	

Place the cucumber in a shallow bowl, sprinkle over the salt, and leave it to stand for 30 minutes. Rinse the salt off under cold running water, and drain the cucumber well; lightly squeeze out any excess water.

Put the cucumber in a bowl with the remaining ingredients, and mix everything together well. Leave the dip to rest in the refrigerator for at least 1 hour before transferring it to a container with a tight-fitting lid. Keep the dip in its container in the refrigerator until you go to the picnic. Pack it upright inside a cool box.

SUGGESTED ACCOMPANIMENT: *crunchy fresh vegetables.*

Red Pepper Dip

Serves 6
Working time: about 15 minutes
Total time: about 1 hour and 15 minutes (includes chilling)

Calories **40**		
Protein **3g**		
Cholesterol **trace**		
Total fat **3g**		
Saturated fat **1g**		
Sodium **130mg**		

2	sweet red peppers (about 200 g/7 oz each), skinned (page 138), seeded, deribbed and roughly chopped	2
175 g	low-fat fromage frais	6 oz
½ tsp	salt	½ tsp
¼ tsp	cayenne pepper	¼ tsp

Place the chopped red peppers in a food processor, and process them until smooth. Pour the pepper purée into a bowl, and stir in the *fromage frais*. Season the dip with the salt and cayenne pepper, mixing well. Leave the dip to rest in the refrigerator for at least 1 hour before transferring it to a container with a tight-fitting lid. Keep the dip in its container in the refrigerator until you are ready to go to the picnic site. Pack it upright inside a cool box.

SUGGESTED ACCOMPANIMENT: *crunchy fresh vegetables.*

Melon and Parma Ham in Poppy Seed Rolls

Makes 6 filled rolls
Working (and total) time: about 20 minutes

6	crusty poppy-seed rolls	6
6 tbsp	cream cheese	6 tbsp
45 g	piece of peeled melon, cut into six slices	1½ oz
12	thin cucumber slices, halved	12
6	paper-thin slices Parma ham (about 45 g/1½ oz)	6
12	watercress sprigs	12

Per filled roll:
Calories **218**
Protein **7g**
Cholesterol **50mg**
Total fat **9g**
Saturated fat **4g**
Sodium **470mg**

Cut the rolls in half and spread 1 tablespoon of the cream cheese evenly over each bottom half. Arrange a melon slice and four pieces of cucumber on the cheese in each roll, and lay a slice of Parma ham on top of the melon. Add two sprigs of watercress to each roll and replace the top halves.

Spicy Cod and Corn in Sourdough Bread

Makes 6 sandwiches
Working time: about 30 minutes
Total time: about 1 hour and 30 minutes

140 g	cod fillet	4½ oz
30 cl	unsalted vegetable stock (recipe, page 139)	½ pint
1 tbsp	mayonnaise	1 tbsp
2 tbsp	thick Greek yogurt	2 tbsp
½ tsp	garam masala	½ tsp
½ tsp	ground turmeric	½ tsp.
12	slices sourdough bread	12
90 g	frozen sweetcorn kernels, blanched in boiling water and drained thoroughly	3 oz
6	unskinned shelled almonds, cut into slivers with a sharp knife	6
½	box mustard and cress, trimmed	½

Per sandwich:
Calories **200**
Protein **11g**
Cholesterol **15mg**
Total fat **7g**
Saturated fat **1g**
Sodium **350mg**

Place the fish in a wide, shallow pan, and pour in sufficient stock to cover it. Cover the pan, and bring the liquid gently to simmering point. Simmer the cod for 3 to 4 minutes, until the flesh flakes easily with a fork. Using a fish slice, transfer the cod to a plate and allow it to cool. Flake the fish gently.

Place the mayonnaise and yogurt in a small bowl, and stir in the garam masala and turmeric. Spread this mixture evenly over six of the bread slices. Divide the flaked cod and the sweetcorn among the six covered slices, and sprinkle on a few almond slivers. Top each filling with some mustard and cress and cover it with a second slice of bread.

Chicken, Celery and Pistachio Nut Baps

Makes 6 filled baps
Working (and total) time: about 25 minutes

6	wholemeal baps	6
6 tbsp	low-fat fromage frais	6 tbsp
175 g	skinned cooked chicken breast, cut into strips	6 oz
1 tbsp	wholegrain mustard	1 tbsp
6	iceberg lettuce leaves, washed and dried	6
2	small sticks celery, trimmed and thinly sliced	2
18	skinned shelled pistachio nuts, finely sliced	18
	cayenne pepper, for garnish	

Per filled bap:
Calories **200**
Protein **15g**
Cholesterol **20mg**
Total fat **4g**
Saturated fat **1g**
Sodium **360mg**

Cut the baps in half and spread each bottom half evenly with 1 tablespoon of the fromage frais. Spread the mustard over the chicken breast strips.

Place a lettuce leaf on top of each covered base and divide the chicken strips, celery slices and pistachio nuts among them. Garnish each filling with a light dusting of cayenne pepper and replace the top halves of the baps.

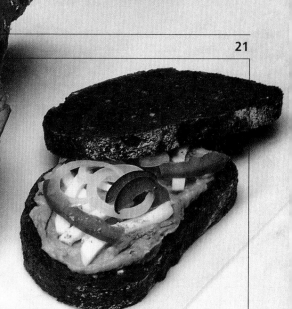

Cottage Cheese, Prawn and Pepper Sandwiches

Makes 6 sandwiches
Working (and total) time: about 25 minutes

200 g	low-fat cottage cheese	7 oz
1 tbsp	tomato paste	1 tbsp
	white pepper	
12	slices wholegrain bread	12
90 g	peeled cooked prawns	3 oz
6	button mushrooms, wiped clean and thinly sliced	6
½	sweet red pepper, seeded, deribbed and sliced into six rings	½
6	chives, finely cut	6

Per sandwich:
Calories **160**
Protein **12g**
Cholesterol **30mg**
Total fat **3g**
Saturated fat **1g**
Sodium **450mg**

Place the cottage cheese in a bowl and stir in the tomato paste and some white pepper. Spread the cheese mixture evenly over six of the slices of bread, and divide the prawns, sliced mushrooms and pepper rings among the covered slices. Scatter some cut chives over each filling, and press a second slice of bread gently on top.

Chinese-Style Beef Sandwiches

Makes 6 sandwiches
Working (and total) time: about 30 minutes

1	granary baguette, about 60 cm (2 feet) long, cut into six equal pieces	1
45 g	polyunsaturated margarine	1½ oz
1½ tsp	finely chopped fresh ginger root	1½ tsp
2 tbsp	low-sodium soy sauce or shoyu	2 tbsp
6	slices cold cooked lean beef (about 175 g/6 oz)	6
1	slice fresh pineapple, peeled, cored and chopped	1
45 g	skinned shelled peanuts, roughly chopped	1½ oz
3	spring onions, trimmed, white parts sliced, green parts cut lengthwise into slivers	3

Per sandwich:
Calories **335**
Protein **16g**
Cholesterol **20mg**
Total fat **14g**
Saturated fat **4g**
Sodium **480mg**

Cut open the baguette pieces. In a small bowl, stir together the margarine, ginger root and soy sauce, and spread this mixture evenly over the bottoms of the baguette pieces. Place a slice of beef loosely on each covered base, then cover them with the chopped pineapple and peanuts, and the spring onions. Replace the top halves of the baguette pieces.

Avocado and Mozzarella Salad in Rye Bread

Makes 6 sandwiches
Working (and total) time: about 25 minutes

1	small avocado, halved, stoned and peeled	1
2 tbsp	fresh lemon juice	2 tbsp
	white pepper	
6	fresh basil leaves, shredded	6
12	slices dark rye bread	12
45 g	low-fat mozzarella, sliced	1½ oz
1	large tomato, halved, seeded and sliced	1
1	small onion, cut into rings	1
1	black olive, stoned and thinly sliced	1

Per sandwich:
Calories **225**
Protein **8g**
Cholesterol **5mg**
Total fat **6g**
Saturated fat **2g**
Sodium **400mg**

Put the avocado flesh in a bowl and mash it with a fork. Add the fresh lemon juice, and some white pepper together with the shredded basil leaves, and mix them in thoroughly with the fork.

Spread six pieces of bread evenly with the avocado mixture, then top each one with some of the cheese, tomato, onion and olive slices. Press a second piece of bread gently on to each filled base.

EDITOR'S NOTE: *The fillings on these pages may be teamed with any bread of your choice; each recipe provides sufficient filling for six sandwiches or rolls. The filled sandwiches and rolls should be loosely wrapped in greaseproof paper or plastic film and chilled until required. To avoid crushing them, carry them to the picnic site in rigid containers, packed upright inside a cool box.*

Mushroom-Stuffed Beef Fillet in a Crusty Loaf

Serves 12
Working time: about 1 hour
Total time: about 11 hours (includes chilling)

Calories **240**
Protein **23g**
Cholesterol **45mg**
Total fat **13g**
Saturated fat **3g**
Sodium **265mg**

1 kg	beef fillet in one piece, trimmed of fat	2½ lb
250 g	oyster or field mushrooms, wiped clean and finely sliced	8 oz
1 tsp	unsalted butter	1 tsp
⅛ tsp	salt	⅛ tsp
1 tbsp	Dijon mustard	1 tbsp
1 tbsp	finely chopped fresh tarragon	1 tbsp
	freshly ground black pepper	
600 g	large spinach leaves, stalks removed	1¼ lb
1	white bloomer loaf (about 400 g/14 oz)	1
2 tsp	safflower oil	2 tsp
3 tbsp	soured cream	3 tbsp
1½ tbsp	grainy mustard	1½ tbsp

To make a pocket in the fillet, use a sharp knife to slit into the meat from one side, cutting about two thirds of the way through the meat and stopping about 1 cm (½ inch) short of each end. Place the fillet on a work surface with the slit facing upwards. Using a meat bat or a rolling pin, lightly pound the edges of the meat to open up the pocket a little. Set the fillet aside while you prepare the mushroom stuffing.

Place the mushrooms, butter, salt and Dijon mustard in a non-stick saucepan. Cover the pan and cook the mixture over gentle heat for about 5 minutes, until the mushrooms are exuding their juices. Remove the lid and cook for a further 5 to 10 minutes, until all the moisture has evaporated. Cool the mushroom mixture a little, then stir in the tarragon.

Sprinkle the cut surfaces of the meat generously with black pepper, and pack the mushroom stuffing into the prepared pocket. Close up the slit and tie the fillet neatly with string at 1 cm (½ inch) intervals. Grind a little more pepper over the fillet. Preheat the oven to 240°C (475°F or Mark 9).

Cook the spinach leaves in a saucepan of rapidly boiling water until they are just tender — 1 to 2 minutes. Drain the spinach, refresh it under cold running water and drain it again thoroughly, pressing out as much water as possible without tearing the leaves. Place the leaves on paper towels to dry. When they are dry, lay them out on a large piece of plastic film, overlapping them, to form a rectangle large enough to wrap round the beef fillet.

Slice through the bloomer loaf on one of its long sides, cutting about half way through and leaving the other side intact to serve as a hinge. Open out the loaf a little and hollow it to make a cavity; you will need to remove about 200 g (7 oz) of crumb to make sufficient space for the wrapped fillet.

Brush the fillet all over with the oil and place it in a roasting pan. Roast the fillet for 25 minutes for medium-rare meat; for well-done meat, cook it for another 10 minutes. Remove the meat from the oven and allow it to rest for 15 minutes. Cut off and discard the string and place the fillet in the centre of the spinach rectangle. Blend the soured cream and grainy mustard and spread this mixture all over the fillet. Using the plastic film to lift them, wrap the spinach leaves round the coated fillet. Place the wrapped fillet inside the hollowed-out loaf and close up the loaf firmly.

Wrap the stuffed loaf in foil and place it in a large loaf tin or a terrine into which it will fit snugly; if necessary, pack the tin with crumpled foil. Place a brick or a similar weight on top of the loaf, and leave it to cool completely. Place the loaf in the refrigerator, still weighted if space allows, and chill it for at least 8 hours, or overnight.

Carry the loaf to the picnic site wrapped in its foil, inside a cool box. To serve, cut the loaf into slices with a sharp, long-bladed knife.

SUGGESTED ACCOMPANIMENT: *fresh tomatoes.*

Mediterranean Lamb Baguettes

Makes 24 slices
Working time: about 30 minutes
Total time: about 3 hours (includes chilling)

Per slice:
Calories **95**
Protein **7g**
Cholesterol **20mg**
Total fat **4g**
Saturated fat **2g**
Sodium **115mg**

3	small baguettes (about 125 g/4 oz each)	3
1 tbsp	virgin olive oil	1 tbsp
1	large garlic clove, finely chopped	1
500 g	lean lamb from the leg or loin, trimmed of fat and minced	1 lb
1 tbsp	tomato paste	1 tbsp
1 tbsp	sun-dried tomato paste, or 15 g (½ oz) sun-dried tomatoes, softened in hot water and finely chopped	1 tbsp
125 g	courgettes, blanched and coarsely grated	4 oz
15 g	black olives, stoned and finely chopped	½ oz
30 g	capers, rinsed	1 oz
1 tsp	finely chopped fresh summer savory, or ½ tsp dried summer savory	1 tsp
¼ tsp	salt	¼ tsp
	freshly ground black pepper	
45 g	unsalted butter	1½ oz
	summer savory sprigs, for garnish (optional)	

Cut each baguette lengthwise along one side, leaving the other side intact. Open up the baguettes and hollow them out, reserving the crumbs.

Heat the oil in a heavy frying pan, add the garlic, and cook over medium heat until soft — about 5 minutes. Add the lamb and cook it, stirring frequently, until no pink meat remains — about 15 minutes. Stir in the tomato and sun-dried tomato pastes, then add the courgettes, olives and capers. Stir well, reduce the heat to low, and cook the ingredients gently for another 2 minutes. Add the chopped savory, the salt and some black pepper, and cook the mixture for 30 seconds more. Set the pan aside, and allow the contents to cool to room temperature — about 20 minutes.

Meanwhile, if the breadcrumbs are not already fairly fine, process them in a blender or food processor.

When the lamb mixture has cooled, stir in the breadcrumbs. Open up the baguette shells, and butter the inside of each one. Divide the stuffing among the baguettes, packing it firmly into the hollowed-out cavities. Close the loaves, completely surrounding the filling, and wrap each one tightly in foil. Chill the stuffed baguettes in the refrigerator for at least 2 hours.

Take the baguettes on a picnic still wrapped in their foil and packed inside a cool box, and slice them just before serving. Alternatively, you can preslice the baguettes at home, then re-form them and wrap them tightly in foil again. Garnish the slices with a few sprigs of summer savory, if you wish.

SUGGESTED ACCOMPANIMENT: *a salad of Mediterranean tomatoes, rocket leaves and capers, dressed with an olive oil and red wine vinaigrette.*

EDITOR'S NOTE: *Select lightly cooked, soft loaves for this recipe. Wrapped, stuffed baguettes keep well in the refrigerator for up to 48 hours. They may also be frozen for up to two months. To thaw a stuffed baguette, remove it from the freezer and allow it to stand, wrapped in its foil, at room temperature for 2 hours. Place the thawed baguette, still in its foil, in a preheated 220°C (425°F or Mark 7) oven for 10 to 15 minutes, to crisp it.*

Crab and Avocado Stacked Sandwiches

Serves 6
Working time: about 35 minutes
Total time: about 2 hours (includes chilling)

Calories **270**
Protein **14g**
Cholesterol **30mg**
Total fat **10g**
Saturated fat **2g**
Sodium **520mg**

1	small wholemeal tin loaf, crusts removed	1
1	small white tin loaf, crusts removed	1
1	small black rye tin loaf, crusts removed	1
Crab filling		
100 g	quark	3 ½ oz
175 g	brown crab meat, picked over	6 oz
1 tbsp	tomato paste	1 tbsp
½ tsp	muscovado sugar	½ tsp
1 tsp	sherry vinegar	1 tsp
⅛ tsp	cayenne pepper	⅛ tsp
Avocado filling		
75 g	watercress leaves, blanched, drained and squeezed dry	2 ½ oz
125 g	avocado, peeled and stoned, sprinkled with 1 tsp fresh lemon juice to prevent discoloration	4 oz
100 g	low-fat fromage frais	3 ½ oz
1 tbsp	finely chopped fresh lemon balm	1 tbsp
⅛ tsp	white pepper	⅛ tsp

Cut off and discard the rounded tops of the loaves. Slice each loaf lengthwise into three equal rectangles. Trim all the bread rectangles so that they are exactly the same size, and set them aside.

To prepare the crab filling, first mash the quark with a fork to soften it, then mix in the crab meat, tomato paste, sugar, sherry vinegar and cayenne pepper. Place the mixture in the refrigerator and chill it until it is firm — about 1 hour.

To make the avocado filling, chop the watercress leaves finely and place them in the bowl of a food processor. Add the avocado, and process the mixture until it is smooth. Add the *fromage frais*, the chopped fresh lemon balm and the white pepper, and apply a few quick, short bursts of power to amalgamate the ingredients. Chill the mixture in the refrigerator until it is firm — 30 minutes to 1 hour.

Divide the crab filling among the three rye bread rectangles, and spread it right up to the edges. Spread the avocado filling over the wholemeal bread rectangles in the same way. Lay each wholemeal slice on a rye slice, and top the stacks with the white bread slices. Wrap the sandwiches in plastic film or greaseproof paper, and chill them for at least 30 minutes. Pack the sandwiches in a cool box to take them to the picnic site.

Unwrap the stacked sandwiches just before they are to be eaten, and cut them into slices using a sharp, serrated bread knife.

Wholemeal Loaf Filled with Smoked Chicken Salad

Serves 8
Working time: about 1 hour
Total time: about 9 hours (includes chilling)

Calories **190**
Protein **22g**
Cholesterol **45mg**
Total fat **5g**
Saturated fat **2g**
Sodium **400mg**

1	round wholemeal loaf, about 18 cm (7 inches) in diameter	1
15 g	unsalted butter	½ oz
125 g	sorrel leaves, washed and dried, stalks discarded, leaves deveined	4 oz
4	garlic cloves, crushed	4
500 g	boned and skinned cooked smoked chicken breasts, cut crosswise into thin slices, or one 1.5 kg (3 lb) cooked smoked chicken, skinned and boned, meat cut into thin slices	1 lb
4	firm small tomatoes (about 275 g/9 oz), thinly sliced	4
¼	cucumber, thinly sliced	¼
½ tsp	salt	½ tsp
	freshly ground black pepper	

Cut a lid, about 12 cm (5 inches) in diameter, from the top of the loaf. Scoop out most of the crumb from the centre, leaving a crusty shell about 1 cm (½ inch) thick. Using the back of a dessertspoon, spread the butter inside the shell and on the underside of the lid.

Lay about one quarter of the sorrel leaves in the base of the hollowed-out loaf, and spread them with one quarter of the crushed garlic. Pack one third of the sliced chicken on top, followed by one third of the tomato and cucumber slices. Season with a little of the salt and plenty of freshly ground black pepper. Repeat the layers with the remaining ingredients, finishing with a layer of sorrel and garlic.

Place the buttered lid over the top layer of filling, and wrap the loaf in foil. Set a bread board on top of the loaf, and weight it down with a 1 kg (2 lb) weight from a kitchen scale. Chill the loaf overnight.

Transport the filled loaf to a picnic, still wrapped in its foil, inside a cool box. To serve, remove the foil and cut the loaf into wedges, using a sharp knife.

EDITOR'S NOTE: *The bread removed from the centre of the loaf may be used to make fresh breadcrumbs.*

Cheese and Bacon Granary Bars

Serves 6
Working time: about 30 minutes
Total time: about 1 hour and 30 minutes (includes cooling)

Calories **315**
Protein **12g**
Cholesterol **30mg**
Total fat **10g**
Saturated fat **6g**
Sodium **315mg**

45 g	lean bacon, rind removed, minced	1 ½ oz
150 g	granary flour	5 oz
150 g	plain flour	5 oz
3 tsp	baking powder	3 tsp
⅛ tsp	salt	⅛ tsp
45 g	unsalted butter	1 ½ oz
45 g	mature Cheddar cheese, finely grated	1 ½ oz
1 tbsp	finely grated Parmesan cheese	1 tbsp
1 tbsp	chopped fresh oregano, or 1 tsp dried oregano	1 tbsp
1 tbsp	fresh lemon juice	1 tbsp
15 cl	skimmed milk	¼ pint
Salad filling		
150 g	low-fat fromage frais	5 oz
¼	crisp lettuce, sliced	¼
¼	cucumber, thinly sliced	¼
6	spring onions, sliced	6

Preheat the oven to 230°C (450°F or Mark 8), and grease and flour a baking sheet.

Put the bacon in a non-stick frying pan and dry-fry it over medium heat, stirring it frequently, until it is lightly browned — 2 to 3 minutes. Transfer the bacon to paper towels to drain and cool.

Put the granary flour in a mixing bowl and sift in the plain flour, baking powder and salt. Using your fingertips, rub in the butter until the mixture resembles fine breadcrumbs. Stir in the bacon, the Cheddar and Parmesan cheeses, and the oregano. Add the lemon juice to the milk then, using a round-bladed knife, gradually mix sufficient liquid into the dry ingredients to make a soft, but not sticky, dough.

Transfer the dough to a floured work surface and, with floured hands, shape it into a rectangle measuring about 25 by 10 cm (10 by 4 inches). Using a metal spatula, lift the dough on to the prepared baking sheet. With a sharp knife, mark the top of the dough rectangle crosswise into six bars, cutting down about 5 mm (¼ inch) into the dough. Bake the dough until it is well risen, firm to the touch and a light golden-brown in colour — about 20 minutes. Allow the bread to cool on a wire rack.

Cut the bread into the six marked bars and split each one in half. Fill the bars with the *fromage frais* and the lettuce, cucumber and spring onion slices. Wrap the filled bars individually in foil or plastic film, and pack them in a rigid plastic container. Place the container in a cool box to take to the picnic.

EDITOR'S NOTE: *The baked bread may be frozen, unfilled, for up to two months. Wrap it tightly in plastic film and foil before putting it in the freezer. Thaw at room temperature for 2 hours.*

Turkey and Ham-Filled Buns

Makes 8 filled buns
Working time: about 45 minutes
Total time: about 2 hours and 15 minutes
(includes proving and cooling)

Per filled bun:
Calories **250**
Protein **19g**
Cholesterol **30mg**
Total fat **4g**
Saturated fat **1g**
Sodium **370mg**

1 tsp	virgin olive oil	1 tsp
1	onion, chopped	1
350 g	lean boneless turkey, coarsely chopped	12 oz
8 cl	dry white wine	3 fl oz
175 g	celeriac, peeled and coarsely grated	6 oz
175 g	lean cooked ham, trimmed of fat and cut into 5 mm (¼ inch) dice	6 oz
1 tbsp	chopped fresh thyme, or 1 tsp dried thyme	1 tbsp
3 tbsp	chopped parsley	3 tbsp
2 tbsp	grated horseradish	2 tbsp
	freshly ground black pepper	
Sesame buns		
350 g	strong plain flour	12 oz
½ tsp	caster sugar	½ tsp
½ tsp	salt	½ tsp
1½ tsp	easy-blend dried yeast	1½ tsp
15 cl	skimmed milk	¼ pint
1	egg white	1
	skimmed milk, for glazing	
4 tsp	sesame seeds	4 tsp

First make the dough for the buns. In a large bowl, mix together the flour, sugar, salt and yeast. Heat the milk in a saucepan until it is hot to the touch — about 43°C (110°F) — then pour it into the dry ingredients together with the egg white. Stir to create a soft dough, adding a little warm water if the mixture is too dry. Turn the dough on to a floured surface and knead it gently until it is smooth — about 10 minutes. Place the dough in a clean bowl, cover the bowl with plastic film, and leave the dough to rise in a warm place until it has doubled in size — about 30 minutes.

Meanwhile, make the turkey and ham filling. Heat the oil in a heavy-bottomed saucepan, add the onion and cook it over medium heat until it is soft — about 3 minutes. Add the turkey and cook it, stirring continuously, for about 5 minutes, or until it is cooked through. Blend the turkey with the onion mixture and wine in a food processor until it is finely chopped but not puréed. Transfer the mixture to a bowl and beat in the celeriac, ham, thyme, parsley, horseradish and some pepper. Leave the mixture to cool completely.

Lightly grease a large baking sheet. On a floured work surface, knock back the risen dough to its original size and divide it into eight equal pieces. Roll out one piece into a round about 15 cm (6 inches) in diameter. Brush the edges of the round with water and spoon one eighth of the turkey filling into the centre. Bring the edges of the dough up over the filling and pleat and press them together neatly to seal the filling inside the bun. Place the bun, seam side down, on the baking sheet. Use the remaining dough and filling to make another seven buns and place them on the baking sheet, leaving a 5 mm (¼ inch) gap between the buns. Cover the buns with lightly greased plastic film and leave them to rise for 20 minutes. Meanwhile, preheat the oven to 200°C (400°F or Mark 6).

Glaze the tops of the buns lightly with skimmed milk and sprinkle them with the sesame seeds. Bake the buns for about 20 minutes, or until they turn a deep golden colour. Cool them on a wire rack.

Take the buns on a picnic wrapped in foil inside a rigid container. Carry the container in a cool box.

SUGGESTED ACCOMPANIMENT: *a salad of shredded white and green cabbage and flat-leaf parsley, with a dressing of crème fraîche.*

Individual Tomato Pizzas

Serves 4
Working time: about 45 minutes
Total time: about 3 hours (includes rising and cooling)

Calories **345**
Protein **10g**
Cholesterol **55mg**
Total fat **9g**
Saturated fat **3g**
Sodium **135mg**

250 g	strong white flour	8 oz
¼ tsp	salt	¼ tsp
15 g	unsalted butter	½ oz
1 tsp	easy-blend dried yeast	1 tsp
1 tbsp	safflower oil	1 tbsp
250 g	onions, thinly sliced	8 oz
2	garlic cloves, crushed	2
500 g	tomatoes, skinned (page 138) and sliced	1 lb
1 tbsp	tomato paste	1 tbsp
1 tbsp	chopped fresh basil, or 1 tsp dried basil	1 tbsp
1 tsp	chopped fresh marjoram, or ¼ tsp dried marjoram	1 tsp
90 g	button mushrooms, trimmed and sliced	3 oz
	freshly ground black pepper	
¼	sweet green pepper, seeded, deribbed, blanched for 2 minutes and cut into long, narrow strips	¼
4	quail's eggs, hard boiled, each cut into four slices (optional)	4
1	large black olive, stoned and cut into thin slivers	1

Sift the flour and ⅛ teaspoon of the salt into a mixing bowl, and rub in the butter until the mixture resembles fine breadcrumbs. Sprinkle on the dried yeast, and mix it in thoroughly. Heat some water in a small pan until it is hot to the touch — about 43°C (110°F). Using a wooden spoon, mix sufficient warm water — about 15 cl (¼ pint) — into the dry ingredients to form a pliable dough. Turn out the dough on to a lightly floured surface, and knead it for 5 to 10 minutes, until it is smooth. Put the dough into a large, oiled polythene bag, and fold over the top of the bag but do not seal it. Set the dough aside in a warm place to rise for about 1 hour, until it has doubled in size.

Meanwhile, prepare the topping. Heat the oil in a heavy-bottomed saucepan, and fry the onions and garlic gently until the onions are soft but only very lightly coloured. Add the tomatoes and tomato paste, and continue cooking for another 5 to 8 minutes, until the tomatoes have broken down. Add the herbs, the mushrooms, the remaining salt and some pepper, and cook the mixture for a further 1 to 2 minutes, until the mushrooms are soft. Set the filling aside to cool.

Lightly grease four 15 to 18 cm (6 to 7 inch) flan tins, and place them on a baking sheet. Knock back the risen dough, and knead it again until it is smooth. Divide the dough into quarters. Keeping the unrolled dough covered with plastic film while you are working to prevent it from drying out, roll out each piece of dough in turn to a thickness of about 5 mm (¼ inch). Line each of the tins with a portion of the rolled-out dough. Divide the cooled tomato mixture among the bases, spreading it in an even layer. Set the pizzas aside to rise in a warm place, uncovered, for 10 to 15 minutes, until they are puffy. Meanwhile, preheat the oven to 220°C (425°F or Mark 7).

Bake the pizzas for about 20 minutes, or until their edges are lightly browned. Remove the pizzas from their tins and leave them to cool on a wire rack. When they are cool — after about 1 hour — arrange the strips of blanched green pepper, the slices of quail's egg if you are using them, and the olive slivers in a decorative pattern on top of the pizzas. Return the pizzas to their tins, and wrap each one loosely in a sheet of greaseproof paper to take on a picnic.

Artichoke Filled with Seafood in a Dill Dressing

Serves 4
Working time: about 1 hour
Total time: about 4 hours (includes marinating)

Calories **230**			
Protein **28g**	1	garlic clove, halved	1
Cholesterol **100mg**	3 tbsp	fresh lemon juice	3 tbsp
Total fat **11g**	4	globe artichokes	4
Saturated fat **3g**	250 g	salmon trout fillets	8 oz
Sodium **480mg**	4	shelled scallops, bright white connective tissue removed	4
	1	shallot, thinly sliced	1
	3 tbsp	dry vermouth	3 tbsp
	1 tsp	safflower oil	1 tsp
		freshly ground black pepper	
	2	fresh thyme sprigs	2
	125 g	white crab meat, picked over and flaked	4 oz
	2 tsp	chopped fresh dill	2 tsp
	1	lemon, finely grated rind of half, the other half sliced, for garnish	1
	4	thin slices smoked salmon (about 45 g/1 ½ oz)	4
		dill sprigs, for garnish (optional)	

Pour 4 litres (7 pints) of water into a large, non-reactive saucepan, and add the garlic and 1 tablespoon of the lemon juice. Using a stainless steel knife, cut off and discard the top third and the stem of an artichoke; trim away the small or discoloured leaves at the base, and use kitchen scissors to trim off the prickly tips of the leaves. Rinse the artichoke well, then drop it immediately into the pan of acidulated water. Prepare the remaining artichokes in the same way.

Bring the pan of artichokes to the boil, cover the pan and simmer them for 40 to 45 minutes, until they are tender. Drain the artichokes and refresh them under cold running water, then drain them again and leave them upside down on a clean tea towel to dry.

Meanwhile, preheat the oven to 190°C (375°F or Mark 5), and lightly grease a sheet of foil measuring about 35 by 30 cm (14 by 12 inches). Place the trout fillets and scallops on the sheet of foil with the shallot, 1 tablespoon of the lemon juice, 2 tablespoons of the vermouth, the oil, some pepper and the sprigs of thyme. Wrap the foil over to enclose the fish in a parcel. Place the parcel on a baking sheet and put it in the oven for 15 minutes. Leave the fish to cool in its parcel.

Open the parcel carefully and drain off and reserve the cooking liquid. Skin the trout fillets and remove any bones, then flake the flesh into neat pieces; put the flaked trout in a bowl. Slice the scallops and add them to the bowl, together with the crab meat. Strain the reserved cooking liquid and mix into it the remaining lemon juice and vermouth, the dill and the lemon rind. Add this to the fish and toss the ingredients lightly. Cover the bowl and marinate the fish in the refrigerator for at least 2 hours, stirring it gently from time to time.

Form the smoked salmon slices into neat rolls. Remove the choke from each cooled artichoke by spreading apart the top leaves and pulling out the smaller inner leaves, then scraping away the hairy choke with a teaspoon, to expose the artichoke heart. Spoon the marinated fish mixture into the prepared artichokes, and top each one with a smoked salmon roll. Cover the filled artichokes loosely with plastic film and chill them until required.

Pack the artichokes, wedged upright, into a rigid container. Cut the lemon slices in half and pack them and the dill sprigs, if you are using them, in a separate small, plastic container. Transport both to the picnic in a cool box. To serve, garnish the filled artichokes with the halved lemon slices and dill sprigs.

Ginger and Coriander Fish Balls

Makes 16 fish balls
Working time: about 35 minutes
Total time: about 2 hours (includes chilling)

Per fish ball:
Calories **70**
Protein **11g**
Cholesterol **25mg**
Total fat **3g**
Saturated fat **1g**
Sodium **150mg**

4 cm	piece fresh ginger root, finely chopped	1½ inch
3	shallots, finely chopped	3
2 tbsp	dry vermouth	2 tbsp
1 tbsp	fresh lemon juice	1 tbsp
250 g	thinly sliced smoked halibut or smoked cod fillet	8 oz
500 g	fresh cod fillet, skinned, chopped into 2.5 cm (1 inch) cubes and chilled	1 lb
1½	egg whites, chilled	1½
¼ tsp	salt	¼ tsp
1 tbsp	chopped fresh coriander	1 tbsp
	white pepper	
2 tbsp	safflower oil	2 tbsp
16	small coriander sprigs	16
1	lemon, cut into wedges, for garnish (optional)	1
	Oriental or other salad leaves, for garnish	

Put the ginger and shallots in a small, non-reactive saucepan with the vermouth and lemon juice. Simmer the mixture gently until only half the liquid remains — about 2 minutes. Leave the mixture to cool.

Meanwhile, select the best slices of smoked halibut and cut from them 16 ribbons, each measuring about 7.5 by 1 cm (3 by ½ inch). Store the ribbons in the refrigerator until required.

Dice the rest of the smoked fish finely. Put the diced smoked fish and the ginger and shallot mixture in the refrigerator, together with a food processor bowl and blade and a mixing bowl. Chill for at least 30 minutes.

Using the chilled equipment, process the diced smoked fish with the cubed fresh cod, the egg whites and the salt until the mixture forms a coarse-textured ball. Transfer the ball to the mixing bowl. Add the chopped coriander and some white pepper, and mix them in well. Cover the bowl with plastic film and return it to the refrigerator for 30 minutes.

Pour enough water into a saucepan to fill it to a depth of 2.5 cm (1 inch). Line a steamer with a sheet of foil large enough to form a cover when the edges are folded over. Oil the foil with a little of the safflower oil.

Divide the chilled fish mixture into 16 portions. Lightly oil your hands and a board with the remaining safflower oil and roll each portion into a ball on the board. Wrap a ribbon of smoked fish round each ball, and arrange the balls in the steamer with the ribbon join underneath. Place a coriander sprig on top of each ball, and fold the foil over the balls to cover them.

Bring the saucepan of water to the boil. Cover the steamer and place it over the pan of boiling water. Reduce the heat to low and steam the balls gently for 10 to 15 minutes, until they are spongy and firm to the touch. Remove the foil package from the steamer and transfer the fish balls to a plate to cool.

Pack the fish balls in a rigid plastic container, together with the lemon wedges, if you are using them, and put the salad leaves in a plastic bag. Transport them to the picnic site inside a cool box. Serve the fish balls on a bed of leaves.

Seafood and Tagliatelle Salad

Serves 8
Working time: about 45 minutes
Total time: about 1 hour

Calories **315**
Protein **26g**
Cholesterol **300mg**
Total fat **7g**
Saturated fat **1g**
Sodium **420mg**

1 kg	baby squid, cleaned and skinned, tentacles reserved	2 lb
2 tsp	white wine vinegar	2 tsp
12	peppercorns	12
2	bay leaves	2
1 tsp	salt	1 tsp
350 g	green tagliatelle	12 oz
250 g	peeled cooked prawns	8 oz
1	sweet red pepper, seeded, deribbed and cut into long julienne	1
8	large cooked prawns, peeled, heads and tails left on, for garnish	8
Lemon vinaigrette		
¼ tsp	salt	¼ tsp
2½ tbsp	fresh lemon juice	2½ tbsp
½	lemon, grated rind only	½
3 tbsp	virgin olive oil	3 tbsp
¼	garlic clove, very finely chopped	¼
¼ tsp	very finely chopped chili pepper (caution, page 63)	¼ tsp
2 tbsp	chopped parsley	2 tbsp

First make the vinaigrette. Put all the ingredients into a screw-top jar and shake the jar well to combine them. Refrigerate the vinaigrette until required.

Slice the squid pouches into rings, and cut the tentacles in half crosswise. Bring 1 litre (2 pints) of water to the boil in a saucepan with the vinegar, peppercorns, bay leaves and salt. Add the squid to the pan, and cook it in the boiling water for 2 minutes. Drain the squid well, and set it aside to cool; discard the bay leaves and peppercorns.

Add the tagliatelle to 3 litres (5 pints) of boiling water with 1 teaspoon of salt. Start testing the pasta after 10 minutes, and cook it until it is *al dente*. Drain the pasta and rinse it under cold running water, then drain it again. Place the squid, pasta, small prawns, red pepper strips and vinaigrette in a large bowl, and toss them until they are thoroughly combined.

Carry the tossed salad and the large prawns to a picnic in separate plastic containers inside a cool box. At the picnic, turn the salad on to a platter and serve garnished with the large prawns.

Chicken, Mango and Penne Salad

Serves 6
Working time: about 40 minutes
Total time: about 1 hour (includes cooling)

Calories **435**
Protein **30g**
Cholesterol **60mg**
Total fat **8g**
Saturated fat **5g**
Sodium **160mg**

4	skinned and boned chicken breasts, (about 500 g/1 lb)	4
2 tsp	low-sodium soy sauce or shoyu	2 tsp
350 g	penne (or other short, tubular pasta)	12 oz
250 g	mange-tout, stems and strings removed	8 oz
2	large mangoes	2
Coriander and coconut dressing		
17.5 cl	plain low-fat yogurt	6 fl oz
1 tbsp	chopped fresh coriander	1 tbsp
¼ tsp	salt	¼ tsp
	freshly ground black pepper	
3 tbsp	desiccated coconut	3 tbsp

In a bowl, mix together all the ingredients for the yogurt dressing. Set the dressing aside.

Put the chicken breasts in a saucepan, and pour in 60 cl (1 pint) of water and the soy sauce; slowly bring the liquid to a simmer. Partially cover the saucepan, and poach the chicken breasts gently until the flesh is firm and opaque all the way through when pierced with the tip of a sharp knife — 10 to 15 minutes. Remove the chicken breasts from the liquid with a slotted spoon, and set them aside to cool. When they are cold, carve them into slices.

While the chicken is cooling, bring 3½ litres (6 pints) of water to the boil in a large saucepan. Add 2 teaspoons of salt and the penne. Start testing the pasta after 10 minutes, and cook it until it is *al dente*. Drain the pasta, refresh it under cold running water, and drain it again thoroughly. Blanch the mange-tout in a saucepan of boiling water, then refresh them under cold running water and drain them well. Peel the mangoes, and cut the flesh into slices.

Toss the chicken, penne and mange-tout in the yogurt dressing, and pack the mixture in a rigid plastic container to take on the picnic. Put the mango slices in another rigid container. Transport both containers to the picnic site in a cool box, and combine their contents when serving.

Minted Potato and Turkey Salad

Serves 4
Working time: about 30 minutes
Total time: about 40 minutes

Calories **275**
Protein **21g**
Cholesterol **40mg**
Total fat **9g**
Saturated fat **2g**
Sodium **55mg**

500 g	small new potatoes, scrubbed and cut into 1 cm (½ inch) chunks	1 lb
2 tbsp	safflower oil	2 tbsp
2 tbsp	fresh lemon juice	2 tbsp
1 tbsp	white wine vinegar	1 tbsp
½	lemon, grated rind only	½
½ tsp	grainy mustard	½ tsp
1	garlic clove, crushed	1
⅛ tsp	salt	⅛ tsp
	freshly ground black pepper	
½ tsp	sugar	½ tsp
175 g	broccoli florets	6 oz
1	red-skinned dessert apple	1
300 g	cooked skinless turkey breast, cut into 1 cm (½ inch) cubes	10 oz
125 g	carrots, julienned	4 oz
3	spring onions, trimmed and sliced diagonally into 2.5 cm (1 inch) pieces	3
	mint sprigs, for garnish	

Cook the potatoes in a pan of simmering water until they are tender but not too soft — about 10 minutes.

Meanwhile, prepare the dressing. In a small bowl, whisk together the oil, 1 tablespoon of the lemon juice, the vinegar, lemon rind, mustard, garlic, salt, plenty of black pepper and the sugar.

Drain the potatoes thoroughly and put them in a large mixing bowl. While the potatoes are still hot, add the dressing and toss them well. Set the potatoes aside and leave them to cool.

Parboil the broccoli florets in a saucepan of boiling water for 1 to 2 minutes, then drain them, rinse them under cold running water and drain them again very thoroughly. Quarter and core the dessert apple, cut it into thin slices and toss the slices in the remaining tablespoon of lemon juice. Add the broccoli florets, apple slices, turkey cubes, carrot sticks and spring onions to the cooled potatoes. Toss all the ingredients together and transfer them to a container with a tight-fitting lid for carrying to the picnic site. Put the mint sprigs into a plastic bag, and take a small pair of scissors to the picnic as well.

At the picnic, transfer the salad to a serving bowl. Use the scissors to cut one or two mint sprigs into strips over the salad. Finally, garnish the salad with a few whole mint sprigs.

Sesame Chicken Breasts with Jellied Beetroot

Serves 8
Working time: about 30 minutes
Total time: about 4 hours and 15 minutes (includes setting)

Calories **245**
Protein **21g**
Cholesterol **50mg**
Total fat **9g**
Saturated fat **2g**
Sodium **205mg**

60 cl	dry white wine	1 pint
2 tsp	caster sugar	2 tsp
1 tbsp	powdered gelatine	1 tbsp
500 g	cooked beetroot, peeled, sliced and cut into 4 cm (1½ inch) long batons	1 lb
8	skinned and boned chicken breasts (about 125 g/4 oz each)	8
75 g	sesame seeds, toasted	2½ oz
10	green cardamom pods, seeds only, lightly crushed	10
2 tsp	ground cumin	2 tsp
1½ tsp	chili powder	1½ tsp
½ tsp	salt	½ tsp
	freshly ground black pepper	
1	egg white	1
8 tsp	soured cream, for garnish	8 tsp

Put the wine and sugar in a non-reactive saucepan, and bring the wine just to the boil. Pour it into a heat-proof bowl and sprinkle on the gelatine, whisking well until the gelatine has dissolved. Leave the gelatine solution to cool slightly, then stir in the beetroot. Turn the mixture into a 1 litre (1¾ pint) rigid plastic container with a tight-fitting lid. Refrigerate it for at least 3 hours, or overnight, until the jelly has set.

Preheat the oven to 180°C (350°F or Mark 4), and lightly grease a baking dish. Wipe the chicken breasts on paper towels. Mix together the sesame seeds, crushed cardamom seeds, cumin, chili powder, salt and some black pepper, and spread this mixture out on a plate. In a small bowl, lightly whisk the egg white. Dip each chicken breast into the egg white, then coat it in the sesame-seed mixture, pressing the seeds and spices on with the back of a spoon. Place the coated breasts, skinned side up, in the baking dish and bake them for about 25 minutes, until they are just cooked through. (The juices should run clear when a skewer is inserted into the thickest part of a breast.) Set the breasts aside and leave them to cool.

Pack the chicken breasts in a rigid container and spoon the soured cream into a small, lidded plastic pot. Put the lid on the jellied beetroot and transport all three containers to the picnic in a cool box.

At the picnic site, cut each chicken breast into slices. Serve the sliced chicken with the jellied beetroot, and garnish each portion of beetroot with a teaspoon of the soured cream.

EDITOR'S NOTE: *To toast sesame seeds, warm them in a heavy frying pan over medium-low heat until they are golden — about 3 minutes.*

Summer Lamb with Broad Bean and Nectarine Salad

Serves 8
Working time: about 35 minutes
Total time: about 14 hours (includes marinating)

Calories **250**
Protein **29g**
Cholesterol **65mg**
Total fat **12g**
Saturated fat **4g**
Sodium **130mg**

2 or 3	eyes of loin of lamb (about 850 g/ 1 ¾ lb), trimmed of fat and sinew	2 or 3
2 tsp	virgin olive oil	2 tsp
1 ½ tsp	pink peppercorns, rinsed, dried and crushed	1 ½ tsp
¼ tsp	salt	¼ tsp
1 tsp	ground cinnamon	1 tsp
1 tsp	ground cumin	1 tsp
½ tsp	ground mace	½ tsp
Broad bean and nectarine salad		
400 g	shelled fresh young broad beans, skinned, or frozen young broad beans, thawed and skinned	14 oz
2	nectarines	2
2 tsp	tarragon vinegar	2 tsp
1 tsp	clear honey	1 tsp
⅛ tsp	salt	⅛ tsp
8	fresh mint leaves, finely chopped	8
1 tbsp	finely chopped fresh tarragon	1 tbsp
1 tbsp	virgin olive oil	1 tbsp
4 tbsp	plain low-fat yogurt	4 tbsp
	pink peppercorns, washed and dried, for garnish	

Brush the pieces of lamb all over with the olive oil, rub them with the crushed peppercorns, and sprinkle them with the salt. Stir together the cinnamon, cumin and mace, and pat each piece of meat all over with the mixture. Put the lamb in the refrigerator and leave it to marinate, loosely covered, for about 12 hours, to allow the flavours to develop.

Remove the lamb from the refrigerator 30 minutes before you plan to cook it, and place it in a roasting pan. Preheat the oven to 230°C (450°F or Mark 8). Roast the lamb, on the top shelf of the oven, for 6 to 9 minutes for rare to medium meat; turn it over once during roasting. Remove the meat from the oven, cover it loosely with foil, and leave it to cool to room temperature. When it has cooled, pour off and reserve the roasting juices. Wrap the meat tightly in the foil, and chill it until required.

To make the salad, cook the broad beans in rapidly boiling water until they are just tender — 6 to 10 minutes. Drain them, and set them aside to cool. Slice each nectarine lengthwise into 16 wedge-shaped segments. Put the beans and the nectarine segments in separate lidded containers.

To make the dressing, put the vinegar in a small bowl. Stir in the honey and salt, then add the mint, tarragon, oil and yogurt, and the reserved roasting juices. Whisk the dressing until all the ingredients are thoroughly amalgamated. Stir the dressing into the beans, and put the lid on the container.

Pack the foil-wrapped meat and the containers of beans and sliced nectarines inside a cool box to take on a picnic. Combine the dressed beans and sliced nectarines at the picnic site, just before serving. If possible, slice the meat there too, on a board and using a sharp knife. Alternatively, the meat may be sliced beforehand, then reassembled into loins and wrapped tightly in foil. Take a small, sealed container of pink peppercorns with you, and garnish each serving with two or three of them.

Pork and Prune Loaf with Minted Onion Relish

Serves 6
Working time: about 45 minutes
Total time: about 8 hours and 45 minutes
(includes cooling and chilling)

Calories **325**		
Protein **38g**		
Cholesterol **80mg**		
Total fat **8g**		
Saturated fat **3g**		
Sodium **225mg**		

1	onion, finely chopped	1
90 g	fresh brown breadcrumbs	3 oz
125 g	ready-to-eat stoned prunes, chopped	4 oz
⅛ tsp	salt	⅛ tsp
¼ tsp	ground mixed spice	¼ tsp
	freshly ground black pepper	
1	egg white, lightly beaten	1
2	pork fillets (about 350 g/12 oz each), trimmed of fat	2
Minted onion relish		
1	dessert apple, peeled, cored and cut into pieces	1
4	onions, sliced	4
8 cl	white wine vinegar	3 fl oz
2 tbsp	light brown sugar	2 tbsp
3 tbsp	chopped mint	3 tbsp
	mint sprig, for garnish	

To make the stuffing for the pork loaf, combine the chopped onion, breadcrumbs and chopped prunes in a mixing bowl. Add the salt, mixed spice and some black pepper, then stir in the lightly beaten egg white.

Preheat the oven to 190°C (375°F or Mark 5). Place the trimmed pork fillets on a board and cut a 10 to 12 cm (4 to 5 inch) "tail" off the narrow end of each fillet. Using a long, sharp knife, slit each larger piece of meat lengthwise, leaving a hinge at one side so that the upper and lower halves remain attached. Slit the two tail pieces in the same way.

Open out one of the larger pieces of fillet and spread half of the stuffing over it. Open out the two fillet tails and arrange them on top of the stuffing, overlapping their narrow ends if necessary. Spread the remaining stuffing over the tails, then open out the last piece of fillet and lay it on top. Tie the layered meat with string at 2.5 cm (1 inch) intervals, then wrap it in a sheet of foil. Put the foil parcel in a baking dish and bake it for 1½ hours. Leave the meat in its foil to cool — 4 to 6 hours — then chill it for at least 2 hours, or overnight.

To make the relish, chop the apple and onions finely in a food processor. Transfer them to a non-reactive saucepan and add the vinegar. Cook the mixture over low heat, stirring frequently, until it is soft and thick — about 20 minutes. Add the sugar and cook until all the liquid has been absorbed — about 10 minutes. Stir in half of the chopped mint and cook for a further minute. Allow the relish to cool to room temperature, then stir in the remaining mint. Pack the relish in a container with a tight-fitting lid and put the mint sprig in a small plastic bag to take to the picnic.

Cut the chilled pork loaf into 12 slices; it can then be reassembled, wrapped in foil and carried to the picnic site in a rigid container, inside a cool box. Serve the slices with the relish, garnished with the mint sprig.

SUGGESTED ACCOMPANIMENT: *crisp lettuce leaves.*

Spiced Fillet of Beef

Serves 12
Working time: about 1 hour
Total time: about 7 hours and 30 minutes
(includes cooling and chilling)

Calories **290**
Protein **30g**
Cholesterol **65mg**
Total fat **14g**
Saturated fat **5g**
Sodium **240mg**

45 g	pine-nuts	1 ½ oz
2 tbsp	virgin olive oil	2 tbsp
1	large onion, finely chopped	1
3	garlic cloves, crushed	3
2 tsp	ground coriander	2 tsp
1 ½ tsp	ground cardamom	1 ½ tsp
1 tsp	ground cumin	1 tsp
3 tsp	paprika	3 tsp
1 ¼ tsp	salt	1 ¼ tsp
⅛ tsp	cayenne pepper	⅛ tsp
	freshly ground black pepper	
150 g	seedless raisins	5 oz
250 g	chestnut mushrooms, chopped	8 oz
1.5 kg	beef fillet in one piece, trimmed of fat	3 lb
2 tbsp	black peppercorns, coarsely crushed	2 tbsp
4 tbsp	finely chopped parsley	4 tbsp

Put the pine-nuts in a dry frying pan and cook them, over medium heat, shaking the pan frequently, for 30 seconds, or until they are lightly browned all over.

Heat 1 tablespoon of the oil in a large, heavy frying pan over medium heat. Add the onion and cook it until it is soft but not browned — about 5 minutes. Stir in the garlic, coriander, cardamom, cumin, 2 teaspoons of the paprika, ¾ teaspoon of the salt, the cayenne and plenty of freshly ground black pepper. Continue cooking for 2 minutes, then stir in the raisins and mushrooms. Cook the mixture, stirring frequently, for a further 10 to 15 minutes, until the raisins are plump. Remove the pan from the heat, stir in the pine-nuts and allow the stuffing to cool for about 30 minutes.

Preheat the oven to 220°C (425°F or Mark 7). Make an incision lengthwise through the centre of the fillet by inserting a long, thin-bladed carving knife into the meat from the middle of one end, and pressing it in as far as possible. Withdraw the knife and insert a well-scrubbed sharpening steel into the slit. Gently rotate the steel, and work it up and down and from side to side until you have created a hole 2.5 to 5 cm (1 to 2 inches) wide. To ensure that the hole is uniform down the length of the fillet, it may be necessary to repeat the process from the other end.

With your fingers, carefully push the cooled stuffing into the fillet until the hole is completely and compactly filled. Tie the stuffed fillet with string at 2.5 cm (1 inch) intervals. Season the meat with the remaining salt and coat it evenly with the crushed peppercorns.

Heat the remaining tablespoon of oil in a large, heavy roasting pan over medium heat. Lightly brown the fillet all over in the hot oil, then transfer the roasting pan to the oven. Cook the fillet for 30 minutes for medium-rare meat, basting it every 10 minutes with the pan juices. For well-done meat, cook the fillet for a further 10 minutes. Allow the fillet to cool at room temperature for 1 hour, then cover it loosely with foil and chill it for at least 4 hours, or overnight.

Before packing the fillet to go on a picnic, remove the string. Coat the meat evenly with the chopped parsley and sprinkle it lightly with the remaining teaspoon of paprika. Wrap the meat in foil and pack it into a long, rigid container. Transport the container to the picnic inside a cool box.

At the picnic, set the fillet on a board and use a sharp carving knife to slice the meat.

Stuffed Pork Fillet with Peppered Pear Salad

Serves 4
Working time: about 1 hour and 20 minutes
Total time: about 9 hours (includes cooling and chilling)

Calories **315**
Protein **28g**
Cholesterol **60mg**
Total fat **12g**
Saturated fat **3g**
Sodium **280mg**

100 g	dried pears	3 ½ oz
1	pork fillet (about 350 g/12 oz), trimmed of fat and connective tissue	1
¼ tsp	salt	¼ tsp
⅛ tsp	freshly ground black pepper	⅛ tsp
⅛ tsp	ground allspice	⅛ tsp
2 tsp	grainy mustard	2 tsp
½ tsp	ground cinnamon	½ tsp
¼ tsp	green peppercorns, rinsed and dried	¼ tsp
1 tbsp	finely chopped fresh tarragon, or 1 tsp dried tarragon	1 tbsp
½ tsp	virgin olive oil	½ tsp
2 tsp	clear honey	2 tsp
1 tsp	dry mustard	1 tsp
Peppered pear salad		
1 tbsp	clear honey	1 tbsp
3 ½ tsp	fresh lemon juice	3 ½ tsp
7.5 cm	piece cinnamon stick	3 inch
1 tsp	green peppercorns, rinsed and dried	1 tsp
4	allspice berries	4
2	fresh pears	2
1 ½ tbsp	virgin olive oil	1 ½ tbsp
⅛ tsp	salt	⅛ tsp
1	soft lettuce heart, leaves washed and dried	1
60 g	watercress leaves, washed and dried	2 oz
8	nasturtium flowers, for garnish	8

Soak the dried pears in 30 cl (½ pint) of hot water until they are soft — about 20 minutes. Meanwhile, use a long, sharp knife to cut a lengthwise slit in the pork fillet to a depth of about 4 cm (1½ inches). Lift the upper section and deepen the cut to within about 8 mm (⅓ inch) of the opposite side. Open out the meat and place it on a sheet of plastic film. Cover the fillet with a second sheet of plastic film. Using the flat, wide side of a wooden mallet, beat out the fillet as thinly as possible. Sprinkle the flattened surface with the salt, pepper and allspice, and set the meat aside.

Remove the dried pears from their soaking liquid; reserve the liquid. Pat the pears dry with paper towels and dice them finely. Mix the diced pears with the grainy mustard, cinnamon, green peppercorns and tarragon, and spread the mixture along the centre of the flattened fillet. Close up the fillet tightly and tie it with string at 2.5 cm (1 inch) intervals.

Preheat the oven to 190°C (375°F or Mark 5). Brush a heavy, non-stick frying pan with the olive oil and brown the stuffed fillet lightly on all sides over high heat. Brush the meat all over with the honey, sprinkle it with the dry mustard, and wrap it in a double thickness of foil. Roast it in the oven for 40 minutes, then allow it

to cool to room temperature in the foil — 4 to 6 hours. Tighten the foil round the meat and chill the meat for at least 2 hours, or until required.

To prepare the salad, put the reserved pear-soaking water in a non-reactive saucepan and add the honey, 3 teaspoons of the lemon juice, the cinnamon stick, peppercorns and allspice berries. Bring the mixture to the boil, then reduce the heat and simmer it for 5 minutes. Meanwhile, peel and quarter the fresh pears; do not core them yet or they will break up during cooking. Add the pears to the pan, cover them and simmer them very gently until they are tender — 10 to 20 minutes, depending on the ripeness of the pears. Carefully remove the pears with a slotted spoon and set them aside. Strain the poaching liquid, return it to the saucepan and boil it rapidly until only 1½ to 2 tablespoons remain. Allow the liquid to cool, then transfer it to a bottle with a tight-fitting stopper. Add the olive oil, the remaining ½ teaspoon of lemon juice and the salt, and shake the bottle well.

To pack the salad for carrying to the picnic site, carefully core the pears and put them in a rigid container. Pour a little of the dressing over them — leave the remaining dressing in its bottle. Place the lettuce leaves on top of the pears, followed by the watercress leaves. Cover the container. Pack the nasturtium flowers for garnish in a separate container.

To prepare the meat for the picnic, cut the stuffed fillet into 12 slices, then reassemble the roll and rewrap it tightly in foil. Pack it in a rigid container and carry it to the picnic inside a cool box.

Arrange three slices of stuffed fillet on each individual plate. Accompany each serving with two pear quarters and a portion of the dressed green salad, and garnish it with two nasturtium flowers. Serve the remaining dressing separately.

Marinated Steak Salad with Vegetable Batons

Serves 6
Working time: about 45 minutes
Total time: about 6 hours (includes marinating)

Calories **290**
Protein **34g**
Cholesterol **80mg**
Total fat **13g**
Saturated fat **5g**
Sodium **110mg**

1 tbsp	safflower oil	1 tbsp
800 g	beef fillet in one piece, trimmed of fat	1 lb 10 oz
1	1 cm (½ inch) piece fresh ginger root, peeled and finely chopped	1
2	garlic cloves, crushed	2
5 tbsp	rice wine or sherry	5 tbsp
3 tbsp	low-sodium soy sauce or shoyu	3 tbsp
	freshly ground black pepper	
250 g	carrots	8 oz
½	cucumber	½
2	sticks celery	2
250 g	canned bamboo shoots	8 oz

Preheat the oven to 220°C (425°F or Mark 7).
Pour the oil into a large, shallow fireproof casserole or roasting pan set over high heat. When the oil is hot, sear the meat until it is well browned on all sides — 3 to 5 minutes. Place the casserole in the oven and cook the fillet for 15 minutes for rare meat, or for up to 30 minutes for medium meat. Remove the fillet from the oven and let it rest and cool for 30 minutes.

In a shallow, rigid container, mix together the ginger, garlic, rice wine, soy sauce and a grinding of black pepper, to make a marinade. Slice the meat as thinly as possible across the grain, and place the slices in the marinade. Cover the container with a lid or with foil and leave the meat to marinate in the refrigerator for at least 4 hours, or overnight, turning it from time to time.

On the day of the picnic, cut the carrots, cucumber, celery and bamboo shoots into 4 to 5 cm (1½ to 2 inch) batons. Mix the prepared vegetables together and put them in a covered container or a plastic bag. Pack the containers of vegetables and marinating meat into a cool box to take to the picnic site.

To serve, transfer the vegetables to individual plates. Lift the slices of fillet from the marinade and lay them over the salad.

Pasta, Corn and Leek Salad

Serves 6 as a side dish
Working time: about 20 minutes
Total time: about 30 minutes

Calories **260**
Protein **10g**
Cholesterol **0mg**
Total fat **4g**
Saturated fat **1g**
Sodium **110mg**

90 g	pasta spirals	3 oz
4	ears of sweetcorn, husked, or 500 g (1 lb) frozen sweetcorn kernels	4
250 g	white parts of leek, cut into thin rounds	8 oz
2	beef tomatoes, cut into thin wedges	2
2	black olives, stoned and diced	2
Mustard-basil dressing		
1 tbsp	fresh lemon juice	1 tbsp
1 tsp	Dijon mustard	1 tsp
100 g	low-fat fromage frais	3½ oz
¼ tsp	salt	¼ tsp
	freshly ground black pepper	
4 tbsp	chopped fresh basil	4 tbsp

Cook the pasta spirals in 1 litre (1¾ pints) of boiling water with 1 teaspoon of salt. Start testing the pasta after 10 minutes and continue cooking it until it is *al dente*. Refresh the pasta under cold running water, then drain it thoroughly.

If you are using fresh sweetcorn, cook it in a saucepan of boiling water for 6 to 10 minutes, until it is just tender. Refresh the ears under cold running water and drain them well. Using a sharp knife, cut off the corn kernels. If you are using frozen sweetcorn, blanch it in boiling water and drain it thoroughly.

Parboil the leeks for 2 to 3 minutes, until they are just tender but still have bite. Refresh them under cold running water and drain them well.

For the dressing, blend the lemon juice and mustard into the *fromage frais*, then stir in the salt, some pepper and the chopped basil. Tip the pasta, sweetcorn and leeks into a lidded plastic container, pour on the dressing and toss the salad gently to combine the ingredients. Chill the salad until required.

Put the container of dressed salad in a cool box to transport it to the picnic site. Pack the tomato wedges and olive dice in separate small containers and carry these in the cool box too. To serve, arrange the tomato wedges round the edge of a serving bowl, pile the salad in the centre and sprinkle over the olive dice.

Artichoke and Asparagus Salad

Serves 8 as a side dish
Working time: about 45 minutes
Total time: about 1 hour

Calories **55**
Protein **3g**
Cholesterol **trace**
Total fat **3g**
Saturated fat **1g**
Sodium **105mg**

1	lemon, cut in half	1
4	globe artichokes	4
500 g	fine asparagus, trimmed	1 lb
1	red lollo lettuce, leaves separated, washed and dried, torn into large pieces	1
4	little gem lettuces, cut into 2.5 by 1 cm (1 by ½ inch) chunks, washed and dried	4
Orange-hazelnut vinaigrette		
2 tbsp	fresh orange juice	2 tbsp
1 ½ tbsp	hazelnut oil	1 ½ tbsp
1 tsp	grainy mustard	1 tsp
½	orange, grated rind only	½
½ tsp	salt	½ tsp
	freshly ground black pepper	

Fill a large, non-reactive saucepan with water. Squeeze the juice from one lemon half into the pan, then add the lemon half itself.

Remove two or three outer layers of leaves from one of the artichokes to expose the tender yellow-green inner leaves. Using a stainless steel knife, slice through the artichoke about 4 cm (1½ inches) above the rounded base and discard the top. Cut off the stem flush with the rounded end of the artichoke and rub the base with the cut surface of the second lemon half. Pare off the dark green bases of the leaves, then trim away the light green parts from the upper half of the artichoke, moistening the cut surfaces with the lemon half as you work. With a teaspoon, scrape out and discard the hairy choke from the centre of the vegetable. Drop the artichoke heart which remains into the pan of acidulated water to preserve its colour. Prepare the remaining artichokes in the same way.

Bring the pan of artichoke hearts to the boil and cook them gently until they can be pierced easily with the tip of a sharp knife — 12 to 15 minutes. Refresh the artichoke hearts under cold running water, then cut each one into 16 pieces.

While the artichokes are cooking, cook the asparagus in a large, shallow pan of boiling water for 2 to 3 minutes, until tender. Refresh it under cold running water and drain it thoroughly. Cut the spears diagonally into 2.5 cm (1 inch) pieces, keeping the tips intact.

Put the red lollo and little gem lettuce, the artichokes and the asparagus in a lidded plastic container in the refrigerator until required. Put all the ingredients for the orange-hazelnut vinaigrette into a screw-topped jar and shake them together well. Store the jar of vinaigrette in the refrigerator too.

When you are ready to leave for the picnic, pack the container of salad and the jar of vinaigrette inside a cool box. At the picnic site, tip the salad into a serving bowl. Pour on the dressing and toss the salad gently just before serving it.

Pear, Fennel and Watercress Salad

Serves 4
Working (and total) time: about 40 minutes

Calories **195**
Protein **6g**
Cholesterol **10mg**
Total fat **11g**
Saturated fat **3g**
Sodium **305mg**

75 g	light rye or other wholegrain bread, crusts removed, cut into 1 cm (½ inch) cubes	2½ oz
2	large ripe dessert pears, cored, diced and placed in acidulated water	2
60 g	Edam cheese, cut into bâtonnets	2 oz
125 g	bulb fennel, trimmed and thinly sliced	4 oz
90 g	watercress, washed and dried, divided into sprigs	3 oz
Lemon dressing		
¼	thin-skinned lemon, roughly chopped	¼
½ tsp	grainy mustard	½ tsp
1 tbsp	clear honey	1 tbsp
2 tbsp	virgin olive oil	2 tbsp

Preheat the oven to 180°C (350°F or Mark 4). Arrange the bread cubes on a baking sheet and toast them in the oven until they are golden-brown and crisp — about 20 minutes. Leave the croûtons to cool.

To prepare the dressing, put the chopped lemon, the mustard, honey and oil in a food processor or blender. Add 2 tablespoons of water and process the ingredients until they form a creamy purée.

Drain the diced pears and place them in a large mixing bowl, together with the cheese and fennel. Add the lemon dressing and toss the ingredients thoroughly. Transfer the dressed ingredients to a large container with a tight-fitting lid. Pack the croûtons and the watercress sprigs in separate containers.

At the picnic site, add the watercress and croûtons to the dressed salad, and toss all the ingredients together. Serve the salad at once.

EDITOR'S NOTE: *The pears, cheese and fennel can be prepared and dressed up to 12 hours in advance and stored in the refrigerator.*

Mushroom Ratatouille Salad

Serves 8 as a side dish
Working time: about 30 minutes
Total time: about 2 hours and 15 minutes (includes cooling)

Calories **75**
Protein **3g**
Cholesterol **0mg**
Total fat **4g**
Saturated fat **1g**
Sodium **110mg**

750 g	aubergines, cut into 2 cm (¾ inch) pieces	1 ½ lb
1 ½ tsp	salt	1 ½ tsp
2 tbsp	virgin olive oil	2 tbsp
2	large onions, cut into fine rings	2
4	garlic cloves, crushed	4
4 tbsp	white wine	4 tbsp
250 g	chestnut mushrooms, sliced	8 oz
3 tbsp	chopped fresh oregano	3 tbsp
2	sweet yellow peppers, blanched and cut into 6 cm (2 ½ inch) long strips	2
500 g	Italian plum tomatoes, skinned, seeded (page 138) and roughly chopped into 1 cm (½ inch) pieces	1 lb
	freshly ground black pepper	
3 tbsp	chopped parsley	3 tbsp

In a bowl, toss the aubergine pieces with 1 teaspoon of the salt. Place the aubergine in a colander and weight it down with a plate small enough to rest on top of the pieces. Let the aubergine drain for 30 minutes, to eliminate its natural bitterness. Rinse the aubergine under cold running water to rid it of the salt, and drain it well. Pat the pieces dry on paper towels.

Heat the oil in a large saucepan. Add the onion and cook it over low heat for about 8 minutes, stirring occasionally, until it is soft but not brown. Mix in the garlic and cook for a further minute. Add the aubergine pieces to the saucepan, pour in the wine and cook them, uncovered, for 15 minutes. Stir in the mushroom slices and the oregano, cover the pan, and cook the mixture for 5 minutes more.

Remove the lid from the pan and add the yellow pepper strips, the tomatoes, the remaining salt and some freshly ground black pepper. Heat the contents through for 2 minutes, stir in the parsley, and set the pan aside for the salad to cool.

Transfer the salad to a rigid plastic container to transport to the picnic site.

Salad of Red Leaves, Beans and Roots

Serves 12 as a side dish
Working time: about 40 minutes
Total time: about 3 hours

Calories **100**
Protein **4g**
Cholesterol **5mg**
Total fat **6g**
Saturated fat **2g**
Sodium **75mg**

175 g	dried red kidney beans, picked over	6 oz
250 g	red cabbage, finely shredded	8 oz
1	small red onion, quartered and finely sliced	1
300 g	raw beetroot, peeled and grated	10 oz
1	head radicchio, leaves washed and dried	1
30 g	blue Stilton cheese, crumbled	1 oz
1 tsp	poppy seeds	1 tsp

Walnut vinaigrette

1 tsp	grainy French mustard	1 tsp
⅛ tsp	Tabasco sauce	⅛ tsp
⅛ tsp	salt	⅛ tsp
⅛ tsp	freshly ground black pepper	⅛ tsp
2 tbsp	red wine vinegar	2 tbsp
4 tbsp	walnut oil	4 tbsp

Rinse the kidney beans under cold running water, then put them into a large saucepan with enough cold water to cover them by about 7.5 cm (3 inches). Discard any beans that float to the surface. Cover the saucepan, leaving the lid ajar, and slowly bring the liquid to the boil. Boil the beans for two minutes, then turn off the heat and soak the beans, covered, for at least an hour. (Alternatively, soak the beans overnight in cold water.)

Rinse the beans and place them in a clean saucepan with enough cold water to cover them by about 7.5 cm (3 inches). Bring them to the boil and boil them for 10 minutes, then rinse them and discard the water. Wash out the pan, replace the beans and cover them again by about 7.5 cm (3 inches) of fresh water, then simmer them until tender — about 1 hour. Check the water level from time to time and add more hot water if necessary. When they are cooked, drain and rinse the beans, and dry them thoroughly.

Put the shredded cabbage in a large bowl with the kidney beans, onion and beetroot. Mix them together well. In a small bowl, whisk together all the ingredients for the walnut vinaigrette. Pour the dressing over the salad and toss it well.

Transfer the salad to a rigid plastic container and chill it in the refrigerator until you are ready to leave for the picnic. Place the radicchio leaves in a plastic bag, and the Stilton in a small sealed container, and chill these too. Fold the poppy seeds in a paper towel.

At the picnic, line a large salad bowl with the radicchio leaves. Pile the salad in the centre and sprinkle the Stilton and poppy seeds over the top.

EDITOR'S NOTE: *This salad may also be made with canned red kidney beans; rinse the beans thoroughly before use.*

Green and White Rice Salad

Serves 12 as a side dish
Working time: about 25 minutes
Total time: about 45 minutes

Calories **105**
Protein **2g**
Cholesterol **0mg**
Total fat **5g**
Saturated fat **1g**
Sodium **123mg**

45 cl	unsalted vegetable stock (recipe, page 139)	¾ pint
175 g	long-grain rice	6 oz
400 g	fresh peas, shelled, or 125 g (4 oz) frozen peas, thawed	14 oz
½	cucumber, cut into 5 mm (¼ inch) dice	½
125 g	courgettes, trimmed and julienned	4 oz
6	spring onions, trimmed and thinly sliced diagonally	6
1 tbsp	finely cut chives	1 tbsp
3 tbsp	chopped parsley	3 tbsp
1	crisp round lettuce, leaves washed and dried	1

Tarragon vinaigrette

½ tsp	French mustard	½ tsp
⅛ tsp	salt	⅛ tsp
⅛ tsp	freshly ground black pepper	⅛ tsp
2 tbsp	tarragon vinegar	2 tbsp
4 tbsp	walnut or virgin olive oil	4 tbsp

Bring the stock to the boil in a small pan and add the rice. Reduce the heat to a simmer and cook the rice, covered, until it is just tender and all the stock is absorbed — 15 to 20 minutes. Set aside to cool.

Blanch the fresh peas in a saucepan of boiling water for about 30 seconds; if you are using frozen peas, add them to boiling water and just bring the water back to the boil. Drain the peas, refresh them under cold running water and drain them again.

Transfer the cooled rice to a large bowl, add the blanched peas, the cucumber and courgettes, and mix the ingredients together well. Stir in the spring onion slices, the chives and the parsley.

To make the dressing, whisk the mustard, salt, black pepper, vinegar and oil together in a small bowl. Pour the dressing over the salad, and toss it thoroughly. Place the dressed salad in a rigid plastic container to take to the picnic, and chill it in the refrigerator until you are ready to leave. Place the lettuce leaves in a plastic bag and chill them too.

At the picnic site, line a large serving bowl with the lettuce leaves and pile the salad in the centre.

Asparagus and Walnut Frittata

A FRITTATA IS AN OPEN ITALIAN OMELETTE WHICH MAY BE MADE WITH ALMOST ANY VEGETABLE OR HERB FILLING. UNLIKE A FRENCH OMELETTE, WHICH HAS A MOIST, CREAMY FILLING AND IS USUALLY FOLDED OVER FOR SERVING, A FRITTATA IS COOKED UNTIL FIRM AND SET. THE COMBINATION OF WHOLE EGGS AND EGG WHITES USED HERE PRODUCES A LIGHT RESULT AND A FAT AND CHOLESTEROL COUNT CONSIDERABLY LOWER THAN A FRITTATA BASED ON WHOLE EGGS.

Serves 6
Working and (total time): about 30 minutes

Calories **150**
Protein **10g**
Cholesterol **120mg**
Total fat **10g**
Saturated fat **3g**
Sodium **205mg**

300 g	asparagus, trimmed	10 oz
3	eggs	3
3	egg whites	3
45 g	Parmesan cheese, freshly grated	1½ oz
45 g	shelled walnuts, toasted and chopped	1½ oz
60 g	day-old wholemeal bread, crusts removed, soaked for 10 minutes in 4 tbsp skimmed milk	2 oz
1 tbsp	chopped fresh basil	1 tbsp
⅛ tsp	salt	⅛ tsp
	freshly ground black pepper	
1 tsp	virgin olive or safflower oil	1 tsp

Bring a large, shallow pan of water to the boil. Cook the asparagus in the boiling water for about 2 minutes, then drain it, refresh it under cold running water, and drain it again well. Cut the asparagus into 5 cm (2 inch) pieces and set them aside.

Whisk the whole eggs and egg whites with the Parmesan and the chopped walnuts. Add the soaked bread, the basil and the asparagus pieces to the egg mixture, and season it with the salt and some black pepper. Mix the ingredients well.

Heat the oil in a non-stick frying pan over medium heat and pour in the egg mixture; distribute the asparagus pieces evenly in the frying pan and flatten the mixture with the back of a wooden spoon. Cook the frittata over medium heat for 5 to 8 minutes, until the underside is firm. Invert the frittata on to a large plate, then slide it back into the frying pan and cook the second side until it, too, is firm and golden-brown — another 5 to 8 minutes. Slide the frittata back on to the plate and leave it to cool.

When you are ready to go to the picnic, wrap the frittata in greaseproof paper and pack it in a rigid container. Serve the frittata cut into wedges.

SUGGESTED ACCOMPANIMENT: *a salad of mixed lettuce leaves dressed with a light vinaigrette.*

EDITOR'S NOTE: *To toast walnuts, spread them out on a baking sheet and place them in a 180°C (350°F or Mark 4) oven for 5 minutes, stirring them from time to time. On other occasions, the frittata may also be served hot.*

Chinese Chicken Pancakes

Makes 12 pancakes
Working (and total) time: about 1 hour and 45 minutes

Per pancake:
Calories **125**
Protein **9g**
Cholesterol **30mg**
Total fat **3g**
Saturated fat **trace**
Sodium **35mg**

175 g	plain flour	6 oz
1 tbsp	sesame oil	1 tbsp
300 g	skinless chicken breast fillets	10 oz
2	shallots, one sliced, the other quartered, sliced lengthwise and separated into slivers	2
¼ tsp	five-spice powder	¼ tsp
	white pepper	
1 tsp	safflower oil	1 tsp
1	large garlic clove, very finely chopped	1
1	large carrot, halved crosswise and julienned	1
2.5 cm	piece fresh ginger root, finely chopped	1 inch
1 tbsp	light brown sugar	1 tbsp
2 tsp	low-sodium soy sauce or shoyu	2 tsp
1 tbsp	dry sherry	1 tbsp
1 tbsp	malt vinegar	1 tbsp
1 tbsp	tomato paste	1 tbsp
15 cl	unsweetened pineapple juice	¼ pint
2 tsp	cornflour	2 tsp
125 g	fresh beansprouts	4 oz
4	spring onions, halved lengthwise and shredded into fine slivers	4
1	sweet red pepper, seeded, deribbed and cut into thin strips	1
6	canned water chestnuts, sliced	6
12	long chives	12

Place the flour in a bowl, add 17.5 cl (6 fl oz) of boiling water and mix well with a wooden spoon to form a dough. Leave the dough to cool for 2 minutes, then knead it on a lightly floured surface until it is smooth. Form the dough into a roll or oblong and cut it into 12 equal pieces. Shape each piece into a ball. Using a floured rolling pin, roll out each ball on a well floured surface into a 15 cm (6 inch) round: flatten the ball with the rolling pin, rotating the dough to keep its circular shape, then roll it out, turning it and pulling it into shape as necessary. Brush off the excess flour from the pancakes, then lightly brush one side of each pancake with a little of the sesame oil and sandwich them together in pairs, oiled side out.

In a non-stick frying pan, cook one pair of pancakes over medium heat for 1½ to 2 minutes on each side, flattening them with a spatula as they cook. Remove them from the pan and gently pull the two pancakes apart, then lay them on a plate, oiled side up. Cook the remaining pairs of pancakes in the same way, separating them when they are cooked and stacking them on the plate. Leave the pancakes to cool, then cover them and chill them until required.

Put the chicken breasts in a small pan with ¼ litre (8 fl oz) of cold water, the sliced shallot, the five-spice powder and some white pepper. Cover the pan and bring the liquid to the boil, then reduce the heat and simmer the chicken gently for 15 minutes. Remove the pan from the heat, turn the chicken pieces over, then leave them to cool in their cooking liquid. Remove the cooled chicken from the pan and cut it into long, thin strips; strain and reserve 15 cl (¼ pint) of the cooking liquid. Cover the chicken and chill it until required.

To prepare the sauce, heat the safflower oil in a non-stick frying pan over medium heat. Add the garlic, shallot slivers, carrot and ginger, and fry them gently for 3 minutes. In a bowl, mix together the sugar, soy sauce, sherry, vinegar, tomato paste and pineapple juice, and add the mixture to the frying pan. Blend the cornflour to a smooth paste with 3 tablespoons of the reserved chicken-cooking liquid, and add the remaining reserved liquid to the pan. Bring the contents of the pan to the boil over medium heat, stir in the cornflour mixture, and simmer for 2 minutes, stirring constantly, until the sauce thickens and clears. Pour the sauce into a bowl and set it aside to cool.

Meanwhile, put the bean sprouts in a heatproof bowl, pour on sufficient boiling water to cover them, and let them soften for 15 seconds. Drain the bean sprouts and refresh them under cold running water, then drain them again thoroughly

Lay out the pancakes, oiled side up, on the work surface. Spread the centre of each one with a little of the sauce. Place a bundle of bean sprouts, chicken strips, spring onion slivers, red pepper strips and water chestnut slices on the sauced area of each pancake, allowing the strips of filling to overhang one edge of the pancake a little. Fold up the opposite section of each pancake over the strips, then fold over the two side sections to enclose the filling. Tie each filled pancake with a long chive to hold it together.

Wrap the pancakes individually in foil or plastic film and arrange them in a rigid container. Pack the remaining sauce in a separate small container to serve with the pancakes as a dipping sauce. Take the pancakes and sauce to the picnic in a cool box.

EDITOR'S NOTE: *For best results, cook the pancakes, chicken and sauce a day in advance, then assemble and wrap the pancakes on the day of the picnic.*

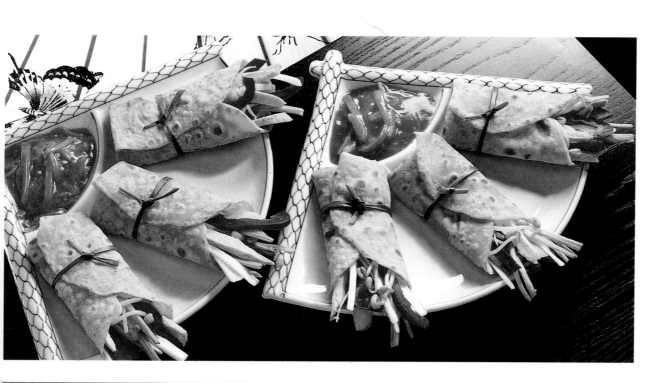

Baked Vegetable Samosas

UNLIKE TRADITIONAL SAMOSAS, WHICH ARE DEEP-FRIED IN OIL,
THESE HEALTHIER ALTERNATIVES ARE OVEN-BAKED. TO
FURTHER REDUCE THE FAT AND CALORIES, THE FILLING IS
ENCASED BY A SPECIAL LIGHT PASTRY WHICH HAS ONLY HALF
THE USUAL FAT CONTENT OF SHORTCRUST.

Makes 8 samosas
Working time: about 1 hour
Total time: about 1 hour and 25 minutes

Per samosa:
Calories **170**
Protein **5g**
Cholesterol **30mg**
Total fat **7g**
Saturated fat **2g**
Sodium **70mg**

1	potato (about 100 g/3½ oz), peeled and quartered	1
1	small carrot, quartered lengthwise	1
1 tsp	safflower oil	1 tsp
2 tsp	fresh lemon juice	2 tsp
1	leek (about 90g/3oz), trimmed, washed thoroughly to remove all grit and finely shredded	1
45 g	frozen peas	1½ oz
1	fresh hot green chili pepper, seeded and finely chopped (caution, page 63)	1
¾ tsp	cumin seeds	¾ tsp
½ tsp	ground turmeric	½ tsp
¾ tsp	ground coriander	¾ tsp
1	small egg, beaten, for glazing	1
1 tbsp	poppy seeds	1 tbsp
Shortcrust pastry		
140 g	plain flour	4½ oz
45 g	brown flour	1½ oz
45 g	polyunsaturated margarine	1½ oz
3½ tbsp	skimmed milk	3½ tbsp

Bring a saucepan of water to the boil. Add the potato and carrot to the pan, reduce the heat and simmer them for 10 minutes. Drain the vegetables, return them to the pan and shake them over low heat for a few seconds, to dry them off. Allow them to cool a little, then chop them and set them aside.

Put the oil, lemon juice, leek, peas, chili pepper, cumin seeds, turmeric and coriander in a small, heavy-bottomed saucepan. Add 1 tablespoon of water to the pan and cook the mixture gently for 3 minutes, stirring it frequently. Stir in the potato and carrot and turn the vegetables on to a plate to cool.

Meanwhile, prepare the pastry. Put the plain flour and brown flour in a mixing bowl and rub in the margarine with your fingertips until the mixture resembles fine breadcrumbs. Add the milk and mix it in, using a round-bladed knife, to form a firm dough. Gather the dough into a ball and knead it on a lightly floured surface until it is smooth. Divide the dough into four equal portions. Form each portion into a ball, then roll out each ball into an 18 cm (7 inch) round. Use a small plate to trim the rounds neatly to size, then cut each round in half.

Preheat the oven to 190°C (375°F or Mark 5). Lightly grease a baking sheet. Divide the vegetable mixture evenly among the semicircles of dough, mounding it on one half only and leaving a narrow border free of filling. Lightly dampen the edges of each semicircle with water, then fold the unfilled section of dough over the filling and press the edges together firmly to form neat triangular parcels. Decorate each rounded edge by gently pressing in the tip of a pointed knife.

Brush the samosas lightly with the beaten egg and sprinkle poppy seeds in two parallel lines across each one. Arrange the samosas on the baking sheet and bake them until they are golden-brown — 20 to 25 minutes. Cool them on a wire rack.

Pack the cold samosas in a covered rigid container to carry them to the picnic site.

SUGGESTED ACCOMPANIMENT: *spring onions; hot lime pickle.*

EDITOR'S NOTE: *If preferred, chopped onion may be substituted for the leek.*

Rump Steak Pasties

Serves 4
Working time: about 50 minutes
Total time: about 2 hours and 50 minutes
(includes cooling)

Calories **365**
Protein **15g**
Cholesterol **20mg**
Total fat **16g**
Saturated fat **4g**
Sodium **230mg**

1 tsp	virgin olive oil	1 tsp
125 g	potatoes, peeled and cut into 5 mm (¼ inch) dice	4 oz
90 g	carrots, cut into 5 mm (¼ inch) dice	3 oz
90 g	swede, peeled and cut into 5 mm (¼ inch) dice	3 oz
1	onion, finely chopped	1
125 g	lean rump steak, trimmed of fat and connective tissue and cut into 1 cm (½ inch) dice	4 oz
1 tbsp	chopped fresh oregano, or 1 tsp dried oregano	1 tbsp
3 tbsp	unsalted veal stock (recipe, page 139) or water	3 tbsp
⅛ tsp	salt	⅛ tsp
	freshly ground black pepper	
1	egg white, beaten	1
Shortcrust pastry		
175 g	plain flour	6 oz
⅛ tsp	salt	⅛ tsp
60 g	polyunsaturated margarine	2 oz

Heat the olive oil in a large, heavy frying pan over medium heat. Add the potatoes, carrots, swede and onion, and cook the vegetables gently until they just begin to soften — about 10 minutes. Remove the pan from the heat and allow the vegetables to cool.

Meanwhile, make the pastry. Sift the flour and salt into a mixing bowl and rub in the margarine with your fingertips until the mixture resembles fine breadcrumbs. Make a well in the centre and pour in 3 tablespoons of cold water. Using a round-bladed knife, mix the ingredients together to form a firm dough. Gather the dough into a ball and knead it on a lightly floured surface until it is smooth. Divide the dough into four equal pieces. Roll out each piece to a round, about 15 cm (6 inches) in diameter then, using a small plate as a guide, trim the edges of each pastry round neatly with a sharp knife. Lay the pastry rounds flat on the work surface.

Add the diced rump steak to the cooled vegetables, then stir in the oregano, veal stock, salt, and some freshly ground black pepper. Place a quarter of the steak and vegetable mixture in the centre of each pastry round, and brush the edges with a little of the beaten egg white. Taking one round at a time, carefully bring two opposite sides together until they meet in the centre of the filling; press the edges together firmly, to seal them. Shape the pastry neatly round the filling, and crimp the joined edges by pinching them between your thumb and forefinger.

Place the pasties on a baking sheet and refrigerate them for 20 minutes. Meanwhile, preheat the oven to 220°C (425°F or Mark 7).

Brush each pasty with the remaining beaten egg white, then bake them for 25 to 30 minutes, or until they are golden-brown. Cool the pasties on a wire rack for at least an hour before packing them in a rigid container to take to the picnic site.

SUGGESTED ACCOMPANIMENTS: *celery sticks; tomatoes.*

Individual
Smoked Trout Flans

Makes 6 flans
Working time: about 25 minutes
Total time: about 1 hour and 10 minutes

Per flan:
Calories **160**
Protein **22g**
Cholesterol **55mg**
Total fat **15g**
Saturated fat **3g**
Sodium **210mg**

175 g	wholemeal flour	6 oz
90 g	polyunsaturated margarine, chilled	3 oz
400 g	skinned smoked trout fillets	14 oz
15 cl	skimmed milk	¼ pint
3 tbsp	grated horseradish	3 tbsp
125 g	low-fat fromage frais	4 oz
125 g	cucumber, peeled, seeded and finely diced	4 oz
1 tbsp	chopped fresh tarragon	1 tbsp
1	lemon, finely grated rind and juice	1
	freshly ground black pepper	
2	egg whites	2
6	lemon wedges, for garnish	6
6	tarragon sprigs, for garnish	6

First make the pastry. Put the flour into a large bowl and rub the margarine into the flour with your fingertips, until the mixture resembles fine breadcrumbs. Using a round-bladed knife, stir in 3 tablespoons of cold water to make a firm dough. Turn the dough on to a lightly floured surface and knead it until it is smooth. Divide the dough into six portions. Roll out the portions thinly and use them to line six fluted flan cases about 10 cm (4 inches) in diameter and 2.5 cm (1 inch) deep. Prick the bases and sides of the cases with a fork and chill them for 20 minutes while you preheat the oven to 200°C (400°F or Mark 6).

Meanwhile, place the trout fillets in a large saucepan with the milk, and poach them gently until the fish is tender and flakes easily with a fork — about 15 minutes. Drain the fillets and discard the milk. Set the fish aside and leave it to cool.

Bake the chilled flan cases for 20 to 25 minutes, or until the pastry is crisp and lightly browned. Reduce the oven temperature to 170°C (325°F or Mark 3).

Flake the flesh of the smoked trout and put it in a mixing bowl. Add the horseradish, *fromage frais*, cucumber, chopped tarragon, the lemon rind and juice and some black pepper, and mix well.

In a separate bowl, whisk the egg whites lightly until they begin to form soft peaks. Using a metal tablespoon, fold the whites into the fish mixture. Fill the pastry cases with the filling and bake the flans until they are set in the centre — about 15 minutes. Allow the flans to cool completely, still in their tins, then refrigerate them until required.

When you are ready to go to the picnic, wrap the flans — still in their tins — in several thicknesses of greaseproof paper. Pack them into a rigid container and place this in a cool box. Put the lemon wedges and tarragon sprigs in small plastic bags, and add them to the cool box. At the picnic, remove the flans from their tins and serve each one garnished with a lemon wedge and a sprig of tarragon.

Courgette and Camembert Quiche

Serves 8
Working time: about 30 minutes
Total time: about 1 hour and 35 minutes

Calories **250**
Protein **8g**
Cholesterol **70mg**
Total fat **13g**
Saturated fat **3g**
Sodium **3mg**

600 g	courgettes, sliced	1¼ lb
1 tsp	polyunsaturated margarine	1 tsp
1	onion, finely chopped	1
1½ tbsp	chopped fresh basil, or 1½ tsp dried basil	1½ tbsp
140 g	firm Camembert, rind removed, cut into small pieces	4½ oz
30 cl	skimmed milk	½ pint
2	eggs, beaten	2
⅛ tsp	salt	⅛ tsp
	freshly ground black pepper	
Shortcrust pastry		
200 g	plain flour	7 oz
⅛ tsp	salt	⅛ tsp
90 g	polyunsaturated margarine, chilled	3 oz

Preheat the oven to 180°C (350°F or Mark 4). Place the sliced courgettes in a lightly oiled baking dish, cover them with foil and bake them until they are tender — about 20 minutes.

Meanwhile, sift the flour and salt for the pastry into a large bowl, then rub in the chilled margarine with your fingertips until the mixture resembles fine bread-crumbs. Using a round-bladed knife, stir in 3 to 4 tablespoons of cold water to make a firm dough. Turn out the dough on to a lightly floured surface and knead it until it is smooth. Roll out the dough and use it to line a 2.5 cm (1 inch) deep 22 cm (9 inch) flan dish. Prick the base and sides of the pastry case with a fork and chill the case for 20 minutes.

Increase the oven temperature to 200°C (400°F or Mark 6). Bake the pastry case for 15 minutes, then remove it from the oven and set it aside. Reduce the oven temperature to 180°C (350°F or Mark 4).

Melt the margarine in a heavy frying pan and gently fry the onion until it is transparent and tender — 5 to 6 minutes. Add the basil and cook for another minute.

Spread half of the onion mixture in the base of the flan case and cover it with half of the courgettes, then add the remaining onion, followed by the rest of the courgettes. Sprinkle the diced cheese on top. In a bowl, whisk together the milk, eggs, salt and some black pepper. Pour this mixture over the layered vege-tables. Bake the quiche until it is set and golden-brown — 30 to 40 minutes. Allow it to cool completely.

Take the quiche to the picnic site in its dish, covered with foil. Cut it into wedges for serving.

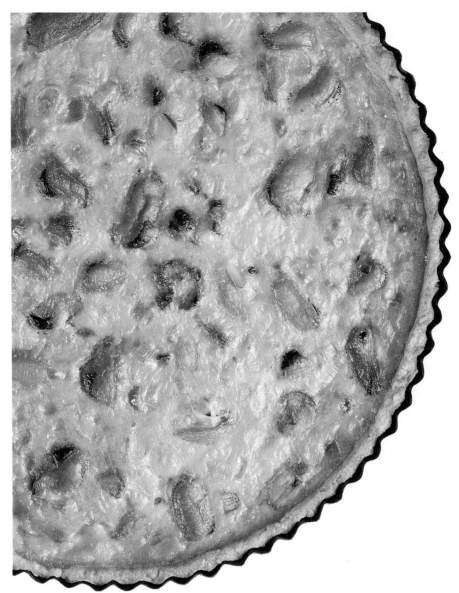

Mussel and Leek Quiche

Serves 12
Working time: about 40 minutes
Total time: about 3 hours (includes chilling)

Calories **150**
Protein **10g**
Cholesterol **80mg**
Total fat **6g**
Saturated fat **2g**
Sodium **135mg**

1.5 kg	mussels, scrubbed and debearded	3 lb
175 g	baby leeks, trimmed to leave 5 cm (2 inches) of green stem, sliced into rings	6 oz
30 cl	dry white wine	½ pint
1 tsp	saffron threads, crushed	1 tsp
2	eggs	2
1	egg yolk	1
2 tbsp	crème fraîche	2 tbsp
15 cl	skimmed milk	¼ pint
Yogurt pastry		
140 g	plain flour	4½ oz
45 g	polyunsaturated margarine, chilled	1½ oz
90 g	thick Greek yogurt	3 oz

First, prepare the yogurt pastry. Put the flour and margarine into a food processor and process them until fine crumbs are formed. Add the yogurt and process again until the mixture forms a firm, slightly wet ball. Scrape down the sides of the bowl and gather all the dough into one ball. Wrap the ball of dough in plastic film and chill it in the refrigerator for 1 hour.

Lightly grease a 25 cm (10 inch) loose-bottomed flan tin. Place the ball of dough in the tin. Using a round-bladed knife and one hand, gently flatten and spread the dough to line the tin, pressing it into a smooth, even layer over the base and sides. Place the flan case in the refrigerator until you are ready to fill it.

For the filling, place the mussels, leeks and wine in a large, heavy-bottomed saucepan. Bring the liquid to the boil over high heat, then cover the pan and steam the mussels for 3 to 5 minutes, or until the shells have opened, shaking the pan occasionally. Tip the contents of the pan into a muslin-lined colander set over a bowl, and allow all the liquid to drain into the bowl. Pour the reserved liquid into a clean pan and add the crushed saffron threads. Boil the liquid until it has reduced to ¼ litre (8 fl oz), then set it aside and allow it to cool. Remove the mussels from their shells, discarding any that have not opened.

Preheat the oven to 180°C (350°F or Mark 4). In a measuring jug, beat the eggs and egg yolk with a fork and whisk in the *crème fraîche*. Add the cooled saffron liquid and the skimmed milk to the measuring jug and whisk the mixture thoroughly.

Arrange the mussels and leeks evenly in the chilled flan case, and pour on the saffron custard. Place the quiche in the oven and immediately increase the setting to 200°C (400°F or Mark 6). Bake the quiche for 15 minutes, then turn the oven setting back to 180°C (350°F or Mark 4) and cook the quiche for a further 25 to 35 minutes, until the custard is set and the pastry is golden-brown. Remove the quiche from the oven and allow it to cool in its tin.

Transport the quiche to the picnic site in its tin and covered with foil, inside a cool box. At the picnic, unmould it on to a platter and cut it into wedges.

EDITOR'S NOTE: *This recipe may also be adapted to make six individual quiches, as shown on page 10. Use the same amount of yogurt pastry to line six 9.5 cm (3¾ inch) flan tins. For the filling, reduce the quantity of mussels to 1 kg (2 lb), and boil the cooking liquid down to 8 cl (3 fl oz). Prepare the saffron custard in the same way, but use only one egg and no additional yolk, 1 tablespoon of crème fraîche, and sufficient skimmed milk to make the quantity up to 17.5 cl (6 fl oz).*

Mushroom Strudel

Serves 6
Working time: about 40 minutes
Total time: about 1 hour and 30 minutes (includes cooling)

Calories **130**
Protein **5g**
Cholesterol **5mg**
Total fat **5g**
Saturated fat **2g**
Sodium **130mg**

2 tsp	virgin olive oil	2 tsp
1	large onion, finely chopped	1
2	garlic cloves, crushed	2
500 g	open mushrooms, wiped clean and finely chopped	1 lb
2 tsp	chopped fresh marjoram, or ½ tsp dried marjoram	2 tsp
1 tsp	Dijon mustard	1 tsp
125 g	fresh wholemeal breadcrumbs	4 oz
½ tsp	salt	½ tsp
	freshly grated nutmeg	
	freshly ground black pepper	
4	sheets phyllo pastry, each about 45 by 30 cm (18 by 12 inches)	4
15 g	unsalted butter, melted	½ oz

Heat the oil in a heavy-bottomed saucepan over medium heat. Add the onion and garlic and cook them for about 5 minutes, or until the onion has softened. Mix in the mushrooms, increase the heat to medium high and cook, stirring, until the mushrooms release their juices — 3 to 4 minutes. Push the mushroom pulp to one side of the pan, then boil the juices rapidly for 5 to 10 minutes, until they have evaporated. Stir the marjoram, mustard, breadcrumbs, salt and some nutmeg and black pepper into the mushroom pulp, and set the mixture aside to cool completely.

Preheat the oven to 200°C (400°F or Mark 6). Keeping the sheets you are not using covered with a damp cloth to prevent them from drying out, lay one sheet of phyllo pastry on the work surface, with a long side towards you, and brush it with a little of the melted butter. Lay a second sheet of pastry on top and brush it with a little more of the butter. Repeat the process with the third and fourth sheets of phyllo. Spoon the mushroom filling down the long side of pastry nearest to you, about 5 cm (2 inches) in from the edge, and pack it down lightly with the back of the spoon to form a sausage shape about 2.5 cm (1 inch) in diameter. Working away from you, roll up the filling inside the pastry. Using two metal spatulas, transfer the strudel to a large, lightly oiled baking sheet. Brush the strudel with the remaining butter and sprinkle it with a little grated nutmeg. Bake it in the oven for 20 to 25 minutes, until it is crisp and golden.

When the strudel is cooked, leave it to cool completely, then transfer it to a shallow, oblong container and cover it with a lid or a sheet of foil. Alternatively, wrap the strudel in a double thickness of foil. Cut the strudel into slices at the picnic site.

SUGGESTED ACCOMPANIMENT: *salad of lettuce, tomato, black olives and onion rings with a parsley and lemon dressing.*

Salmon Phyllo Parcels

Makes 6 parcels
Working time: about 45 minutes
Total time: about 1 hour and 20 minutes (includes cooling)

Per parcel:			
Calories **290**	6	salmon steaks (about 125 g/4 oz each)	6
Protein **27g**	1 tsp	unsalted butter, melted	1 tsp
Cholesterol **70mg**	1/4 tsp	salt	1/4 tsp
Total fat **14g**		freshly ground black pepper	
Saturated fat **4g**	6	sheets phyllo pastry, each about 45 by 30 cm (18 by 12 inches)	6
Sodium **140mg**	12	long chives, six finely cut	12
	Watercress dressing		
	30 g	watercress, leaves only, finely chopped	1 oz
	200 g	quark	7 oz
	1 tbsp	white wine vinegar	1 tbsp
	1/8 tsp	salt	1/8 tsp
	2 tbsp	skimmed milk	2 tbsp

Using a small, sharp knife, trim away the skin from the salmon steaks. Divide each steak into two boneless pieces by cutting down each side of the backbone and round the ribs. Preheat the grill to hot. Tie the two pieces of each steak together with fine string to form six "noisettes" of salmon. Place the tied steaks in a foil-lined grill pan. Brush each one lightly with a little of the melted butter and season them with the salt and some black pepper. Grill the steaks for about 2 minutes on each side, or until the flesh is opaque. Drain the steaks thoroughly on paper towels and leave them to cool — about 30 minutes.

Meanwhile, prepare the watercress dressing. Put the chopped watercress in a mixing bowl, add the quark, vinegar, salt and skimmed milk, and beat the ingredients together until they form a smooth sauce. Place the bowl of dressing in the refrigerator until you are ready to go to the picnic.

Preheat the oven to 200°C (400°F or Mark 6) and lightly grease a baking sheet. Using a 21 cm (8½ inch) plate as a guide, cut two large circles from each sheet of phyllo pastry. Keep the uncut sheets, and the circles as you cut them, covered by damp tea towels to prevent them from drying out. Place one phyllo circle on the work surface and brush it with a little of the melted butter. Place another circle on top, then cover the pair with a damp tea towel. Sandwich the remaining pastry circles together in pairs in the same way, to give a total of six pairs of circles.

Remove the string from the salmon steaks. Place one steak in the centre of each pair of pastry circles and sprinkle the steaks with the finely cut chives. Gather the pastry edges up over the salmon steaks. Tie a long chive firmly round the neck of each parcel, then carefully open out the pastry layers above the chive to create a decorative effect. Place the phyllo parcels on the baking sheet and brush them with the remaining melted butter. Loosely cover the frilly top of each parcel with a piece of foil, to prevent them from burning in the oven. Bake the parcels for 20 minutes, or until they are golden-brown. Cool them on a wire rack, then chill them until required.

When you are ready to leave for the picnic, carefully pack the phyllo parcels in rigid containers and surround them with crumpled paper towels or greaseproof paper to keep them separate and upright. Place the containers in a cool box. Transfer the dressing to a container with a tight-fitting lid, and put it in the cool box too. Serve each parcel with a little dressing.

Veal and Cashew Nut Rolls

Makes 8 rolls
Working time: about 45 minutes
Total time: about 2 hours (includes cooling)

Per roll:
Calories **135**
Protein **16g**
Cholesterol **40mg**
Total fat **4g**
Saturated fat **1g**
Sodium **140mg**

500 g	lean veal, minced	1 lb
250 g	carrots, grated and placed in a sieve to drain	8 oz
60 g	skinned shelled cashew nuts, coarsely chopped	2 oz
60 g	pickled gherkins, coarsely chopped	2 oz
½	lemon, grated rind and juice	½
1 tbsp	chopped parsley	1 tbsp
1 tbsp	chopped fresh sage, or 1 tsp dried sage	1 tbsp
¼ tsp	salt	¼ tsp
	freshly ground black pepper	
4	sheets phyllo pastry, each about 45 by 30 cm (18 by 12 inches)	4
1 tbsp	safflower oil	1 tbsp

Put the minced veal in a large mixing bowl. Add the carrots, nuts, gherkins, lemon rind and juice, parsley, sage, salt and some black pepper. Using a fork or your hand, combine the ingredients thoroughly. Turn the mixture on to a work surface and divide it into eight equal portions. Use your hands to roll each portion into a sausage shape about 11 cm (4½ inches) long.

Preheat the oven to 180°C (350°F or Mark 4). Line a baking sheet with non-stick parchment paper.

Keeping the sheets of phyllo pastry you are not working with covered by a damp tea towel to prevent them from drying out, lay one sheet on the work surface. Brush it with a little of the safflower oil and cover it with a second sheet of phyllo. Cut this double sheet of phyllo crosswise into four equal strips, each measuring 30 by 11 cm (12 by 4½ inches). Cover the strips with a damp tea towel. Repeat the procedure with the remaining two sheets of phyllo.

Lay one of the prepared phyllo strips on the work surface and place a portion of veal and cashew nut stuffing across the strip at one of the short ends. Roll up the pastry and filling tightly. Using a sharp knife, make three diagonal slashes across the top of the roll. Brush the roll with safflower oil and place it on the baking sheet. Use the remaining phyllo strips and stuffing to prepare another seven rolls.

Bake the filled rolls until they are golden-brown — 50 minutes to 1 hour. Cool them on a wire rack, then pack them, in a single layer, into a plastic container lined with paper towels. Put the container in a cool box to take to the picnic site.

SUGGESTED ACCOMPANIMENT: *spring onions and radishes.*

EDITOR'S NOTE: *In this recipe, lamb may be used in place of veal and hazelnuts in place of cashew nuts, if preferred.*

Fresh Fruits in a Watermelon Bowl

Serves 8
Working time: about 45 minutes
Total time: about 2 hours (includes chilling)

Calories **80**
Protein **2g**
Cholesterol **0mg**
Total fat **0g**
Saturated fat **0g**
Sodium **10mg**

1	watermelon (about 3 kg/6½ lb)	1
6	ripe figs, washed, stemmed and cut lengthwise into eighths	6
250 g	seedless red grapes, washed and stemmed	8 oz
2	oranges, juice and grated rind	2
1	lemon, grated rind only	1
1 tbsp	ginger syrup, from a jar of preserved stem ginger	1 tbsp
2 tbsp	clear honey	2 tbsp

Slice off the top of the watermelon, about one fifth of the way down. Using a basting spoon or a large tablespoon, scoop out the flesh from the lid. Remove the seeds and cut the flesh into 2.5 cm (1 inch) cubes and other similar-sized chunks. Reserve the lid.

Run a long-bladed knife round the edge of the large piece of melon, between the flesh and the skin, cutting down deeply and keeping as close as possible to the skin. Make a series of deep parallel cuts, 2.5 cm (1 inch) apart, across the flesh, followed by a series of similar cuts at right angles to the first. Gently scoop out the long, square sections of flesh. Remove the seeds and chop the flesh into cubes. Use the large spoon to scrape the remaining flesh from the walls of the watermelon shell, then seed it and cut it into pieces in the same way as before. Reserve the watermelon shell. Put all the pieces of watermelon flesh into a large, heatproof bowl and add the figs and grapes.

In a small, non-reactive pan, mix together the orange juice and rind, the lemon rind, the ginger syrup and the honey. Bring the liquid slowly to the boil and pour it over the fruit. Stir the fruit and syrup together, then leave the syrup to cool for 5 minutes. Stir again, cover the bowl and chill it for 1 hour. Turn the fruit over occasionally, to encourage it to absorb the syrup.

To pack the salad for a picnic, transfer the chilled fruit to the watermelon shell, replace the lid and wrap the whole assembly tightly in a double layer of plastic film. Wedge the filled watermelon upright in a cool box to carry it to the picnic site.

EDITOR'S NOTE: *If preferred, the watermelon flesh may be scooped from its shell with a melon-baller.*

Goat Cheesecake with Fresh Figs

Serves 8
Working time: about 45 minutes
Total time: about 8 hours (includes chilling)

Calories **165**
Protein **5g**
Cholesterol **30mg**
Total fat **8g**
Saturated fat **3g**
Sodium **140mg**

150 g	soft goat cheese	5 oz
150 g	low-fat fromage frais	5 oz
3 tbsp	clear honey	3 tbsp
1 tsp	fresh lemon juice	1 tsp
½ tsp	finely grated lemon rind	½ tsp
½ tsp	pure vanilla extract	½ tsp
⅛ tsp	pure almond extract	⅛ tsp
1 tbsp	cornflour	1 tbsp
1 tbsp	skimmed milk	1 tbsp
1	egg, separated, yolk lightly beaten, white chilled	1
2	firm fresh figs, stemmed and quartered	2
15 g	flaked almonds	½ oz
Hazelnut crumb base		
75 g	fresh wholemeal breadcrumbs, toasted	2½ oz
30 g	ground hazelnuts, toasted	1 oz
30 g	vanilla sugar	1 oz
¼ tsp	ground cinnamon	¼ tsp
1 tbsp	apricot preserve without added sugar	1 tbsp
1 tsp	polyunsaturated margarine	1 tsp
1 tsp	nut oil (walnut, hazelnut or almond)	1 tsp

First prepare the hazelnut crumb base. Line the base and sides of an 18 cm (7 inch) square baking tin with non-stick parchment paper. In a mixing bowl, combine the toasted crumbs and hazelnuts, the sugar and the cinnamon. Warm the apricot preserve in a small saucepan until it liquefies, whisking it to break up any lumps. Add the margarine and oil to the pan, and stir until the margarine melts. Pour the mixture into the dry ingredients and stir it in thoroughly with a wooden spoon. Turn the crumb mixture into the prepared tin and press it down firmly with the back of a spoon. Chill the base in the refrigerator for at least 1 hour.

To make the filling, put the goat cheese, *fromage frais*, honey, lemon juice, lemon rind, vanilla extract and almond extract into a mixing bowl. Beat the mixture with a wooden spoon until it is smooth. Stir the cornflour into the milk to form a smooth paste. Beat the cornflour paste into the cheese mixture, then beat in the egg yolk. Chill the filling in the refrigerator until it thickens — about 1 hour.

Preheat the oven to 170°C (325°F or Mark 3). Whisk the egg white until it forms soft peaks, and use a metal tablespoon to fold it gently into the chilled filling. Pour the filling over the chilled base and level it with the back of a spoon. Press the fig quarters into the cheese filling, flesh side upwards, positioning them in two straight rows so that each serving will contain a fig quarter. Sprinkle the surface of the cheesecake with the flaked almonds.

Bake the cheesecake until the filling is just firm to the touch in the centre — about 45 minutes. Leave it in the oven, with the door slightly ajar, to cool and set. Once the cake has reached room temperature, remove it from the oven and chill it for at least 4 hours.

Cover the cheesecake with plastic film or foil and carry it to the picnic site in its tin.

EDITOR'S NOTE: *The breadcrumbs and ground hazelnuts may be toasted at the same time. Spread out the crumbs on one end of a baking sheet, and the hazelnuts on the other. Place the baking sheet in a preheated 180°C (350°C or Mark 4) oven. Stir the crumbs and hazelnuts occasionally, but keep them separate. Remove the hazelnuts after 10 minutes and the crumbs after 15 minutes. Leave both to cool.*

Mixed Berry Yogurt Ice

Serves 10
Working time: about 40 minutes
Total time: about 11 hours (includes freezing)

Calories **200**
Protein **5g**
Cholesterol **0mg**
Total fat **1g**
Saturated fat **trace**
Sodium **65mg**

750 g	mixed soft fruits (blackberries, strawberries, blueberries, raspberries, blackcurrants, redcurrants), hulled, stemmed or picked over, as appropriate	1½ lb
350 g	caster sugar	12 oz
3	egg whites	3
60 cl	plain low-fat yogurt	1 pint
2 tbsp	Kirsch	2 tbsp

Purée the soft fruits in a food processor. Pass the purée through a nylon sieve and set it aside.

Put 15 cl (¼ pint) of water and the sugar into a heavy-bottomed saucepan. Set the pan over medium heat and stir the mixture gently with a wooden spoon to dissolve the sugar; brush down any sugar crystals stuck to the sides of the pan with a pastry brush dipped in hot water. Warm a sugar thermometer in a jug of hot water and place it in the pan. Increase the heat, bring the syrup to the boil, and continue to boil it rapidly until the temperature on the thermometer is between 121° and 130°C (250° and 266°F).

While the sugar syrup is cooking, whisk the egg whites in a large bowl until they form stiff peaks.

Whisking all the time, pour the boiling sugar syrup into the egg whites in a thin, steady stream. Continue to whisk the meringue mixture vigorously until it is cool — about 10 minutes — then set it aside for 5 minutes to cool completely.

Measure off 35 cl (12 fl oz) of the fruit purée and transfer the remaining purée to a sealed plastic container to take to the picnic site. Using a metal tablespoon, carefully fold the measured fruit purée into the cooled meringue, then fold in the yogurt and the Kirsch. Turn the mixture into a rigid plastic container, smooth it level and cover it with a lid. Place the container in the freezer, which should be set as low as possible, and leave the mixture to set — 10 to 12 hours. Do not remove the yogurt ice from the freezer until you are ready to leave for the picnic.

To transport the yogurt ice to the picnic site, place it in a cool box lined with ice packs. Put the container of fruit purée in the cool box too. Serve the dessert with the fruit purée.

SUGGESTED ACCOMPANIMENT: *extra soft fruits, carried in a sealed, rigid container to prevent crushing.*

Pear and Banana Bread

Serves 8
Working time: about 30 minutes
Total time: about 4 hours (includes cooling)

Calories **300**
Protein **6g**
Cholesterol **30mg**
Total fat **8g**
Saturated fat **2g**
Sodium **160mg**

125 g	sun-dried bananas, finely chopped	4 oz
60 g	polyunsaturated margarine	2 oz
90 g	dark brown sugar	3 oz
250 g	brown flour	8 oz
2 tsp	baking powder	2 tsp
⅛ tsp	salt	⅛ tsp
1	egg, beaten	1
1	pear, peeled, cored and finely chopped	1
Pear and apple glaze		
2 tbsp	clear honey	2 tbsp
2 tbsp	pear and apple spread	2 tbsp

Put the bananas in a saucepan with 20 cl (7 fl oz) of water. Bring the liquid to the boil, then reduce the heat, cover the pan and simmer the bananas until they are soft — 30 to 35 minutes. Using a slotted spoon, transfer the bananas to a plate and allow them to cool for 10 minutes. Strain and reserve the cooking liquid.

Preheat the oven to 180°C (350°F or Mark 4). Lightly grease a 16 by 11 by 7.5 cm (6½ by 4½ by 3 inch) loaf tin. Purée the bananas in a food processor, then add the margarine and sugar and process again until the mixture is light and fluffy. Transfer this mixture to a mixing bowl and sift in the flour, baking powder and salt. Add the egg and the pear to the bowl, and mix all the ingredients together thoroughly with a wooden spoon. The batter should be of a soft, dropping consistency; if it is too dry, add a tablespoon or two of the reserved banana-cooking liquid.

Pour the mixture into the prepared tin, level it with the back of a spoon and bake it until a thin skewer inserted in the centre comes out clean — 50 minutes to 1 hour. (If the top of the loaf appears too brown towards the end of the cooking time, cover it with foil or greaseproof paper.) Turn out the loaf on to a wire rack and let it cool for about 1 hour.

To make the glaze, stir together the honey and the pear and apple spread in a small saucepan. Bring the mixture to the boil, reduce the heat and simmer it until it is thick and syrupy — 3 to 4 minutes. Allow the glaze to cool for 5 minutes. Using a pastry brush, paint the glaze lightly over the top of the bread. Set the glazed loaf aside to cool for another hour before wrapping it in foil and packing it in a rigid container, ready to take to the picnic site.

EDITOR'S NOTE: *Sun-dried bananas and pear and apple spread are available from most wholefood shops.*

2 *Poussin halves, marinated in rum, honey and lime juice and coated in crushed coriander seeds and pepper, cook over hot coals (recipe, page 83).*

New Ways with an Ancient Art

Barbecues not only greatly extend the range of foods that can be enjoyed outdoors, they also make the cooking of the food an integral feature of the meal in which all the guests can share. The 45 recipes in this chapter confirm that 20th-century tastes and innovations, allied with time-honoured culinary knowledge, have re-established this traditional technique as one of the most rewarding means of preparing food.

Ever since food was first cooked on open fires, the mainstay of outdoor cooking has been meat. The lean prime cuts used in this chapter are naturally tender, but even the best steaks or chops, when trimmed of fat and grilled without oily basting liquids, can dry out over a barbecue's searing heat. For this reason, most of the recipes call for the meat to be marinated for several hours beforehand. Acidic marinades tenderize the meat, reducing cooking time to a minimum. Yogurt-based marinades are especially useful for low-calorie cooking. Not only does yogurt help tenderize the meat, it can also form a protective coating, allowing thick or unevenly shaped cuts, such as the butterflied leg of lamb on page 67, to cook without drying out.

Even sausages, those frequently fatty and salty standbys of outdoor cookery, can remain part of a nutritious barbecue when they are made at home. Use only lean meat, and keep the texture slightly coarse; too smooth a consistency can cause a lean sausage to dry out during cooking.

Poultry is another staple of the barbecue menu. Threaded on skewers, marinated cubes of chicken grill to perfection over white-hot coals. For even cooking on a grill rack, a whole bird can be split and flattened *(pages 84 and 85)*. Alternatively, you can spit-roast a whole chicken *(page 82)*, a task made immeasurably easier by the electric rotisserie. Make room for a drip pan underneath the spit by raking the hot coals to the sides of the barbecue firebox.

Seafood is particularly delicious when cooked over coals. Firm-fleshed fish or shellfish, such as the monkfish, scallops and prawns on page 92, can be skewered and cooked as kebabs. More delicately textured fish can be wrapped in foil or vine leaves *(pages 90 and 95)* or grilled whole enclosed in a fish basket *(page 96)*. Most seafood cooks quickly over medium-hot coals; the higher temperature required to sear meat will dry out a fish's naturally tender flesh.

Vegetarians will find recipes here too. Kebabs of cheese, fruit and vegetables *(page 98)* or marinated mixed vegetables baked in foil *(page 100)* make a delicious alternative to a main dish of meat or fish. And there is no need to go indoors for dessert. Round off an outdoor meal with apples and chestnuts baked in foil *(page 102)* before extinguishing the fire.

Mexican Beef Brochettes

Serves 4
Working time: about 25 minutes
Total time: about 5 hours
(includes marinating)

Calories **250**
Protein **27g**
Cholesterol **55mg**
Total fat **15g**
Saturated fat **4g**
Sodium **155mg**

500 g	rump steak, in one or two slices about 1 cm (½ inch) thick, trimmed of fat	1 lb
2	bay leaves	2
	dried bamboo leaves, for garnish (optional)	
¼ tsp	salt	¼ tsp
	lime wedges, for garnish	
Coriander marinade		
30 g	finely chopped onion	1 oz
1	garlic clove, crushed	1
1 to 2	red chili peppers, seeded and finely chopped (caution, box, opposite)	1 to 2
½ tsp	ground cumin	½ tsp
½ tbsp	chopped fresh oregano, or ½ tsp dried oregano	½ tbsp
½ tsp	paprika	½ tsp
½ tsp	ground cinnamon	½ tsp
6	cloves	6
1 tbsp	sesame seeds	1 tbsp
2 tbsp	finely chopped fresh coriander	2 tbsp
1 ½ tbsp	safflower oil	1 ½ tbsp
1 tbsp	fresh lime juice	1 tbsp

In a shallow dish, combine all the ingredients for the marinade. Cut the rump steak into strips about 15 cm (6 inches) long and 6 mm (¼ inch) wide, and stir them into the marinade together with the bay leaves. Cover the dish and put the meat in the refrigerator to marinate for at least 4 hours, or overnight, turning it once or twice during this time. Remove the beef from the refrigerator at least 30 minutes before cooking.

Soak eight wooden skewers in water for 10 minutes. Thread the meat strips on to the skewers, sprinkling on any remaining marinade. Cook the brochettes over hot coals for 5 to 8 minutes, turning them frequently.

Transfer the brochettes to a serving plate lined with dried bamboo leaves, if you are using them. Sprinkle the brochettes with the salt and serve them garnished with the lime wedges.

SUGGESTED ACCOMPANIMENT: *a salad of mixed beans and sweetcorn kernels.*

Steakburgers with Parsnips and Brown Ale

Serves 12
Working (and total) time: about 50 minutes

Calories **130**
Protein **17g**
Cholesterol **35mg**
Total fat **5g**
Saturated fat **2g**
Sodium **125mg**

20 cl	strong brown ale	7 fl oz
750 g	lean steak, trimmed of fat and minced	1 ½ lb
1	onion, finely chopped	1
300 g	parsnips, peeled and finely grated	10 oz
2 tsp	chopped fresh thyme	2 tsp
2 tbsp	chopped parsley	2 tbsp
45 g	fresh wholemeal breadcrumbs	1 ½ oz
1 tbsp	grainy mustard	1 tbsp
½ tsp	salt	½ tsp
	freshly ground black pepper	

In a small, heavy-bottomed pan, bring the ale to the boil, then reduce the heat and boil gently until it has reduced to 4 tablespoons — about 5 minutes. Put the steak in a large bowl and add the onion, parsnips, thyme, parsley, breadcrumbs, mustard, salt and some pepper. Pour in the ale. Using a wooden spoon, work the mixture together to combine the ingredients.

Divide the mixture into 12 equal portions. Shape each portion into a ball between your palms, then flatten the balls into burger shapes on a chopping board. Lightly oil the barbecue rack and cook the steakburgers over medium-hot coals for 7 to 8 minutes on each side, until they are just cooked through.

SUGGESTED ACCOMPANIMENTS: *barbecued sliced red onions; field mushrooms.*

Chili Peppers — a Cautionary Note

Both dried and fresh hot chili peppers should be handled with care. Their flesh and seeds contain volatile oils that can make skin tingle and cause eyes to burn. Rubber gloves offer protection — but the cook should still be careful not to touch the face, lips or eyes when working with chilies.

Soaking fresh chilies in cold, salted water for an hour will remove some of their fire. If canned chilies are substituted for fresh ones, they should be rinsed in cold water in order to eliminate as much of the brine used to preserve them as possible.

Mustard Steaks with Yogurt Sauce and Chicory Salad

Serves 4
Working time: about 20 minutes
Total time: about 45 minutes

Calories **325**			
Protein **45g**	4	sirloin steaks (about 150 g/5 oz each), trimmed of fat	4
Cholesterol **100mg**	2 tbsp	grainy mustard, tarragon flavoured if possible	2 tbsp
Total fat **14g**			
Saturated fat **6g**	2	garlic cloves, crushed	2
Sodium **125mg**	15 cl	plain low-fat yogurt	¼ pint
		freshly ground black pepper	

Chicory salad

90 g	button mushrooms, wiped and trimmed	3 oz
2 tbsp	fresh lemon juice	2 tbsp
175 g	chicory, trimmed and thinly sliced	6 oz
1	box mustard and cress	1
4	spring onions, trimmed and sliced	4
½	sweet orange or red pepper, sliced and blanched	½

Starting at the untrimmed side of each steak, cut a pocket almost through to the opposite side. Coat the insides of the pockets with half of the mustard, then rub the steaks all over with half of the crushed garlic. Put the steaks in a dish and set them aside in a cool place, covered, to marinate for 30 minutes.

Meanwhile, make the yogurt sauce. Put the yogurt, the remaining mustard and garlic, and plenty of black pepper in a bowl, and mix them together thoroughly.

For the salad, slice the mushrooms and put them in a bowl with the lemon juice. Toss the mushrooms well and leave them to stand for 10 minutes. Add the chicory, mustard and cress, spring onions and sweet pepper, and mix them together well. Cover the salad and chill it until required.

Brush the barbecue rack with oil and cook the mustard steaks over hot coals for 3 to 5 minutes on each side. Serve the steaks with the salad and sauce.

Barbecued Escalope of Veal

Serves 4
Working time: about 25 minutes
Total time: about 4 hours and 25 minutes
(includes marinating)

Calories **150**
Protein **53g**
Cholesterol **30mg**
Total fat **7g**
Saturated fat **5g**
Sodium **220mg**

8	small thin-cut veal escalopes (about 45 g/1 ½ oz each), trimmed of fat	8
4 tbsp	plain low-fat yogurt	4 tbsp
1 tbsp	virgin olive oil	1 tbsp
1 tbsp	balsamic vinegar	1 tbsp
1 tbsp	grainy mustard	1 tbsp
	white pepper	
8	fresh sage leaves, finely chopped	8
¼ tsp	salt	¼ tsp
	coarsely crushed white peppercorns (optional)	

Lay an escalope on the work surface between two sheets of plastic film. Using the smooth side of a meat-bat or a rolling pin, pound the meat until it is about 1.5 mm (¹⁄₁₆ inch) thick. Repeat this process with the other escalopes. In a small bowl, whisk together the yogurt, oil, vinegar, mustard, pepper and chopped sage leaves. Brush the escalopes with the marinade and place them in a shallow dish; reserve any remaining marinade. Cover the dish, and leave the escalopes to marinate for 4 to 6 hours at room temperature, or for 12 to 24 hours in the refrigerator. The escalopes should be removed from the refrigerator about 1 hour before you plan to cook them.

Cook the escalopes over hot coals for 45 seconds on each side, basting them with any remaining marinade. Sprinkle the cooked escalopes with the salt and, if you like, with crushed white peppercorns. Serve the escalopes immediately.

SUGGESTED ACCOMPANIMENTS: *a salad of pink grapefruit segments and young spinach leaves; radicchio hearts with a balsamic vinaigrette.*

Peppercorn-Crusted Fillet with Three Sauces

Serves 16
Working time: about 1 hour and 30 minutes
Total time: about 2 hours and 15 minutes

Calories **290**
Protein **33g**
Cholesterol **72mg**
Total fat **16g**
Saturated fat **6g**
Sodium **480mg**

3	garlic cloves, crushed	3
2.2 kg	beef fillet in one piece, trimmed of fat	4½ lb
125 g	black peppercorns, crushed	4 oz
2 tbsp	virgin olive oil	2 tbsp
Spinach sauce		
15 g	polyunsaturated margarine	½ oz
1	leek, trimmed, washed thoroughly to remove all grit, sliced	1
1	shallot, chopped	1
2	garlic cloves, roughly chopped	2
500 g	young spinach, washed and stemmed	1 lb
1 tbsp	fresh lemon juice	1 tbsp
½ tsp	salt	½ tsp
60 g	crème fraîche	2 oz
Pumpkin sauce		
500 g	pumpkin, peeled, seeds removed, flesh cubed	1 lb
30 cl	unsalted chicken stock (recipe, page 139)	½ pint
1 tsp	molasses	1 tsp
20 g	Parmesan cheese, grated	¾ oz
1 tbsp	cut chives	1 tbsp
¼	small nutmeg, grated	¼
1 tsp	salt	1 tsp
100 g	thick Greek yogurt	3½ oz
Parsnip and apple sauce		
400 g	young parsnips, trimmed and cubed	14 oz
3	dessert apples, peeled, cored and chopped, placed in acidulated water	3
1	cinnamon stick	1
½	lemon, rind only, cut into wide strips	½

30 g	polyunsaturated margarine	1 oz
1 tsp	salt	1 tsp
1 tbsp	finely chopped chervil	1 tbsp

Rub the garlic all over the beef. Place the peppercorns on a plate and roll the fillet in them until evenly coated; press the peppercorns firmly into the fillet to form a crust. Place the beef on a large platter, cover it and set it aside while you prepare the sauces.

For the spinach sauce, melt the margarine in a large pan. Add the leek, shallot and garlic, and cook them gently until just soft — about 5 minutes. Add the spinach with water still clinging to its leaves, then cook the vegetables for 1 minute, turning the spinach continuously to prevent it sticking and to coat it in the cooking juices. Cover the pan and cook the vegetables gently for about 5 minutes more, stirring occasionally, until they are tender. Remove the pan from the heat and cool the mixture slightly, then transfer it to a food processor or blender, with the cooking juices. Process it to a smooth purée. Add the lemon juice and salt, process for 10 seconds, then add the *crème fraîche*. Process again very briefly, then pour the sauce into a small pan ready to be reheated before serving.

For the pumpkin sauce, put the pumpkin in a large pan and add the stock. Bring the stock to simmering point, then simmer the pumpkin until it is soft — 15 to 20 minutes. Remove the pan from the heat, allow the pumpkin to cool slightly, then transfer it to a food processor or blender, with the cooking liquid. Add the molasses, Parmesan, chives, nutmeg and salt, and process the mixture until it forms a smooth purée. Add the yogurt and process for a few more seconds. Sieve the sauce into a small pan, then set it aside.

To make the third sauce, place the parsnips and apples in a large pan. Add the cinnamon stick and lemon rind. Pour in 30 cl (½ pint) of water, and bring it to a simmer over medium heat. Simmer the parsnips and apples for 10 to 15 minutes, or until they are soft. Discard the cinnamon stick and all but 2.5 cm (1 inch) of the lemon rind. Transfer the parsnips, apples, reserved lemon rind and the cooking liquid to a food processor or blender. Add the margarine and salt, then process the mixture until smooth. Sieve the sauce into a pan, stir in the chervil and set it aside.

Brush the olive oil over the beef's peppercorn crust, reserving any excess to baste the meat as it cooks. Set the barbecue rack close to medium-hot coals, and cook the meat for 15 minutes to seal it, turning it frequently and basting it with any remaining oil. Raise the rack and cook the meat for a further 15 minutes for rare beef, or 20 minutes for rare to medium meat. During the latter stage of the cooking, keep the thin end of the fillet away from the hottest part of the barbecue to prevent it from overcooking.

While the beef is cooking, gently reheat the sauces without letting them boil. Transfer the peppercorn-crusted fillet to a board or serving platter, and carve it into thick slices. Serve the sauces separately.

Aromatic Leg of Lamb

TURNING THE LAMB AND BASTING IT AT REGULAR INTERVALS
DURING COOKING KEEPS THE JUICES WITHIN THE MEAT
AND ENSURES A SUCCULENT JOINT.

Serves 12
Working time: about 1 hour
Total time: about 27 hours (includes marinating)

Calories **250**
Protein **21g**
Cholesterol **80mg**
Total fat **12g**
Saturated fat **5g**
Sodium **170mg**

15 cl	plain low-fat yogurt	¼ pint
1 tbsp	fresh lemon juice	1 tbsp
1 tbsp	ground coriander	1 tbsp
2 tsp	ground cinnamon	2 tsp
1 tsp	ground cardamom	1 tsp
1 tsp	ground ginger	1 tsp
½ tsp	ground cloves	½ tsp
	freshly ground black pepper	
1 tbsp	virgin olive oil	1 tbsp
2.5 kg	leg of lamb, boned, trimmed of fat and opened out flat	5 lb
½ tsp	salt	½ tsp
1 tbsp	black poppy seeds	1 tbsp
1 tbsp	white sesame seeds	1 tbsp
1	pitta-style flat bread (optional)	1
Citrus-yogurt sauce		
400 g	thick Greek yogurt	14 oz
1	lemon, finely grated rind only	1
2 tbsp	fresh lemon balm, finely chopped	2 tbsp

In a small bowl, stir together the low-fat yogurt, lemon juice, coriander, cinnamon, cardamom, ginger, cloves and some black pepper to form a light paste. Spread the paste all over the lamb. Place the lamb in a large, flat dish, cover it and leave the meat to marinate in the refrigerator for at least 24 hours, or up to three days. Remove the meat from the refrigerator at least 2 hours before you plan to cook it.

Lay the meat out to form a rough rectangle. Thread two metal skewers through the meat, each about 7.5 cm (3 inches) from the edge of a long side; this will keep the meat flat while it is cooking. Set the barbecue rack at its lowest position and brush it lightly with oil. Sear each side of the joint over hot coals for 5 to 8 minutes, or until the surface is caramelized and lightly charred. Remove the meat from the rack and adjust the rack to its highest position. Return the meat to the rack. Brush one side with a little oil, sprinkle on a little of the salt and half of the poppy seeds and sesame seeds, and cook the lamb for a further 3 minutes. Turn the meat over, brush it with oil, sprinkle on the remaining salt, poppy seeds and sesame seeds, and grill the meat for 3 minutes. Turn the joint four more times, brushing it each time with any remaining marinade or with a little oil, and grilling it for a further 3 minutes after each turn. The meat should be crisp and dark on the outside, but still tender and pink inside. For more well-done meat, cook it for a further 4 to 6 minutes, turning it once and brushing on more oil as necessary to prevent it drying out. If you like, place the cooked joint on a round of flat bread set on a carving surface:

the bread will catch the meat juices and may be served in chunks with the meat. Remove the skewers, cover the meat lightly with foil and allow it to rest for 5 to 10 minutes before carving.

Meanwhile, make the yogurt sauce. Set 1 teaspoon of the lemon rind aside, and stir the remainder into the yogurt, together with the chopped lemon balm. Sprinkle the reserved lemon rind over the yogurt. Serve the meat accompanied by the sauce.

SUGGESTED ACCOMPANIMENT: *salad of crisp mixed lettuce leaves with blanched sliced courgettes and mange-tout.*

EDITOR'S NOTE: *Throwing cinnamon sticks and bay leaves on to the coals for the last 5 to 10 minutes of barbecuing will enhance the flavour of the meat.*

Caucasian Lamb Kebabs with Fruity Pilaff

Serves 6
Working time: about 1 hour and 15 minutes
Total time: about 25 hours (includes marinating)

Calories **390**
Protein **29g**
Cholesterol **65mg**
Total fat **12g**
Saturated fat **4g**
Sodium **150mg**

2 tsp	safflower oil	2 tsp
1	small onion, finely chopped	1
400 g	red-skinned plums or damsons, stoned and chopped	14 oz
1 tbsp	red wine vinegar	1 tbsp
1 tbsp	clear honey	1 tbsp
1 tsp	ground cinnamon	1 tsp
¼ tsp	ground allspice	¼ tsp
	freshly ground black pepper	
600 g	lean loin of lamb, trimmed of fat and cut into 4 cm (1½ inch cubes)	1¼ lb
1 tbsp	chopped fresh basil	1 tbsp
15 cl	thick Greek yogurt	¼ pint
Fruity pilaff		
150 g	long-grain rice	5 oz
60 g	large black raisins	2 oz
60 g	dried pears, chopped	2 oz
60 g	dried apricots, chopped	2 oz
12.5 cl	unsweetened white grape or apple juice	4 fl oz
1 tsp	safflower oil	1 tsp
¼ tsp	salt	¼ tsp
¼ tsp	powdered saffron	¼ tsp
1	cinnamon stick	1
1 tsp	clear honey	1 tsp
1	fresh peach or nectarine, stoned and diced	1
15 g	skinned almonds, toasted	½ oz
7 g	mint, chopped	¼ oz

Heat the oil in a heavy frying pan, add the onion and cook it over medium heat for 5 minutes, until it is soft. Add the plums, vinegar, honey, cinnamon, allspice and some black pepper, and simmer the plums until they are very soft — about 20 minutes. Purée the contents of the pan in a food processor or blender.

Place the lamb cubes in a shallow dish. Reserve 6 tablespoons of the plum purée; stir the chopped basil into the remaining purée and pour it over the lamb, turning the cubes of meat to coat them evenly. Cover the lamb loosely and place it in the refrigerator to marinate for about 24 hours.

Two hours before cooking the dish, rinse the rice, then pour 30 cl (½ pint) of cold water over it and leave it to soak. Remove the lamb from the refrigerator to allow it to reach room temperature. At the same time, place the raisins, dried pears and dried apricots in a bowl and pour in the grape juice.

When you are ready to cook the rice, drain it and place it in a large saucepan with an equal volume of cold water. Add the oil, salt and saffron, and bring the liquid to the boil. Stir the rice, reduce the heat, then simmer the rice gently, tightly covered, for about 20 minutes, or until the grains have absorbed all the liquid; do not stir the rice while it is cooking.

Meanwhile, transfer the dried fruit and grape juice to a non-reactive saucepan. Add the cinnamon stick and the honey, cover the pan and simmer the dried fruit until it is soft — about 10 minutes. Remove the lid and reduce the liquid until only a small amount of coating syrup remains. Discard the cinnamon stick.

Stir the cooked dried fruit and its syrup into the rice, together with the diced peach. Allow the rice to cool a little, then stir in the toasted almonds and the chopped mint. Cover the saucepan loosely and set it aside while you cook the lamb.

Lightly oil six long skewers. Thread the lamb cubes on to the skewers, reserving any excess marinade. Oil the rack lightly and cook the kebabs over medium-hot coals for about 15 minutes, turning them frequently and occasionally basting them with any remaining marinade. Rest the cooked kebabs on a warmed serving platter for 5 minutes. Meanwhile, place the yogurt in a serving bowl and gently drop the reserved plum purée on to the surface.

To serve, spoon some fruit pilaff on to a plate. Arrange the lamb cubes from one skewer on top of the pilaff and dribble some of the yogurt over the meat.

EDITOR'S NOTE: *Pilaff is traditionally served warm, rather than hot or cold. It may be prepared in advance and gently reheated in a shallow foil tray set over the barbecue rack, provided it is stirred frequently.*

To toast almonds, place them on a baking sheet under the grill until they are golden; turn or shake them constantly while they are toasting.

Spit-Roasted Moroccan Lamb

Serves 12
Working time: about 30 minutes
Total time: about 6 hours and 30 minutes
(includes marinating)

Calories **275**
Protein **37g**
Cholesterol **100mg**
Total fat **14g**
Saturated fat **5g**
Sodium **85mg**

2 kg	lean leg of lamb, skin and all visible fat removed	4 lb
4	garlic cloves, each cut lengthwise into eight slivers	4
3 tbsp	safflower oil	3 tbsp
1 tbsp	ground cumin	1 tbsp
2 tbsp	ground coriander	2 tbsp
2 tsp	ground cinnamon	2 tsp
2 tbsp	chopped mint	2 tbsp

Cut off and discard the knuckle from the leg of lamb. Make deep incisions about 5 cm (2 inches) apart all over the joint, and insert the garlic slivers into the cuts. Place the joint in a large dish. Mix together the oil, cumin, coriander, cinnamon and mint, and rub half of the mixture over the lamb, coating it completely. Set the remaining spice and mint mixture aside. Cover the meat and leave it to marinate in the refrigerator for at least 4 hours, or overnight. Remove the meat from the refrigerator about 2 hours before you plan to cook it, to allow it to reach room temperature.

Fix the joint diagonally on to a rotating spit so that the weight is evenly distributed and the spit will turn easily. Roast the meat, rotating it, over very hot coals. Start carving slices from the lamb after 15 to 20 minutes, leaving the rest of the joint on the spit to continue cooking. Baste the area from which you have carved the slices with the reserved spice and mint marinade. Continue to carve slices from the lamb about every 10 minutes as it cooks.

SUGGESTED ACCOMPANIMENTS: *warmed pitta bread in which to serve the slices of meat; a salad of cucumber, mint and yogurt.*

Lamb Skewers with Plantain

Serves 4
Working time: about 30 minutes
Total time: about 1 hour

Calories **425**	500 g	lean lamb (from the eye of loin or fillet), trimmed of fat	1 lb
Protein **31g**			
Cholesterol **80mg**	1 tbsp	virgin olive oil	1 tbsp
Total fat **16g**	3 drops	Angostura bitters	3 drops
Saturated fat **5g**	1	garlic clove, finely chopped	1
Sodium **160mg**	1 tsp	coarsely chopped fresh thyme leaves	1 tsp
	¼ tsp	salt	¼ tsp
		freshly ground black pepper	
	2	ripe plantains (about 325 g/11 oz each)	2

Cut the trimmed lamb into disc-shaped slices about 1 cm (½ inch) thick. Squeeze each disc of lamb into a crescent shape and skewer it lengthwise so that the skewer maintains the crescent form; divide the crescents among four skewers. Place the skewers on a tray or a large, flat plate and set them aside.

In a small bowl, combine the olive oil, Angostura bitters, chopped garlic and thyme, salt and some freshly ground black pepper. Brush the lamb skewers with this marinade and leave them, covered, in a cool place for 30 minutes, or up to 3 hours.

Meanwhile, prepare the plantain skewers. Top and tail the plantains, and place them in a large saucepan of boiling water. Boil the plantains, uncovered, for 20 minutes, then drain them and allow them to cool. When they are cool enough to handle, peel them and cut each one lengthwise into four slices. Cut each slice of plantain into 5 cm (2 inch) long pieces. Fold over each piece of plantain so that its ends almost meet, and thread the slices on to four skewers. Brush the plantain skewers lightly with oil.

Place the lamb and the plantain skewers on the barbecue rack over hot coals and cook them for 6 minutes, turning them once as they cook.

SUGGESTED ACCOMPANIMENT: *radicchio salad.*

Lamb Burgers with Basil and Parmesan Sauce

Serves 8
Working time: about 40 minutes
Total time: about 1 hour

Calories **215**
Protein **28g**
Cholesterol **75mg**
Total fat **9g**
Saturated fat **4g**
Sodium **95mg**

750 g	lean leg of lamb, trimmed of fat, minced	1½ lb
3	onions, chopped	3
250 g	courgettes, coarsely grated	8 oz
90 g	fresh wholemeal breadcrumbs	3 oz
¼ tsp	salt	¼ tsp
	freshly ground black pepper	
½ tsp	virgin olive oil	½ tsp
15 cl	unsalted vegetable stock (recipe, page 139)	¼ pint
15 g	basil leaves, roughly chopped	½ oz
30 g	Parmesan cheese, freshly grated	1 oz

Put the minced lamb in a bowl. Add a third of the chopped onions, the courgettes, breadcrumbs, salt and some freshly ground black pepper. Using a wooden spoon or your hands, work the ingredients together until they are thoroughly combined. Divide the mixture into 16 equal portions, then shape each portion into a burger about 6 cm (2½ inches) in diameter and 1 cm (½ inch) thick. Place the burgers on a baking sheet and set them aside.

Heat the oil in a small saucepan over medium heat. Add the remaining chopped onions and cook them gently for about 3 minutes, until they are beginning to soften. Pour the stock into the pan and bring it to the boil, then cover the pan and reduce the heat. Simmer the liquid for 4 to 5 minutes, until the onion is tender. Stir in the basil and cheese, and season the sauce with some pepper. Cook the sauce for a further minute, then transfer it to a food processor or blender and process it until it is smooth. Pour the sauce back into the saucepan, and set it aside ready to be reheated very gently just before serving.

Lightly oil the barbecue rack, and cook the burgers over hot coals for 7 to 8 minutes on each side. Serve them at once, with the reheated sauce.

SUGGESTED ACCOMPANIMENT: *sweet yellow pepper and pasta salad, sprinkled with toasted pine kernels.*

Shoulder of Lamb with Anchovy Stuffing

Serves 10
Working time: about 45 minutes
Total time: about 12 hours (includes marinating)

Calories **185**
Protein **24g**
Cholesterol **65mg**
Total fat **9g**
Saturated fat **3g**
Sodium **290mg**

15 g	fresh rosemary sprigs, woody stems trimmed	½ oz
15 g	parsley	½ oz
3	garlic cloves	3
½	lemon, grated rind and juice	½
60 g	canned anchovy fillets in oil	2 oz
	freshly ground black pepper	
1 kg	shoulder of lamb, skinned and boned, trimmed of all fat	2½ lb

Lemon sauce

1 tbsp	virgin olive oil	1 tbsp
1	small onion, finely chopped	1
1 tbsp	plain flour	1 tbsp
45 cl	unsalted chicken or vegetable stock (recipes, page 139)	¾ pint
1	lemon, finely grated rind and juice	1
2 tbsp	chopped parsley	2 tbsp

Place the rosemary sprigs in a food processor with the parsley, garlic, lemon rind and juice, anchovies with their oil, and some freshly ground black pepper. Process the ingredients until they form a smooth paste.

Wipe the lamb with paper towels to remove any watery juices. Lay the meat out flat on the work surface, boned side uppermost, and spread the paste evenly over the meat. Fold the two opposite sides of the meat over the filling so that they meet in the centre; secure them in place with long metal skewers, to prevent the paste from running out. Cover the lamb and leave it in the refrigerator to marinate for at least 8 hours, or up to 24 hours. Remove the meat from the refrigerator about 2 hours before you plan to cook it, to allow it to reach room temperature.

Lightly oil the barbecue rack, and cook the lamb over medium-hot coals for about 2 hours, turning it frequently. Test the meat by inserting a skewer into the centre — the juices will run clear when the lamb is well cooked. (For meat that is slightly pink in the middle, reduce the cooking time to between 1 ¼ to 1 ½ hours.)

About 20 minutes before the lamb is ready, prepare the sauce. Heat the oil in a small, heavy-bottomed saucepan. Add the onion and cook it over medium heat until it is transparent — about 5 minutes. Stir in the flour and cook the paste for 1 minute, stirring continuously. Gradually pour in the stock, again stirring continuously, and bring the sauce to the boil. Reduce the heat and simmer the sauce for 10 minutes, then stir in the lemon rind and juice, and simmer the sauce for 5 minutes more. Remove the pan from the heat. Stir the parsley into the sauce just before you serve it.

Carve the lamb into thick slices, and pour a little of the sauce over each serving.

SUGGESTED ACCOMPANIMENTS: *small new potatoes, parboiled for 10 to 15 minutes until just tender, then skewered, brushed with clear honey and heated on the barbecue for 3 to 4 minutes; oakleaf lettuce.*

Lamb Noisettes with Tomato and Olive Relish

Serves 4
Working time: about 30 minutes
Total time: about 5 hours and 30 minutes
(includes marinating)

Calories **225**
Protein **28g**
Cholesterol **70mg**
Total fat **10g**
Saturated fat **4g**
Sodium **180mg**

4	long thick rosemary twigs	4
4	lean large noisettes of lamb (about 100 g/3 ½ oz each), trimmed of fat	4
1	onion, thinly sliced	1
2	garlic cloves, chopped	2
1 tsp	chopped fresh oregano, or ¼ tsp dried oregano	1 tsp
¼ tsp	salt	¼ tsp
	freshly ground black pepper	
15 cl	medium white wine	¼ pt
Tomato and olive relish		
1 tsp	virgin olive oil	1 tsp
1	small onion, finely chopped	1
8	black olives, stoned and finely chopped	8
2 tsp	white wine vinegar	2 tsp
½ tsp	caster sugar	½ tsp
2 tsp	chopped fresh thyme, or ½ tsp dried thyme	2 tsp
2 tbsp	medium white wine, or water	2 tbsp
5	tomatoes, skinned, seeded (page 138), coarsely chopped and drained	5

Push a rosemary twig through each noisette, then place the noisettes in a shallow dish large enough to hold them in a single layer. Sprinkle the onion, garlic, oregano, salt and some pepper evenly over the lamb, then pour on the wine. Cover the dish, and put the lamb in the refrigerator to marinate for about 4 hours; turn the noisettes several times during this period. Remove the lamb from the refrigerator about 1 hour before cooking, to allow it to reach room temperature.

To make the tomato and olive relish, heat the oil in a small saucepan. Add the onion and cook it very gently for about 8 minutes, stirring occasionally, until it is softened but not browned. Stir in the olives, vinegar, sugar, thyme, wine and tomatoes. Remove the pan from the heat and set it aside.

Lightly oil the barbecue rack, and cook the noisettes over hot coals for 6 to 8 minutes on each side, until they are firm to the touch and browned. Meanwhile, reheat the relish for about 2 minutes, and transfer it to a small bowl. Remove the strings from the noisettes and serve them accompanied by the relish.

EDITOR'S NOTE: *If the rosemary twigs are too soft to push through the lamb, pierce the meat first with a metal skewer.*

Pork and Apple Kebabs

Serves 4
Working time: about 45 minutes
Total time: about 2 hours and 45 minutes
(includes marinating)

Calories **300**
Protein **35g**
Cholesterol **80mg**
Total fat **12g**
Saturated fat **4g**
Sodium **100mg**

30 cl	dry cider	½ pint
6	black peppercorns, crushed	6
½ tsp	ground cloves	½ tsp
2 tsp	finely chopped fresh sage	2 tsp
2 tsp	chopped fresh rosemary	2 tsp
500 g	pork tenderloin, trimmed of fat, cut into 2.5 cm (1 inch) cubes	1 lb
1 tbsp	safflower oil	1 tbsp
2	crisp dessert apples	2

Pour the cider into a large bowl. Add the peppercorns, cloves, sage and rosemary, and stir well. Add the pork cubes to the bowl, turning them to coat them evenly. Cover the pork, and set it aside to marinate for at least 2 hours at room temperature.

Remove the cubes of pork from the marinade and reserve the marinade. Lightly oil four skewers. Core the apples and cut each one into six wedges; dip each piece of apple in the reserved marinade. Thread pieces of pork and apple alternately on to each of the four skewers, starting and ending with a cube of pork. Stir the oil into the remaining marinade and baste the kebabs with this mixture.

Place the kebabs on the barbecue rack and cook them, over hot coals, for 15 to 20 minutes, until they are cooked through; turn the kebabs and baste them with marinade several times during cooking.

SUGGESTED ACCOMPANIMENT: *celery, walnut and raisin salad with a yogurt and parsley dressing.*

Skewers of Spiced Pork, Aubergine and Pepper

Serves 12
Working time: about 30 minutes
Total time: about 2 hours and 30 minutes
(includes marinating)

Calories **155**
Protein **22g**
Cholesterol **50mg**
Total fat **6g**
Saturated fat **2g**
Sodium **100mg**

1 kg	lean pork fillets, trimmed of all fat, cut into 1 cm (½ inch) medallions	2 lb
3	aubergines, cut into 2.5 cm (1 inch) thick slices and quartered	3
3	sweet green peppers, seeded, deribbed and cut into 2.5 cm (1 inch) squares	3
1 tbsp	safflower oil	1 tbsp
Garlic and cumin marinade		
2	green chili peppers, seeded and finely chopped (caution, page 63)	2
1	small onion, thinly sliced	1
2.5 cm	piece fresh ginger root, finely chopped	1 inch
4	garlic cloves, crushed	4
3	bay leaves	3
1	lime, grated rind and juice	1
2	cinnamon sticks, halved	2
1 tbsp	whole cloves	1 tbsp
2 tsp	ground cumin	2 tsp
¼ tsp	ground turmeric	¼ tsp
1 tbsp	garam masala	1 tbsp

½ tsp	salt	½ tsp
	freshly ground black pepper	
15 cl	plain low-fat yogurt	¼ pint

In a bowl, mix together the marinade ingredients. Add the pork medallions, tossing them in the marinade to coat them well. Cover the bowl and chill the meat in the refrigerator for 2 to 4 hours.

Remove the pork medallions from the marinade and discard the bay leaves, cloves and pieces of cinnamon stick. Thread the pork on to 12 skewers, pushing the skewers through the circumference of each medallion. Thread the pieces of aubergine and sweet green pepper alternately on to 12 more skewers. Brush the vegetable kebabs with the safflower oil.

Oil the barbecue lightly and cook the pork and the vegetable kebabs over hot coals for 3 to 4 minutes on each side, until the meat is lightly browned and cooked through and the peppers and aubergines are tender. Serve the kebabs immediately.

Piquant Pork Chops

Serves 4
Working time: about 15 minutes
Total time: about 9 hours (includes marinating)

Calories **205**
Protein **30g**
Cholesterol **70mg**
Total fat **7g**
Saturated fat **3g**
Sodium **85mg**

1	lime, juice only	1
2 tsp	honey	2 tsp
1 tsp	Tabasco sauce	1 tsp
1 tbsp	red wine vinegar	1 tbsp
75 g	unsalted tomato paste	2½ oz
1 tsp	allspice	1 tsp
	freshly ground black pepper	
4	pork loin chops (about 175 g/6 oz each), trimmed of fat	4

Mix the lime juice, honey, Tabasco sauce, vinegar, tomato paste, allspice and some freshly ground black pepper together in a large bowl. Add the pork chops, and turn them so that they are evenly coated with the marinade. Place the chops in the refrigerator and leave them to marinate for 8 hours, or overnight. Remove them from the refrigerator about an hour before you plan to cook them.

Lightly oil the barbecue rack, and cook the pork chops over hot coals for about 6 minutes on each side, basting them with any remaining marinade.

SUGGESTED ACCOMPANIMENT: *pineapple, cucumber and fennel salad with chopped mint.*

Pork Sheftalias
with Oregano

SHEFTALIAS, MEAT BALLS WRAPPED IN CAUL, ARE A POPULAR
GREEK AND CYPRIOT BARBECUE TREAT.

Serves 6
Working time: about 25 minutes
Total time: about 4 hours and 45 minutes
(includes marinating)

Calories **190**
Protein **25g**
Cholesterol **55mg**
Total fat **5g**
Saturated fat **2g**
Sodium **220mg**

500 g	lean pork, trimmed of fat and minced	1 lb
1	large onion	1
4 tsp	chopped fresh oregano, or 1 teaspoon dried oregano	4 tsp
2 tbsp	chopped flat-leaf parsley	2 tbsp
3 tbsp	red wine	3 tbsp
	freshly ground black pepper	
90 g	fresh breadcrumbs	3 oz
¼ tsp	salt	¼ tsp
1	egg white	1
150 g	caul	6 oz

Put the pork in a bowl and coarsely grate the onion over it. Mix in the oregano, parsley, wine and plenty of pepper. Cover the bowl and put the meat in the refrigerator to marinate for at least 4 hours, or overnight.

Add the breadcrumbs and salt to the marinated pork and mix them in well. In a separate bowl, whisk the egg white until it is fluffy but not stiff, then fold it into the pork and breadcrumb mixture. Shape the mixture into 18 balls. Cut the caul into 18 pieces, each about 12 cm (5 inches) in diameter. Loosely wrap a piece of caul round each ball. Lightly oil the barbecue rack, and cook the sheftalias over hot coals for about 20 minutes, or until they are cooked inside and firm but slightly spongy when pressed; turn the pork balls every 3 to 4 minutes during cooking.

SUGGESTED ACCOMPANIMENTS: *a lightly dressed salad of cucumber, tomatoes, iceberg lettuce and flat-leaf parsley; hot pitta bread.*

EDITOR'S NOTE: *Caul is a weblike fatty membrane that surrounds a pig's stomach. It is available from butchers either fresh or dry-salted. If the latter, rinse before use.*

Pork Rolls with Fennel

Serves 4
Working time: about 1 hour and 30 minutes
Total time: about 10 hours (includes marinating)

Calories **310**
Protein **38g**
Cholesterol **85mg**
Total fat **16g**
Saturated fat **4g**
Sodium **150mg**

2	pork fillets (about 275 g/9 oz each), trimmed of fat	2
2 tbsp	virgin olive oil	2 tbsp
1 tsp	fennel seeds, crushed	1 tsp
1	garlic clove, crushed	1
2	lemons, finely grated rind and juice	2
	freshly ground black pepper	
1	fennel bulb (about 250 g/8 oz), finely chopped, feathery leaves reserved	1
⅛ tsp	salt	⅛ tsp
1 tsp	clear honey	1 tsp

Make a slit down the length of each pork fillet, slicing three quarters of the way through the middle of the meat. Open out each fillet into a rectangular shape and lay it flat on a piece of plastic film; cover each fillet with a second piece of plastic film. Using a wooden meat mallet, beat out the fillets into oblongs about 5 mm (¼ inch) thick. Lay both pieces of meat in a large, rectangular dish. In a small bowl, mix the oil with the fennel seeds, garlic, lemon rind and 4 tablespoons of water. Add some black pepper and mix in the chopped fennel. Spread the mixture evenly over the pork, cover the dish and leave the meat to marinate in the refrigerator for at least 6 hours, or overnight.

Remove the pieces of pork from the dish, scrape off all the marinade ingredients into a bowl, and set the bowl aside. Lay the pork fillets on a work surface and arrange the reserved fennel leaves evenly over them, setting aside a few for garnish. Sprinkle the salt over the chopped fennel mixture in the bowl, then use a slotted spoon to drain the fennel and spread it evenly over the pork; reserve the marinade juices that are left in the bowl. Roll up each fillet to enclose the fennel and tie it with string. Lay the rolls, end to end, on a 40 by 30 cm (16 by 12 inch) double-thickness sheet of foil. Wrap the foil round the pork rolls, folding the edges together to seal the packages.

Place the foil packages on the barbecue rack over hot coals and cook them for 40 minutes, turning them over every 10 minutes; take care not to split the foil as you turn the packages. Remove the cooked pork from the foil, and transfer the cooking juices in the foil to a small bowl. Stir in the lemon juice, the honey and the reserved marinade juices, then brush a little of this mixture over each roll. Cook the pork rolls on the barbecue, without the foil, for a further 10 minutes, basting them frequently with the juices and turning them until they are golden-brown all over. Cut each roll into four thick slices. Serve the slices garnished with the remaining fennel leaves.

SUGGESTED ACCOMPANIMENT: *barbecued tomatoes and courgettes, or other seasonal vegetables.*

EDITOR'S NOTE: *If there are no feathery leaves on the fennel bulbs, spread about 30 g (1 oz) of watercress leaves over the pork fillets instead; garnish the slices of pork with sprigs of watercress.*

Mustard-Marinated Rabbit with Brandied Peaches

Serves 6
Working time: about 35 minutes
Total time: about 7 hours (includes marinating)

Calories **470**
Protein **24g**
Cholesterol **75**
Total fat **10g**
Saturated fat **4g**
Sodium **35mg**

2	garlic cloves, crushed	2
1 kg	rabbit, jointed in six portions, trimmed of fat and membrane	2 lb
6	juniper berries	6
30 cl	red wine	½ pint
1 tbsp	virgin olive oil	1 tbsp
1 tbsp	grainy mustard	1 tbsp
1 tsp	light brown sugar	1 tsp
2 tbsp	soured cream	2 tbsp
Spiced brandied peaches		
175 g	light brown sugar	6 oz
30 cl	brandy	½ pint
30 cl	fruity white wine	½ pint
½	large lemon, juice and pared rind	½
2 tbsp	ground mixed spice	2 tbsp
1	cinnamon stick	1
1 tsp	grated nutmeg	1 tsp
6	firm peaches, halved and stoned	6

Smear the garlic evenly over the rabbit pieces and place them in a dish. Toast the juniper berries in a heavy frying pan over high heat until they release their aroma — about 2 minutes. Add them to the wine together with the oil, mustard, sugar and cream, and whisk the ingredients together with a fork. Pour the marinade over the rabbit and set the meat aside to marinate for 6 to 8 hours, turning it every hour.

About an hour before you cook the rabbit, poach the peaches. Place the sugar, brandy, wine, lemon juice and rind, mixed spice, cinnamon and nutmeg in a pan just large enough to take the 12 peach halves. Bring the liquid to the boil and add the peaches, skin side down. Reduce the heat, cover the pan and simmer the peaches gently for 15 minutes, turning them once. Set the pan of peaches aside.

Remove the rabbit pieces from their dish and reserve the marinade. Cook the rabbit joints over hot coals for 25 to 30 minutes, turning them several times and basting them with the marinade.

Just before serving, use a slotted spoon to remove the peaches from their pan. Place two, skin side down, on each of six serving plates. Strain the syrup into a jug and pour 1 tablespoon over each peach half. Serve the rabbit with the poached peaches.

SUGGESTED ACCOMPANIMENT: *a mixture of long-grain rice and wild rice.*

Bitter-Sweet Duck Breast Salad

Serves 6
Working time: about 30 minutes
Total time: about 8 hours and 30 minutes
(includes marinating)

Calories **145**		
Protein **14g**		
Cholesterol **75mg**		
Total fat **9g**		
Saturated fat **2g**		
Sodium **215mg**		

4	dried bay leaves	4
½ tsp	salt	½ tsp
12	juniper berries	12
1 tsp	mixed peppercorns	1 tsp
2 tsp	coriander seeds	2 tsp
500 g	duck breast fillets, skinned, all visible fat removed	1 lb
4 tsp	virgin olive oil	4 tsp
250 g	chicory, separated into leaves, washed and dried	8 oz
100 g	watercress, trimmed, washed and dried	3½ oz
2	small oranges, rind finely shredded, fruit segmented	2
15 g	shelled walnuts	½ oz
2 tsp	walnut oil	2 tsp
2½ tbsp	fresh orange juice	2½ tbsp

Using a mortar and pestle, pound the bay leaves to a powder with the salt. Add the juniper berries, peppercorns and coriander seeds, and crush the spices to a fine powder. Rub this mixture over the duck breasts, then place them in a dish. Cover the dish and leave the duck to marinate in the refrigerator for at least 8 hours, or up to 24 hours.

Remove the duck from the refrigerator at least 1 hour before cooking. Wipe the meat with paper towels to remove any liquid, excess salt and most of the spices. Brush the duck with 1 teaspoon of the olive oil, and lightly oil the barbecue rack.

Put the chicory, watercress, orange segments and walnuts in a salad bowl. In a small screw-top jar, mix the walnut oil with 2 teaspoons of the olive oil and 1½ tablespoons of the orange juice. Set aside.

Mix together the remaining olive oil and orange juice, and brush a little of this mixture over the duck breasts. Cook the duck over medium-hot coals for 2 minutes, then turn the breasts and continue to cook them for a further 3 to 4 minutes, until the meat is lightly browned on the outside but still slightly pink in the middle. Turn the duck breasts every 1 to 2 minutes during cooking, brushing them lightly with the orange juice and olive oil mixture.

Leave the cooked duck to rest for 2 to 3 minutes, then slice the meat into strips and add them to the chicory and watercress. Add the finely shredded orange rind. Shake the jar of dressing, pour it over the salad and toss all of the ingredients together.

EDITOR'S NOTE: *To segment an orange, first cut off all the peel and pith. Hold the fruit over a bowl to catch the juice, then use a serrated knife to cut between the membranes dividing the segments. Cut in towards the centre of the fruit, removing each segment in turn. (Squeeze all the juice from the remaining core and membranes before discarding them.)*

Spit-Roasted
Savoury Chicken

Serves 8
Working time: about 35 minutes
Total time: about 7 hours (includes marinating)

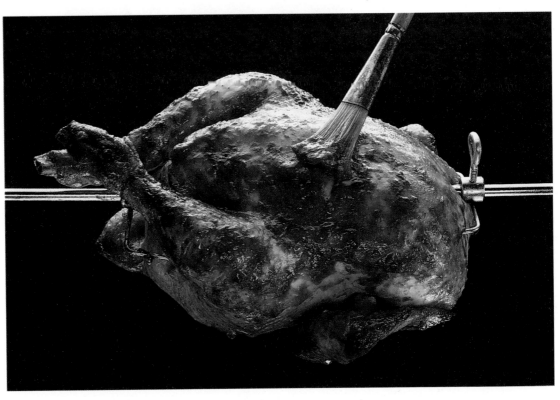

Calories **195**
Protein **24g**
Cholesterol **90mg**
Total fat **9g**
Saturated fat **2g**
Sodium **85mg**

2 tbsp	safflower oil	2 tbsp
1	small onion, grated	1
500 g	tomatoes, skinned, seeded, (page 138) and chopped	1 lb
½	lemon, strained juice only	½
2 tbsp	Worcester sauce	2 tbsp
1 tsp	Tabasco sauce	1 tsp
1 tsp	dry mustard	1 tsp
2 tbsp	dark brown sugar	2 tbsp
1.75 kg	roasting chicken	3½ lb

Heat the oil in a heavy saucepan over low heat. Add the onion and cook for 2 minutes, until it is softened but not browned. Stir in the tomatoes, lemon juice, Worcester sauce, Tabasco sauce, mustard and sugar. Cover the pan and simmer the ingredients for 15 minutes, stirring occasionally, until the tomatoes are reduced to a purée. Remove the pan from the heat and pour the marinade into a bowl, then set it aside until it is cool — about 1 hour.

Put the chicken in a large bowl and pour the cooled marinade over it. Cover the bowl and leave the chicken to marinate for at least 4 hours, at room temperature, turning it several times.

Push a barbecue spit rod into the marinated chicken through the neck flap just above the breast bone, and out just above the tail. Secure the spit rod with the holding forks and attach the spit to the barbecue, on the turning mechanism. Rearrange the coals to leave room for a drip tray immediately below the chicken; set the drip tray in place.

Cook the chicken for 1¼ to 1½ hours, or until it is tender and the juices run clear when a thigh is pierced with a skewer. Baste the chicken frequently while it is cooking, first with the marinade, then with the cooking juices from the drip tray.

Poussins with Rum

Serves 4
Working time: about 30 minutes
Total time: about 1 hour and 20 minutes
(includes marinating)

Calories **190**
Protein **27g**
Cholesterol **90mg**
Total fat **4g**
Saturated fat **1g**
Sodium **120mg**

2	small poussins (about 350 g/12 oz each)	2
2 tbsp	dark rum	2 tbsp
1	lime, juice only	1
1 ½ tbsp	clear honey	1 ½ tbsp
1	garlic clove, crushed	1
⅛ tsp	salt	⅛ tsp
1 tbsp	coriander seeds	1 tbsp
½ tsp	black peppercorns	½ tsp

Using either a pair of poultry shears or strong kitchen scissors, halve each poussin lengthwise by cutting through the backbone and breastbone. Cut off and discard the leg tips and the parson's nose. Wash the poussin halves under running water and pat them dry.

In a small bowl, mix together the rum, lime juice, honey, garlic and salt. Place the poussin halves in a shallow dish just large enough to accommodate them. Rub the rum mixture all over the poussins, then set them aside in a cool place, covered, and leave them to marinate for 30 minutes.

Using either a mortar and pestle or a coffee grinder, coarsely crush the coriander seeds and the black peppercorns. Remove the poussin halves from the marinade and reserve the marinade. Thread two of the poussin halves on to each of two long metal skewers, piercing the legs and wings. Brush the skewered poussins with a little of the remaining rum marinade, then press the crushed coriander seeds and peppercorns all over the skin side of the birds.

Lightly oil the barbecue rack. Cook the poussins over hot coals for 20 to 25 minutes, turning the birds every 5 minutes, until the juices run clear when a skewer is inserted into a thigh.

SUGGESTED ACCOMPANIMENT: *a salad of mixed blanched vegetables, garnished with chopped parsley.*

Yogurt Chicken Drumstricks

Serves 8
Working time: about 30 minutes
Total time: about 3 hours and 30 minutes
(includes marinating)

Calories **160**
Protein **26g**
Cholesterol **90mg**
Total fat **6g**
Saturated f6 **2g**
Sodium **190mg**

16	chicken drumsticks (about 1.5 kg/3 lb), skinned	16
½ tsp	salt	½ tsp
1	lemon, grated rind and juice	1
3 tbsp	paprika	3 tbsp
½ tsp	Tabasco sauce	½ tsp
15 cl	plain low-fat yogurt	, pt
	freshly ground black pepper	
	crisp salad leaves, for garnish	

Cut two deep, diagonal slits in opposite sides of each drumstick. In a small bowl, stir the salt and the grated lemon rind into the lemon juice, then rub the mixture over each drumstick and into the slits. Place the drumsticks on a wire rack set over a baking tray, and sieve 1 tablespoon of the paprika evenly over the upper side of the drumsticks.

In another bowl, mix together the Tabasco sauce, yogurt and some black pepper. Using a brush, coat the paprika-sprinkled side of each drumstick with the yogurt mixture. Turn the drumsticks over, sieve another tablespoon of paprika over them, and coat them with the remaining yogurt mixture. Set the drumsticks aside for 3 hours, until the yogurt begins to dry.

Lightly oil the barbecue rack. Cook the drumsticks over hot coals for 15 to 20 minutes, turning them every 5 minutes. After the last turn, sprinkle the remaining paprika over the drumsticks. Serve the drumsticks immediately, garnished with crisp salad leaves.

SUGGESTED ACCOMPANIMENT: *mushroom and sweet red pepper salad.*

Spatchcocked Poussin with Hot Tropical Fruits

Serves 4
Working time: about 1 hour and 15 minutes
Total time: about 15 hours (includes marinating)

Calories **450**
Protein **33g**
Cholesterol **90mg**
Total fat **13g**
Saturated fat **3g**
Sodium **105mg**

2	poussins (about 350 g/12 oz each)	2
4 tbsp	sweet white wine	4 tbsp
1 tbsp	honey	1 tbsp
1 tsp	Sichuan peppercorns	1 tsp
2 tsp	five-spice powder	2 tsp
1 tsp	dry mustard	1 tsp
2	garlic cloves	2
2.5 cm	piece fresh ginger root, peeled	1 inch
½	lime, juice only	½
1 tbsp	grapeseed or safflower oil	1 tbsp
	lime wedges, for garnish	
Peppered fruits		
125 g	light brown sugar	4 oz
1	lime, peel of whole cut into fine strips, and juice of half	1
5 cm	piece fresh ginger root, cut in half	2 inch
½ tsp	fresh green peppercorns, crushed, or bottled peppercorns, rinsed and crushed	½ tsp
1	chili pepper, seeded and cut into strips (caution, page 63)	1
½	small pineapple, peeled, cored and cut into eight chunks	½
1	small mango, peeled, stoned and cut into eight chunks	1
1	small banana, cut into eight pieces	1
½	avocado, peeled, stoned and cut into 12 pieces	½

Lay one poussin on the work surface, breast down. Using a sharp knife, cut through the cartilage on each side of the backbone from the tail towards the neck; use a sawing motion to cut through the rib cage. Pull the backbone free and discard it. Turn the bird over and position it with its legs towards you. Place the heel of your hand on the breast and press down hard to break the breastbone, rib cage, collarbones and wishbone, so that the bird lies flat. Slip your fingers under the skin at the neck and loosen the skin all over the bird, including the thigh. Repeat with the other bird.

In a small saucepan, warm the wine with the honey and peppercorns until the honey has dissolved. Stir in the five-spice powder and mustard, then remove the pan from the heat. Place the garlic in a press and squeeze out the juice and a minimum of pulp into the wine mixture. Place the ginger in the garlic press and squeeze as much ginger juice as possible into the saucepan. Add the lime juice and stir well. Place the birds in a large, shallow dish and pour the prepared wine marinade over them. Cover the dish and leave the poussins in the refrigerator to marinate for at least 12 hours, or up to 24 hours, turning them from time to time to coat them evenly in the marinade.

About 1½ hours before barbecuing the poussins, remove the birds from the refrigerator and prepare the peppered fruits. In a saucepan, dissolve the sugar in 30 cl (½ pint) of water. Add the strips of lime peel and the ginger. Bring the liquid to the boil and boil it for 5 minutes. Remove the pan from the heat, add the peppercorns and chili pepper, and leave the syrup to cool. Strain the cooled syrup into a dish. Add the lime juice and the pineapple and mango chunks, turning them to coat them with syrup. After 30 minutes, submerge the banana and avocado pieces in the syrup and set the fruits aside until required.

About 10 minutes before barbecuing the poussins, put eight wooden or bamboo skewers to soak in cold water. Pat the poussins dry with paper towels and thread two lightly oiled metal skewers through each bird: one skewer through both wings and the second through both thighs. Drain the fruit and thread the pieces on to the soaked skewers. Boil the syrup rapidly until it is reduced to 2 to 3 tablespoons, and brush a little of the reduced syrup over the skewered fruits; reserve the remaining syrup.

Lightly oil the barbecue rack. Cook the poussins for 20 minutes over medium-hot coals; start with the skin side down and turn the birds once or twice during cooking. Brush the underside of the poussins with a little of the grapeseed oil and the leftover marinade, as necessary. About 2 minutes before the poussins finish cooking, glaze the skin side of each bird with the remaining reduced fruit syrup. Remove the poussins from the heat and leave them to stand for 3 to 5 minutes before removing the skewers.

Meanwhile, barbecue the skewered fruit until the pieces are lightly caramelized — 5 to 6 minutes. Just before serving, glaze the cooked fruit with a little more of the reduced syrup. Serve the poussins and fruits hot, garnished with lime wedges.

SUGGESTED ACCOMPANIMENT: *brown rice.*

EDITOR'S NOTE: *For a slightly less spicy syrup in which to marinate the fruit, remove the strips of chili 10 minutes after the syrup has been set aside to cool.*

Chicken Satay, Thai-Style

SATAY, SKEWERS OF MEAT GRILLED OVER CHARCOAL,
ARE ENJOYED ALL OVER SOUTH-EAST ASIA. THIS CHICKEN
VERSION IS DISTINGUISHED BY THE INCLUSION OF THE
TYPICALLY THAI SPICES GALANGAL, LEMON GRASS AND
CORIANDER STALKS.

Serves 6
Working time: about 1 hour
Total time: about 2 hours and 30 minutes
(includes marinating)

Calories **260**
Protein **22g**
Cholesterol **80g**
Total fat **14g**
Saturated fat **4g**
Sodium **95mg**

1 kg	chicken thighs, skinned and boned	2 lb
1 tsp	tamarind concentrate	1 tsp
2	garlic cloves, chopped	2
6	red Oriental shallots, chopped	6
2.5 cm	piece galangal	1 inch
1 tbsp	dark brown sugar	1 tbsp
1	lime, juice only	1
1 tbsp	safflower oil	1 tbsp
4 tsp	nam pla	4 tsp
Pineapple and cucumber relish		
½	slightly under-ripe pineapple	½
½	cucumber, peeled	½
¼ tsp	salt	¼ tsp
¼ tsp	sugar	¼ tsp
2	limes, juice only	2
6	red Oriental shallots, sliced into rings	6
1	red chili pepper, seeded and thinly sliced into rings (caution, page 63)	1
Peanut and coconut dipping sauce		
60 g	unsalted dry-roasted peanuts, coarsely crushed	2 oz
1	garlic clove, chopped	1
12	red Oriental shallots, chopped	12
2	lemon grass bulbs, chopped	2
4	coriander stalks, chopped	4
1	red chili pepper, seeded and chopped	1
1 tsp	safflower oil	1 tsp
¼ litre	coconut milk	8 fl oz
1 tbsp	nam pla	1 tbsp
1 tsp	dark soy sauce	1 tsp
2 tsp	dark brown sugar	2 tsp
½ tsp	shrimp paste (optional)	½ tsp

Cut the chicken across the grain into long ribbons about 5 mm (¼ inch) thick and 2 cm (¾ inch) wide. Place the strips in a large, shallow dish.

Pound the tamarind concentrate, garlic, shallots, galangal and sugar to a thick paste using a pestle and mortar. Add the lime juice, oil and nam pla, and stir them in. Pour this mixture over the chicken strips and turn them over to coat them thoroughly. Cover the dish

and leave the chicken to marinate in the refrigerator for at least 1 hour, or overnight, stirring occasionally.

For the relish, remove the flesh from the pineapple half with a grapefruit knife, leaving a 1 cm (½ inch) thick shell. Cover the shell with plastic film and put it in the refrigerator until needed. Remove any brown eyes from the flesh and discard the central core if it is fibrous. Cut the flesh into 2 cm (¾ inch) chunks. Halve the cucumber lengthwise; remove the seeds with a spoon and discard them. Cut the cucumber into chunks. Mix the salt, ¼ teaspoon of the sugar and the lime juice in a bowl. Add the pineapple, cucumber, shallots and chili, and toss them well; add more sugar if the pineapple is too sharp for your taste. Cover the dish with plastic film and place it in the refrigerator for at least 1 hour, or overnight, stirring the contents several times during this period.

Soak twenty-four 25 cm (10 inch) bamboo skewers in water for 10 minutes. Thread each chicken strip on to a skewer as if you were sewing with a needle, then gather up the chicken slightly so that the meat on each skewer measures about 12 cm (5 inches) in length. Reserve the marinade.

Next, make the peanut and coconut sauce. Pound the peanuts, garlic, Oriental shallots, lemon grass, coriander and chili to a smooth paste using the pestle and mortar. Heat the safflower oil in a wok or heavy frying pan and gently fry the paste until it is light brown. Add the coconut milk, nam pla, soy sauce, sugar and shrimp paste, if you are using it, and bring the ingredients to the boil. Remove the wok from the heat and cover it with a lid.

Lightly oil the barbecue rack, and cook the satay over hot coals for 8 to 10 minutes, turning them once and brushing them several times with the reserved marinade. Spoon the pineapple and cucumber relish into the pineapple shell. Transfer the peanut and coconut sauce to serving bowls. Serve the satay immediately, with the dipping sauce and the relish.

SUGGESTED ACCOMPANIMENT: *triangles of toasted thin bread.*

EDITOR'S NOTE: *Red Oriental shallots have a coppery red skin and pink flesh, and are smaller and rounder than their European counterparts. Oriental shallots are available in most Chinese groceries, although European shallots or red onions may be substituted.*

An Array of Home-Made Sausages

Shop-bought sausages, an old barbecue favourite, often contain a high percentage of fat, salt and preservatives. By making sausages yourself, however, you can choose the cut of meat and trim it of all fat, vary the ingredients and experiment with interesting combinations of herbs and spices. Meat may even be omitted entirely. Do not over-chop or over-mince sausage meat, as too smooth a texture will dry out during cooking. Aim for a coarse texture, achieved either by patient hand-chopping using two sharp, heavy knives or by using a meat mincer. Good results can also be achieved with a food processor, but chill the container and blade for at least 30 minutes and hand-chop the meat into 2 cm (¾ inch) cubes before processing it; never put more than 500 g (1 lb) at a time into the processor bowl and stop the machine as soon as the meat is chopped, just before it forms a ball.

Use natural lamb sausage casings, which are obtainable from good butchers. Before filling them, soak the casings in acidulated water for about 1 hour, until they are soft and elastic, then cut them into 1 metre (3 foot) lengths. Rinse each length by rolling one end over a tap spout or funnel and running cold water through it. Discard any punctured casings and lay out the rest to drain.

To fill the casings, roll one length on to the sausage-making attachment of a mincer. Leave about 10 cm (4 inches) hanging loose and tie a knot in the end. Fill the mincer's bowl with the stuffing and turn the handle. As the casing fills, gradually slip it off the nozzle; make sure the stuffing is loosely packed. Alternatively, use a food processor with a sausage-making attachment, or gather the casing round the neck of a funnel and press the filling through the funnel with a pestle.

When only about 10 cm (4 inches) of casing remains unfilled, slip the casing off the sausage-making attachment or funnel and knot it. Roll the casing on a work surface in order to even out the stuffing. To form links, twist the casing through three or four turns at 12 cm (5 inch) intervals.

Chicken Sausages with Ricotta and Spinach

Makes 12 sausages
Working time: about 1 hour
Total time: about 1 hour and 15 minutes

125 g	spinach, washed, centre stems removed	4 oz
45 g	sorrel, washed, centre stems removed	1½ oz
675 g	chicken (leg or thigh), minced	1 lb 6 oz
175 g	low-fat ricotta cheese	6 oz
4	shallots, finely chopped	4
1 tbsp	chopped parsley	1 tbsp
1 tbsp	chopped fresh tarragon	1 tbsp
¾ tsp	salt	¾ tsp
	freshly ground black pepper	
125 g	low-fat fromage frais	4 oz
2 metres	lamb sausage casings, soaked	7 feet

Per sausage:
Calories **105**
Protein **16g**
Cholesterol **45mg**
Total fat **3g**
Saturated fat **1g**
Sodium **160mg**

Blanch the spinach and sorrel, and refresh them under cold water; drain and chop them. Wrap them in a piece of muslin or paper towel, squeeze them dry and place them in a bowl. Mix in the chicken, ricotta, shallots, herbs, salt, some pepper and half of the *fromage frais*. Add more *fromage frais* until the mixture is loose enough to be squeezed through a piping bag but stiff enough to be moulded into a walnut-sized ball.

Fill the casings with the mixture following the instructions *(text, left)* and form links. Cut between the links to separate the sausages. Prick each sausage several times. Oil the barbecue rack lightly and cook the sausages over medium-hot coals for 10 to 15 minutes, until golden-brown, turning frequently.

SUGGESTED ACCOMPANIMENT: *salad of radicchio, red onion and diakon radish.*

Lamb Sausages with Yogurt and Thyme

Makes 12 sausages
Working time: about 1 hour
Total time: about 1 hour and 15 minutes

60 g	couscous	2 oz
675 g	lean leg of lamb, trimmed of fat and minced	1 lb 6 oz
150 g	thick Greek ewe's milk yogurt	5 oz
1 tbsp	virgin olive oil	1 tbsp
175 g	sweet red or orange pepper, peeled and finely diced	6 oz
1½ tbsp	fresh thyme leaves	1½ tbsp
1	onion, finely chopped	1
2	garlic cloves, finely chopped	2
4	black olives, stoned, finely diced	4
¾ tsp	salt	¾ tsp
	freshly ground black pepper	
2 metres	lamb sausage casings, soaked	7 feet

Per sausage:
Calories **135**
Protein **16g**
Cholesterol **40mg**
Total fat **6g**
Saturated fat **5g**
Sodium **175mg**

First soak the couscous in 10 cl (3½ fl oz) of water for 10 to 15 minutes, until it has absorbed all the water. Place the soaked couscous in a piece of muslin or paper towel and squeeze out as much water as possible. Place the couscous in a large bowl. Add the lamb, yogurt, olive oil, sweet pepper, thyme, onion, garlic, olives, salt and some black pepper, and mix them well.

Fill the lamb sausage casings with the mixture following the instructions *(text, far left)* and form links. Cut between the links to separate the sausages. Prick each sausage several times. Oil the barbecue rack lightly and cook the sausages over medium-hot coals for 10 to 15 minutes, until golden-brown, turning them frequently.

SUGGESTED ACCOMPANIMENT: *oakleaf lettuce.*

Pork Sausages with Orange and Sage

Makes 12 sausages
Working time: about 1 hour
Total time: about 1 hour and 15 minutes

750 g	neck end of pork, trimmed of excess fat, coarsely chopped	1½ lb
125 g	lean bacon, trimmed of fat and finely diced	4 oz
4 tsp	grated orange rind	4 tsp
2 tbsp	shredded fresh sage leaves	2 tbsp
1	onion, finely chopped	1
1	garlic clove, finely chopped	1
1 tsp	ground ginger	1 tsp
¾ tsp	salt	¾ tsp
	white pepper	
2 tbsp	red vermouth or sherry	2 tbsp
1½ tsp	orange-flavoured liqueur or brandy	1½ tsp
2 tbsp	fresh orange juice	2 tbsp
100 g	fresh breadcrumbs	3½ oz
2 metres	lamb sausage casings, soaked	7 feet
4 tbsp	unsalted chicken stock (recipe, page 139), reduced by boiling to 2 tbsp	4 tbsp

Per sausage:
Calories **170**
Protein **20g**
Cholesterol **45mg**
Total fat **8g**
Saturated fat **4g**
Sodium **325mg**

In a bowl, blend together all of the ingredients except for the casings and 1 tablespoon of the reduced stock. Gradually blend in some or all of the remaining stock until the mixture is loose enough to be squeezed through a piping bag but stiff enough to be moulded into a walnut-sized ball.

Fill the casings with the stuffing following the instructions *(text, far left)* and form links. Cut between the links to separate the sausages. Prick each sausage several times. Oil the barbecue rack lightly and cook the sausages over medium-hot coals for 10 to 15 minutes, turning them frequently, until they are golden-brown.

SUGGESTED ACCOMPANIMENT: *watercress and orange salad.*

Beef Sausages with Five-Spice Powder

Makes 12 sausages
Working time: about 1 hour
Total time: about 1 hour and 15 minutes

600 g	lean blade of beef, trimmed of fat and minced	1¼ lb
150 g	medium oatmeal	5 oz
2	garlic cloves, finely chopped	2
2.5 cm	piece fresh ginger root, finely chopped	1 inch
5	spring onions, finely chopped	5
1½ tbsp	low-sodium light soy sauce or shoyu	1½ tbsp
1½ tbsp	low-sodium dark soy sauce or tamari	1½ tbsp
3 tbsp	rice wine or dry sherry	3 tbsp
1 tsp	clear honey	1 tsp
2 tsp	five-spice powder	2 tsp
¼ tsp	cayenne pepper	¼ tsp
2 metres	lamb sausage casings, soaked	7 feet
8 cl	unsalted veal stock (recipe, page 139) or water	3 fl oz

Per sausage:
Calories **155**
Protein **16g**
Cholesterol **40mg**
Total fat **5g**
Saturated fat **3g**
Sodium **50mg**

In a bowl, blend together all the ingredients except for the casings and half the stock. Mix in some or all of the remaining stock until the mixture is loose enough to be squeezed through a piping bag but stiff enough to be shaped into a walnut-sized ball.

Fill the casings with the stuffing following the instructions *(text, far left)* and form links. Cut between the links to separate the sausages. Prick each of the sausages several times. Oil the barbecue rack lightly and grill the sausages over medium-hot coals for 10 to 15 minutes, turning them frequently, until they are golden-brown.

SUGGESTED ACCOMPANIMENTS: *wild rice; oyster mushroom salad.*

Spicy Potato Sausages with Coriander

Makes 12 sausages
Working time: about 1 hour
Total time: about 2 hours

15 g	unsalted butter	½ oz
1	large onion, finely chopped	1
300 g	mushrooms, finely chopped	10 oz
1 or 2	garlic cloves, finely chopped	1 or 2
3 cm	piece fresh ginger root, finely chopped	1¼ inch
750 g	potatoes, boiled and mashed	1½ lb
1	egg, plus one egg white	1
1 tsp	poppy seeds	1 tsp
1 tsp	mustard seeds, toasted	1 tsp
1½ tbsp	cut chives	1½ tbsp
1½ tbsp	chopped fresh coriander	1½ tbsp
¾ tsp	salt	¾ tsp
¼ tsp	cayenne pepper	¼ tsp
	freshly ground black pepper	
100 g	fromage frais	3 oz
2 metres	lamb sausage casings, soaked	7 feet

Per sausage:
Calories **75**
Protein **3g**
Cholesterol **20mg**
Total fat **2g**
Saturated fat **1g**
Sodium **140mg**

Melt the butter in a pan and fry the onion over medium heat until it is soft — about 5 minutes. Increase the heat, add the mushrooms, garlic and ginger, and fry until the mixture is quite dry — about 3 minutes.

Place the potatoes in a bowl over a pan of simmering water. Add the egg and egg white and stir until the egg thickens. Remove the bowl from the heat and stir in the onion mixture, and all the remaining ingredients except for the casings. Cool, then chill, the filling.

Fill the casings with the mixture following the instructions *(text, far left)* and form links. Cut between the links to separate the sausages. Prick each of the sausages several times. Oil the barbecue rack lightly and cook the sausages gently for 15 to 20 minutes, turning several times, until golden-brown.

SUGGESTED ACCOMPANIMENT: *curly endive and tomato salad.*

Cod Steaks Topped with Tomato and Basil

Serves 4
Working time: about 20 minutes
Total time: about 30 minutes

Calories **170**
Protein **27g**
Cholesterol **75mg**
Total fat **4g**
Saturated fat **1g**
Sodium **120mg**

500 g	tomatoes, skinned, seeded (page 138) and chopped	1 lb
20 g	basil leaves, chopped	¾ oz
3 tbsp	medium-dry sherry	3 tbsp
⅛ tsp	salt	⅛ tsp
	freshly ground black pepper	
2 tsp	virgin olive oil	2 tsp
4	cod steaks (about 150 g/5 oz each), central bones removed	4

In a bowl, mix the chopped tomatoes with the basil and sherry, and season the mixture with the salt and some freshly ground black pepper. Brush the olive oil over four double-thickness rectangles of foil, each one measuring about 32 by 20 cm (13 by 8 inches). Lay a cod steak on each piece of foil and top it with a quarter of the tomato mixture. Wrap the foil round the fish steaks, sealing the edges securely to keep all the cooking juices in the packets.

Cook the cod steaks over hot coals for 3 to 5 minutes on each side, taking care not to split the foil when turning the packets over. Unwrap the packets with the tomato side up and slide the contents of each one on to an individual plate. Remove and discard the thin strips of cod skin and serve the steaks at once.

SUGGESTED ACCOMPANIMENT: *parslied new potatoes.*

Barbecued Fish Steaks
with Red Pepper

Serves 4
Working time: about 45 minutes
Total time: about 1 hour

Calories **215**
Protein **27g**
Cholesterol **75mg**
Total fat **12g**
Saturated fat **2g**
Sodium **215mg**

600 g	grouper or cod fillets, skin left on, cut into four pieces	1 ¼ lb
1 ½ tbsp	virgin olive oil	1 ½ tbsp
2	limes, juice of one, the other cut into wedges, for garnish	2
½ tsp	salt	½ tsp
	freshly ground black pepper	
2	large sweet red peppers	2

Put the fish pieces, skin side down, in a shallow dish. In a small bowl, combine the olive oil, lime juice, salt and some freshly ground black pepper. Reserve 1 tablespoon of this marinade and brush the remainder on the upper side of the steaks. Set the fish aside, covered, to marinate for 30 minutes.

Meanwhile, place the red peppers on the barbecue rack over hot coals. Cook them for 10 to 15 minutes, turning them frequently, until their skins blacken. Remove the cooked peppers from the barbecue and allow them to cool. When they are cool enough to handle, peel off their skins. Slice the skinned peppers thinly and evenly. Toss the slices in the reserved marinade, and set them aside.

Place the fish in an oiled grilling basket and grill it, skin side down, over low coals, for 10 to 15 minutes. Turn the fish over and cook it for a further 5 minutes. Serve the fish immediately, accompanied by the red pepper strips and garnished with the lime wedges.

SUGGESTED ACCOMPANIMENT: *potato and watercress salad.*

Sesame Seafood Kebabs

Serves 4
Working time: about 30 minutes
Total time: about 1 hour and 30 minutes

Calories **195.**
Protein **21g**
Cholesterol **85mg**
Total fat **7g**
Saturated fat **3g**
Sodium **130mg**

¼ litre	dry white wine	8 fl oz
1 tbsp	safflower oil	1 tbsp
1	garlic clove, crushed	1
½	lemon, grated rind and 1 tbsp juice	½
⅛ tsp	salt	⅛ tsp
	freshly ground black pepper	
350 g	monkfish fillets	12 oz
1 tsp	cornflour	1 tsp
1 tbsp	chopped mixed fresh herbs, such as basil, parsley and chives	1 tbsp
1 tbsp	toasted sesame seeds	1 tbsp
4	large raw prawns	4
8	scallops, bright white connective tissue removed	8
	shredded lettuce, for garnish	

In a bowl, mix 15 cl (¼ pint) of the wine with the oil, garlic, lemon rind and juice, salt and some pepper. Pour half of the mixture into a small pan. Cut the fish into 12 equal pieces and add them to the wine mixture remaining in the bowl. Turn the pieces over in the marinade to coat them thoroughly. Cover the bowl and put it in the refrigerator for 1 to 2 hours.

Add the remaining wine to the mixture in the saucepan. Blend the cornflour to a smooth paste with a little cold water. Stir the paste into the liquid in the pan and heat it slowly, stirring continuously, until it boils and thickens. Remove the pan from the heat, then stir in the mixed herbs and the sesame seeds. Cover the pan and set it over very low heat to keep the sauce hot while you cook the kebabs.

Lightly oil four skewers. Drain the fish and thread the pieces on to the skewers, alternating them with the prawns and scallops. Cook the kebabs over medium-hot coals for 3 to 5 minutes on each side; turn them gently, otherwise the pieces of seafood may break.

Spread the shredded lettuce on a large platter and pour the sauce into a warmed jug. Arrange the seafood kebabs on the shredded lettuce and serve them immediately, accompanied by the sauce.

EDITOR'S NOTE: *To toast sesame seeds, sprinkle a layer of seeds in a heavy-bottomed pan, cover the pan and cook the seeds over high heat. When they begin to pop, keep the pan on the heat for 1 minute more but shake it constantly.*

Tarragon-Marinated Side of Salmon with Skewered New Potatoes

Serves 8
Working time: about 1 hour
Total Time: about 14 hours (includes marinating)

Calories **305**
Protein **26g**
Cholesterol **85mg**
Total fat **17g**
Saturated fat **4g**
Sodium **395mg**

1 kg	salmon fillet (either one side or two)	2¼ lb
15 g	fresh tarragon, chopped	½ oz
15 g	salt	½ oz
30 g	light brown sugar	1 oz
1 tbsp	vodka	1 tbsp
1½ tsp	crushed black peppercorns	1½ tsp
350 g	small new potatoes	12 oz
1 tsp	grapeseed or safflower oil	1 tsp
	dried fennel twigs or seeds, to burn on the barbecue (optional)	
	fennel leaves, for garnish	

Wipe the salmon and run a finger along the fillet to feel for remaining small bones: remove these bones with a pair of tweezers. Lay the salmon in a large, shallow dish. In a small bowl, mix the chopped tarragon, salt, sugar, vodka and 1 teaspoon of the crushed peppercorns. Using the back of a metal spoon, spread this tarragon marinade over the flesh side of the salmon. (If you are using two sides of salmon, sandwich the flesh sides together.) Cover the salmon loosely with a damp cloth, and leave it to marinate in the refrigerator for at least 12 hours, or up to 48 hours.

Soak several bamboo skewers in cold water for 10 minutes, then drain them. Cook the new potatoes in boiling water until they are just tender — 10 to 15 minutes. Drain the potatoes and return them to the saucepan. Add the grapeseed oil and the remaining crushed peppercorns, and toss the potatoes to coat them evenly in oil and pepper. Thread the potatoes on to the skewers, and set them aside.

Lightly oil the barbecue rack. Wipe off all the marinade from the salmon and cook it, flesh side down, over hot coals for 1 minute. Turn the salmon over and grill it for a further 6 to 9 minutes, until it is almost cooked through but not quite opaque near the bone. After about 3 minutes, place the skewered potatoes on the grid and heat them through until they are browned. At the same time, throw the dried fennel twigs or seeds on to the coals, if you are using them.

Transfer the cooked side of salmon to a serving platter. Arrange the new potatoes round the salmon and garnish the dish with fennel leaves. To serve the salmon, carve off fine slices, keeping the knife almost parallel with the fillet.

SUGGESTED ACCOMPANIMENT: *cucumber, grape and curly endive salad with a yogurt dressing.*

Barbecued Tuna Steaks

Serves 6
Working time: about 30 minutes
Total time: about 5 hours (includes marinating)

Calories **275**	3	tuna steaks (about 250 g/8 oz each)	3
Protein **35g**	8	spring onions, chopped	8
Cholesterol **80mg**	5 cm	piece fresh ginger root, grated	2 inch
Total fat **16g**	4	garlic cloves	4
Saturated fat **5g**	1	large onion, chopped	1
Sodium **105mg**	1	lime, juice only	1
	4 tbsp	white wine vinegar	4 tbsp
	2 tbsp	virgin olive oil	2 tbsp
	1 tsp	finely crushed black peppercorns	1 tsp
	⅛ tsp	salt	⅛ tsp
	200 g	fromage frais	7 oz
		lime slices, for garnish	

Cut the tuna steaks in half and remove the bone from the middle of each steak. Place the fish in a shallow dish and set it aside while you make the marinade.

Put the spring onions, grated ginger root, garlic cloves and chopped onion in a food processor or blender. Add the lime juice, wine vinegar and olive oil, and process the ingredients to a smooth purée. Stir the crushed peppercorns and the salt into the purée, then pour two thirds of it over the tuna pieces, coating them evenly; reserve the remaining marinade for use in the sauce. Cover the tuna pieces and leave them to marinate in the refrigerator for at least 3 hours, or up to 12 hours. Remove them from the refrigerator at least 1 hour before they are to be cooked, to allow them to reach room temperature.

Before cooking, soak six bamboo skewers in water for 10 minutes. Thread one skewer through each piece of tuna about 2.5 cm (1 inch) from the straight, cut, edge, to keep it flat as it cooks. Cook the tuna over hot coals for 5 to 6 minutes on each side, until it is lightly browned and cooked through.

While the tuna is cooking, stir the remaining marinade into the *fromage frais*. Remove the skewers from the tuna pieces. Serve the tuna with the *fromage frais* sauce, garnished with lime slices.

SUGGESTED ACCOMPANIMENT: *hot herbed bread.*

Leaf-Wrapped Stuffed Herring

THIS RECIPE CALLS FOR HERRING ROE IN THE STUFFING. ASK YOUR FISHMONGER FOR FEMALE FISH WITH SOFT ROE. MALE ROE MAY BE USED AS A SECOND-BEST ALTERNATIVE, BUT IT IS HARDER AND MUST BE BROKEN UP BEFORE USE. IF IT IS THE WRONG SEASON FOR ROE, USE 140 G (4½ OZ) OF CANNED ROE.

Serves 6
Working (and total) time: about 1 hour

Calories **310**
Protein **20g**
Cholesterol **130mg**
Total fat **20g**
Saturated fat **4g**
Sodium **170mg**

1 tsp	unsalted butter	1 tsp
1	small onion, finely chopped	1
6	herrings (about 175 g/6 oz each), gutted and boned, roes reserved	6
1	tart eating apple, peeled, cored, finely diced and put into acidulated water	1
½	lemon, juice only	½
30 g	fresh white breadcrumbs	1 oz
60 g	medium oatmeal	2 oz
1 tbsp	apple juice, cider or water	1 tbsp
2 tbsp	finely chopped fresh dill	2 tbsp
	freshly ground black pepper	
3	cos lettuces	3
¼ tsp	salt	¼ tsp
2 tbsp	Dijon mustard	2 tbsp
12	fresh dill sprigs	12

First make the herring-roe stuffing. Melt the butter in a heavy-bottomed saucepan, add the chopped onion, and cook it gently, stirring occasionally, until it is soft but not browned — about 5 minutes. Add the roe to the saucepan and cook for 2 to 3 minutes, stirring constantly, until all the roe is opaque and broken up. Drain the apple and add it to the roe mixture. Stir in the lemon juice and cook the stuffing gently until the apple is soft but not mushy — about 5 minutes. Remove the saucepan from the heat and allow the stuffing to cool slightly. Mix the white breadcrumbs with 2 tablespoons of the oatmeal, moisten them with the apple juice, cider or water, and add them to the stuffing, together with the chopped dill and some freshly ground black pepper. Mix the stuffing ingredients together well.

Select and wash 24 large lettuce leaves; reserve the lettuce hearts for use in a salad. Keeping the leaves whole, trim out any tough stems. Plunge the leaves into a large saucepan of boiling water, a few at a time, for 2 to 3 seconds, then drain them immediately and refresh them under cold running water. Drain the leaves again and set them aside.

Season the inside of the herrings with the salt and some pepper. Divide the stuffing among the fish, spreading it evenly inside the body cavity. Press the sides of each fish firmly together to enclose the stuffing. Spread 1 teaspoon of the Dijon mustard evenly over the skin of each herring, then coat them in the remaining oatmeal, pressing it gently all over the fish but leaving the head and tail exposed.

For each herring in turn, lay four of the blanched lettuce leaves on the work surface, overlapping them neatly to make an oblong of leaves large enough to wrap round the body of the fish. Place one sixth of the dill sprigs on top of the lettuce and lay the oatmeal-coated herring on the dill sprigs. Wrap the lettuce round the fish, leaving the head and tail exposed but covering the body completely.

Lightly oil the barbecue rack. Lay the herrings on the barbecue, with the joins in the lettuce wrappings underneath (the joins will seal themselves quickly during cooking). Cook the fish for 5 to 10 minutes on each side, according to how plump they are: check that the fish are cooked by cutting into the middle of the plumpest herring. Serve the fish immediately.

SUGGESTED ACCOMPANIMENTS: *baked potatoes; lettuce hearts dressed with soured cream and dill; thinly sliced rye or oatmeal bread.*

EDITOR'S NOTE: *To bone a herring, use a pair of kitchen scissors to snip through the backbone at both ends. Make sure that the belly is slit right down to the tail, then lay the fish, belly side down, on the work surface and press firmly along the length of the body. Turn the fish over and pull away the backbone, starting at the tail end. Use the point of a knife to gently ease away any bones that cling to the fish; pick off any stray bones with a pair of tweezers.*

Whole Anise-Orange Turbot

Serves 4
Working (and total) time: about 25 minutes

Calories **250**
Protein **20g**
Cholesterol **80mg**
Total fat **15g**
Saturated fat **4g**
Sodium **125mg**

1 ½ tsp	ground fennel seeds	1 ½ tsp
1	whole turbot (about 1.5 kg/3 ¼ lb), gilled and bled	1
100 g	thick Greek yogurt	3 ½ oz
1	orange, four slices reserved for garnish, ½ tsp finely grated rind and peel of remainder	1
⅛ tsp	salt	⅛ tsp
⅛ tsp	white pepper	⅛ tsp
6	dried fennel stalks	6
2 tsp	anise-flavoured spirit, such as Pernod	2 tsp
	curly endive leaves, for garnish	

Sprinkle a little of the ground fennel in the gill cavity of the turbot. In a small bowl, mix the yogurt, grated orange rind, salt and pepper with the remaining ground fennel, and set the mixture aside.

Set the rack at its lowest position and oil it lightly. Place the turbot on the rack and grill the fish, dark skin side down, over hot coals for 2½ minutes. Remove the fish and place it on a work surface. Using the point of a sharp knife, cut the skin free at the tail and head ends of the fish. Strip off all the dark skin. Return the fish to the barbecue, placing the white skin side down, and grill the fish for about 1½ minutes. Remove the fish from the barbecue and strip off the white skin.

Lightly oil a grilling basket. Coat one side of the fish with half of the yogurt mixture, and place it, coated side down, on one half of the grilling basket. Spread the remaining yogurt mixture over the second side of the turbot. Close the basket and place the fish on the barbecue with the thick side down (the flesh is thicker on the side which was covered by dark skin). Grill the fish for 2 minutes, then turn the basket over and grill the second side for 1 minute. Repeat this process twice more. Throw the orange peel and fennel stalks on to the coals to produce aromatic smoke. Pour 1 teaspoon of the anise-flavoured spirit over the thick side of the fish and grill it for 2 minutes. Turn the fish and pour the remaining teaspoon of spirit over the thin side. Grill the fish for 1 minute. The flesh should be opaque all over and flake away easily from the bone: test the fish at its thickest part with a small knife. Grill it for a little longer if necessary, but do not overcook it. Serve the turbot at once, on a warmed platter, garnished with the orange slices and curly endive leaves.

SUGGESTED ACCOMPANIMENTS: *barbecued new potatoes; fennel bulbs wrapped in foil and cooked on the barbecue.*

EDITOR'S NOTE: *Turbot are gutted at sea, but ask the fishmonger to remove the gills from the fish. Two small brill may be substituted for the turbot: allow 1 to 2 minutes' grilling on each side before stripping off the skin, then cook the fish for a further 4 minutes, or until it flakes easily.*

Skewered Cheese and Tofu Patties

Serves 4
Working time: about 45 minutes
Total time: about 55 minutes

Calories **240**
Protein **15g**
Cholesterol **30mg**
Total fat **12g**
Saturated fat **5g**
Sodium **435mg**

1 tsp	safflower oil	1 tsp
125 g	onion, finely chopped	4 oz
90 g	fresh white breadcrumbs	3 oz
250 g	smoked tofu	8 oz
125 g	Edam cheese, coarsely grated	4 oz
¼ tsp	freshly ground black pepper	¼ tsp
½ tsp	dry mustard	½ tsp
2 tbsp	chopped parsley	2 tbsp
12	sage leaves, roughly chopped	12
2 tbsp	plain flour	2 tbsp

Soak eight bamboo skewers in water for 10 minutes.

Meanwhile, heat the oil in a small, non-stick frying pan. Add the onion and cook it over medium heat until it is transparent — about 8 minutes. Stir in the bread-crumbs. Remove the pan from the heat and let the mixture cool. Chop the tofu finely in a food processor, then add the cheese, pepper, mustard, parsley and sage. Add the breadcrumb mixture and process briefly, until all the ingredients are evenly combined.

Divide the mixture into 24 equal portions. Mould each portion into a small barrel-shaped patty. Thread these patties on to the bamboo skewers: take a patty in one hand and thread a skewer gently through it lengthwise, holding it firmly in shape as you do so. Keep the remaining patties covered with a damp cloth while you are working, to prevent them from drying out. Sprinkle the flour on the work surface and care-fully roll the skewers in it, so that all the patties are coated evenly in flour; brush off any excess flour.

Place a griddle or baking sheet on the barbecue and brush it lightly with oil. Arrange the skewers on the griddle and cook the patties for 6 to 8 minutes, turning them frequently, until they are golden-brown all over. Serve the cheese and tofu patties immediately.

SUGGESTED ACCOMPANIMENT: *a salad of shredded cos lettuce hearts and onion rings, with a yogurt and parsley dressing.*

Greek Vegetable,
Fruit and Cheese Kebabs

Serves 8
Working time: about 1 hour
Total time: about 2 hours

Calories **170**			
Protein **7g**	125 g	aubergine, cut into eight 2.5 cm (1 inch) cubes	4 oz
Cholesterol **25mg**	¼ tsp	salt	¼ tsp
Total fat **10g**	8	new potatoes (about 350 g/12 oz), scrubbed	8
Saturated fat **5g**			
Sodium **335mg**	2	onions, quartered	2
	2	sweet red or orange peppers, seeded, each cut into eight squares	2
	1	small cucumber, cut into eight thick slices	1
	8	large button mushrooms, wiped clean	8
	2	nectarines, quartered and stoned	2
	200 g	halloumi or feta cheese, cut into eight cubes	7 oz
	2 tbsp	virgin olive oil	2 tbsp
		fresh vine leaves, for garnish (optional)	
	Minted sauce		
	30 cl	plain low-fat yogurt	½ pt
	3 tbsp	chopped mint	3 tbsp
	1	garlic clove, crushed (optional)	1

Sprinkle the aubergine with the salt and set it aside for 30 minutes. Meanwhile, cook the potatoes and onions in a pan of simmering water for 15 to 20 minutes, until just tender. Drain them and leave them to cool.

Rinse the aubergine and put it in a pan of boiling water. Return the water to the boil, reduce the heat and simmer the aubergine for 2 minutes. Add the cucumber, cook for 1 minute, then add the peppers and cook for 2 minutes. Drain and cool the vegetables.

To make the sauce, combine the yogurt, mint, and garlic if you are using it, in a serving bowl.

Put the cooked vegetables, mushrooms, nectarines and cheese on a tray and sprinkle them with the oil. Lightly oil eight metal skewers; thread each skewer with one of each item. Oil the rack and cook the kebabs over hot coals for about 15 minutes, turning them frequently, until tender and lightly charred.

Serve the kebabs at once, on platters lined with vine leaves if you wish, and accompanied by the sauce.

Chick-Pea Croquettes with Sesame Sauce

Serves 6
Working time: about 40 minutes
Total time: about 2 hours and 35 minutes
(includes soaking)

Calories **265**
Protein **14g**
Cholesterol **45mg**
Total fat **12g**
Saturated fat **3g**
Sodium **210mg**

175 g	dried chick-peas, picked over	6 oz
1 tbsp	safflower or peanut oil	1 tbsp
1	small onion, finely chopped	1
2	garlic cloves, crushed	2
2 tsp	ground cumin	2 tsp
1 tsp	ground coriander	1 tsp
60 g	Cheddar cheese, grated	2 oz
30 g	fresh wholemeal breadcrumbs	1 oz
2 tbsp	chopped parsley	2 tbsp
1 tbsp	chopped mint	1 tbsp
1 tbsp	fresh lemon juice	1 tbsp
1	egg, beaten	1
⅛ tsp	salt	⅛ tsp
	freshly ground black pepper	
1	egg white, beaten	1
60 g	dry wholemeal breadcrumbs	2 oz
6	firm tomatoes (about 500 g/1 lb), quartered	6

Sesame sauce

2 tbsp	light tahini	2 tbsp
1 ½ tbsp	fresh lemon juice	1 ½ tbsp
1 tbsp	low-sodium soy sauce or shoyu	1 tbsp

Rinse the chick-peas under cold running water, then put them in a large, heavy-bottomed saucepan and pour in enough cold water to cover them by about 7.5 cm (3 inches). Discard any peas that float to the surface. Cover the saucepan, leaving the lid ajar, and slowly bring the liquid to the boil over medium-low heat. Boil the chick-peas for 2 minutes, then turn off the heat and soak them for at least 1 hour. (Alternatively, soak the peas overnight in cold water.)

Drain the chick-peas, then return them to the pan and cover them with at least twice their volume of fresh water. Bring the liquid to the boil, reduce the heat to maintain a strong simmer, and cook the peas until they are tender — about 1 hour.

Meanwhile, make the sauce. In a bowl, mix the tahini and lemon juice, then gradually add the soy sauce and 4 tablespoons of water, stirring well. Put 12 wooden skewers in water to soak for about 10 minutes.

Heat the oil in a heavy frying pan over medium heat, and fry the onion with the garlic until it is tender — about 5 minutes. Add the cumin and coriander, and cook the mixture for a further 2 to 3 minutes.

Process the chick-peas in a food processor until smooth. Transfer the chick-peas to a bowl and add the onion mixture, cheese, fresh breadcrumbs, herbs, lemon juice, beaten whole egg, salt and some pepper. Mix the ingredients together well, then form the mixture into 36 equal-sized balls. Dip each one in the beaten egg white and coat it with dry breadcrumbs.

Thread three croquettes on to each of the 12 skewers, alternating them with tomato quarters. Place the skewers over hot coals and cook them for about 3 minutes on each side, or until they are golden-brown. Serve the croquettes hot with the sesame sauce.

minutes. Rinse the aubergine slices thoroughly and pat them dry with paper towels.

Add the lemon juice to a pan of boiling water. Drop the okra into the pan, cook them for 5 seconds, then add the fennel wedges and cook them for 10 seconds. Drain the vegetables, refresh them under cold running water and drain them again. When the okra are cool, halve them lengthwise. Put the aubergine, fennel, okra, courgettes and pepper strips in a large bowl.

To prepare the marinade, heat the olive oil gently in a pan and fry the shallots until they are golden-brown — about 8 minutes. Add the garlic and fry it for 20 seconds, then remove the pan from the heat. Stir in the sun-dried tomato quarters and leave the mixture to infuse and cool for about 15 minutes. Add the rest of the marinade ingredients to the pan and mix in the reserved fennel top. Pour the marinade over the vegetables, toss them gently and cover the bowl. Leave the vegetables to marinate for at least 1 hour, or overnight in the refrigerator, turning them several times.

Cut six rectangles of foil each measuring about 60 by 30 cm (24 by 12 inches) and fold them in half crosswise. Pile one sixth of the marinated vegetables in the centre of a foil square. To make a parcel, bring the top and bottom edges of the square together, fold them over twice to seal them, then fold in the sides of the square. Make five more parcels in the same way.

Cook the parcels over medium-hot coals for 20 to 30 minutes. Unfold the parcels to serve the vegetables.

Marinated Mixed Vegetables Cooked in Foil

Serves 6
Working time: about 35 minutes
Total time: about 2 hours and 15 minutes

Calories **75**
Protein **2g**
Cholesterol **0mg**
Total fat **5g**
Saturated fat **1g**
Sodium **45mg**

1	small aubergine (about 175 g/6 oz), stem removed, cut diagonally into 1 cm (¾ inch) thick slices	1
1 tbsp	salt	1 tbsp
1 tbsp	fresh lemon juice	1 tbsp
175 g	small young okra	6 oz
1	small fennel bulb, cut into six wedges, feathery top reserved and chopped	1
175 g	courgettes, sliced diagonally into 2 cm (¾ inch) pieces	6 oz
1	sweet red pepper (about 175 g/6 oz), seeded, deribbed and cut into 12 strips	1
1	sweet orange pepper (about 175 g/6 oz), seeded, deribbed and cut into 12 strips	1
Herb and lemon marinade		
2 tbsp	virgin olive oil	2 tbsp
12	small shallots	12
1	garlic clove	1
6	sun-dried tomatoes, drained and quartered	6
1	lemon, juice only	1
1 ½ tsp	chopped parsley	1 ½ tsp
1 ½ tsp	fresh thyme leaves	1 ½ tsp
1 ½ tsp	chopped fresh oregano	1 ½ tsp
2	stoned black olives, sliced into thin rings	2
¼ tsp	salt	¼ tsp
	freshly ground black pepper	

Place the aubergine slices in a colander, sprinkle the salt over them and set them aside to drain for 30

Barbecued Vegetables

VEGETABLES, BARBECUED WHOLE OR HALVED, OR QUARTERED AND SKEWERED, MAKE A DELICIOUS AND SIMPLE ACCOMPANIMENT TO ANY MEAT OR FISH DISH. THE SELECTION AND QUANTITIES SHOWN BELOW ARE SIMPLY SUGGESTIONS THAT YOU MAY IMPROVISE UPON. MOST VEGETABLES ARE SUITABLE FOR BARBECUING, ALTHOUGH FIRM VEGETABLES, SUCH AS SHALLOTS, FENNEL AND SWEETCORN, NEED TO BE BLANCHED FIRST, AND THE FLAVOUR OF SOME CAN BE ENHANCED BY MARINATION. COOK THE VEGETABLES OVER MEDIUM-HOT COALS; ONIONS AND FENNEL NORMALLY TAKE 10 TO 15 MINUTES, SHALLOTS 5 TO 10 MINUTES, AND PEPPERS 20 TO 25 MINUTES.

Serves 24
Working time: about 40 minutes
Total time: about 1 hour and 40 minutes
(includes marinating)

Calories **50**
Protein **1g**
Cholesterol **0mg**
Total fat **4g**
Saturated fat **1g**
Sodium **50mg**

48	shallots, blanched	48
3	fennel bulbs, trimmed, halved and blanched	3
10	baby sweetcorn, trimmed, cut in half crosswise and blanched	10
24	cherry tomatoes, stalks removed	24
4	sweet green peppers	4
4	sweet yellow peppers	4

2 tbsp	safflower oil	2 tbsp
3	red onions, halved	3
3	white onions, halved	3
Marinade for shallots		
½ tbsp	virgin olive oil	½ tbsp
1 tbsp	fresh lemon juice	1 tbsp
1 tbsp	very finely chopped parsley	1 tbsp
⅛ tsp	salt	⅛ tsp
	white pepper	
Marinade for fennel		
1 tbsp	virgin olive oil	1 tbsp
1	garlic clove, crushed	1
1 tbsp	chopped fresh marjoram	1 tbsp
⅛ tsp	salt	⅛ tsp
	white pepper	

In a large bowl, mix together the ingredients for the shallot marinade. Add the shallots to the mixture, and stir them to coat them thoroughly. Cover the bowl and leave the shallots to marinate for 1 hour.

Meanwhile, in a small bowl, mix together the ingredients for the fennel marinade. Lay the fennel in a shallow dish and brush the marinade all over it. Cover the dish and leave the fennel to marinate for 1 hour.

Thread the pieces of blanched sweetcorn and the cherry tomatoes alternately on to skewers. Thread the marinated shallots on to separate skewers.

Brush the peppers with a little of the safflower oil and place them on the barbecue rack. Cook them for 20 to 25 minutes over medium-hot coals, turning them frequently until they are blistered and evenly tender. After 10 minutes, place the halved red and white onions and the fennel bulbs on the grid. Brush the onions with the remaining safflower oil, and the fennel with any remaining marinade. Cook the onions and fennel for 10 to 15 minutes, turning them once, until they are lightly browned and tender.

Five to 10 minutes before these vegetables are ready, place the skewered shallots, tomatoes and baby sweetcorn on the barbecue; turn the skewers once or twice during cooking. Move the vegetables to the edges of the barbecue as they finish cooking. Serve all the vegetables freshly cooked.

Baked Apples with Ginger

THESE APPLES MAY BE BAKED ON THE RACK ABOVE THE COALS,
OR IN THE ASHES. IF BAKED IN THE ASHES, DOUBLE-WRAP THEM
IN FOIL AND COOK THEM FOR 30 TO 40 MINUTES.

Serves 8
Working time: about 30 minutes
Total time: about 1 hour and 15 minutes

Calories **165**
Protein **2g**
Cholesterol **5mg**
Total fat **3g**
Saturated fat **1g**
Sodium **85mg**

8	firm eating apples (about 150 g/5 oz each)	8
100 g	peeled cooked chestnuts or shelled hazelnuts, roughly chopped	3½ oz
75 g	fresh wholemeal breadcrumbs	2½ oz
60 g	seedless raisins, chopped if large	2 oz
30 g	stem ginger, finely diced	1 oz
2 tbsp	fresh lemon juice	2 tbsp
2 tbsp	maple syrup	2 tbsp
1 tsp	ground mixed spice	1 tsp
15 g	unsalted butter, melted	½ oz
125 g	thick Greek yogurt (optional)	4 oz

Wash the apples and core them, making the hole
through the centre of the apple about 2.5 cm (1 inch) in
diameter. Keeping the apples whole, score the skin
round the circumference of each with a sharp knife.

Place the chestnuts, breadcrumbs, seedless raisins,
ginger, lemon juice, maple syrup and mixed spice in a
large bowl. Knead these ingredients lightly with one
hand to amalgamate them.

Cut eight squares of foil, each one large enough to
wrap round an apple. Brush one side of the foil
squares with the melted butter. Place an apple in the
centre of the buttered side of each foil square, and
press an eighth of the stuffing into the hollowed centre
of the apple. Wrap the apples in the foil.

Arrange the wrapped apples on the rack over
medium-hot coals and cook them for about 45
minutes. Test the apples by piercing them with a thin
skewer: if it meets little resistance, they are done.

Serve the baked apples hot, with a little thick Greek
yogurt, if you are using it.

EDITOR'S NOTE: *To peel and cook chestnuts, first cut a cross in
the hull of each chestnut, then cook them in a saucepan of
boiling water for 10 minutes. Shell and peel the chestnuts,
then return them to the saucepan and simmer them for 20 to
30 minutes, until they are tender.*

Barbecued Bananas with Raspberry Coulis

Serves 8
Working (and total) time: about 20 minutes

Calories **110**
Protein **3g**
Cholesterol **0mg**
Total fat **trace**
Saturated fat **trace**
Sodium **10mg**

200 g	fresh raspberries, or frozen raspberries, thawed	7 oz
2 tbsp	icing sugar	2 tbsp
½ tsp	arrowroot	½ tsp
2	passion fruits, strained juice only, or 2 tbsp Kirsch	2
8	ripe large bananas	8

In a blender or food processor, blend the raspberries with the icing sugar until they are reduced to a purée. Press the purée through a nylon sieve to remove all the seeds, then pour it into a saucepan. Stir the arrowroot into the purée and heat it gently, stirring continuously, until it boils and thickens. Remove the pan from the heat and stir in the passion fruit juice or Kirsch.

Either cover the sauce and keep it warm or set it aside to cool while you barbecue the bananas.

With a sharp knife point, cut the skin along the length of a banana in two places on opposite sides; do not cut into the flesh. Peel off the top half of the skin, leaving the flesh and bottom half of the skin intact. Half-peel the remaining bananas in the same way.

Place the bananas, skin side down, on the barbecue rack, 10 to 15 cm (4 to 6 inches) above medium-hot coals. When the skins have blackened — after about 5 minutes — carefully turn the bananas over and cook them for a further minute.

Serve the bananas hot, in their skins, with a little of the raspberry coulis — either hot or cold — poured over them. Serve the remaining coulis separately.

Fruit Rings Cooked in Foil

Serves 6
Working (and total) time: about 30 minutes

Calories **85**
Protein **1g**
Cholesterol **0mg**
Total fat **0g**
Saturated fat **0g**
Sodium **5mg**

2	red-skinned apples, cored, each cut into six rings and dropped into acidulated water	2
2	ripe pears, peeled, cored, each cut into six rings and dropped into acidulated water	2
2	oranges, peeled, each cut crosswise into six slices	2
1	grapefruit, peeled and cut crosswise into six slices	1
2 tbsp	light brown sugar	2 tbsp

Cut six rectangles of foil measuring about 45 by 30 cm (18 by 12 inches), and fold them in half crosswise.

Drain the apple and pear rings. In the centre of each rectangle of foil, pile two rings each of apple, pear and orange, and one slice of grapefruit. Sprinkle 1 teaspoon of sugar over each pile of fruit, then fold the sides of the foil up and pinch the edges to enclose the fruit in six neat parcels.

Put the parcels on the grid over medium-hot coals and cook for 4 minutes. Serve hot, in the parcels, or on individual plates with the juices poured over.

Rum-Flavoured Soft Fruit Brochettes

Serves 6
Working time: about 20 minutes
Total time: about 30 minutes

Calories **125**
Protein **1g**
Cholesterol **0mg**
Total fat **trace**
Saturated fat **trace**
Sodium **5mg**

3 tbsp	dark rum	3 tbsp
3 tbsp	light brown sugar	3 tbsp
2 tbsp	fresh lemon juice	2 tbsp
3	kiwi fruit, peeled and quartered	3
6	dark-skinned plums, halved and stoned	6
3	small nectarines, quartered	3
2	bananas, peeled, each cut into six chunks	2
12	strawberries, hulled	12
1	orange, juice only	1
1 tbsp	clear honey	1 tbsp

Put the rum, sugar and lemon juice in a large, shallow dish. Add the kiwi fruit, plums, nectarines and bananas to the liquid, and turn them to coat them evenly. Leave the fruits to marinate for about 10 minutes. Meanwhile, soak six bamboo skewers in water for 10 minutes. Juxtaposing different fruits, thread two strawberries and two pieces of each of the other fruits on to each of the skewers; reserve the marinade. Set the skewers aside while you prepare a rum sauce.

Pour the marinade into a small pan and stir in the orange juice and honey. Bring the sauce slowly to the boil, and boil it until it is reduced by half — about 5 minutes. Set the sauce aside to cool.

Lightly oil the barbecue rack. Brush the kebabs with a little of the rum sauce and cook them over medium-hot coals for 4 minutes, turning them once. Serve the fruit kebabs immediately with any remaining rum sauce poured over them.

EDITOR'S NOTE: *Any soft fruit, such as orange, grapefruit, peach or mango, may be substituted for those listed above.*

3

Menus to Match the Occasion

Ideally, every picnic and barbecue should be planned as an entity, so that all the courses not only suit the occasion but also complement the other dishes. This chapter suggests menus for four very different types of outdoor meal — two of the menus are for picnics, and two are for barbecues.

The first menu is for an occasion as formal as a picnic can be — a meal that might be enjoyed at the races, say, or after an alfresco concert. The robust American barbecue *(page 123)*, on the other hand, invites you to an easy-going cookout with just a nip of autumn in the air. Two menus owe their inspiration to regional cuisines: the Middle Eastern picnic, a tempting selection of hors-d'oeuvre and snacks (page 116), and the Caribbean fish barbecue *(page 112)*, impart the romance of tropical sunshine or sultry nights to any suburban garden.

Whether in the park or on the patio, truly carefree meals require careful planning. Common sense dictates that as much preparation as possible be done substantially in advance, and a brief introduction to each menu suggests which dishes may be prepared ahead. Some, such as the trout in aspic *(page 109)*, needs to be made the day before a midday picnic. The lettuce and nasturtium flower salad *(page 110)*, however, is best made shortly before packing the picnic and should only be dressed just before serving.

Because the party atmosphere is not conducive to strict self-control, it is especially important to serve fresh, healthy food. These menus reveal the possibility of creating meals that are low in saturated fats and sodium, while still retaining all the fun of a feast.

A silver platter of trout stuffed with crab and ginger, and glazed with aspic, forms a dramatic centrepiece to this elegant picnic. Salads of sweet peppers and rice, and lettuce and nasturtium flowers, accompany the trout; the main dish is preceded by a chilled soup with croûtons, and a passion fruit and raspberry roulade completes the meal.

Prepare the ingredients for the lettuce and nasturtium flower salad on the day of the picnic, and keep them chilled until you are ready to leave. The other dishes may be made ahead of time, and stored in the refrigerator until you need to pack them.

When packing the picnic hamper, remember to include a tureen and ladle for the soup, and suitable serving vessels for the two salads and the fruit roulade. To avoid breakages in transit, use plenty of tissue paper when you are wrapping the china and glassware, and keep silver cutlery safe from scratches by rolling individual place settings in napkins.

If you plan to serve champagne or another chilled wine, take an ice bucket with you, and fill a wide-necked food flask with ice cubes. The ice cubes will remain frozen for up to 8 hours, and can be transferred to the ice bucket at the picnic site.

Put the melon and cucumber in a heavy-bottomed saucepan with the salt and half of the chervil. Cover the pan and set it over low heat. Cook the cubes gently for 15 to 20 minutes, until they have softened and the juices are flowing. Add the chicken stock and continue cooking for a further 20 minutes.

Purée the contents of the pan in a food processor or blender, then pour the soup into a clean bowl and set it aside to cool. Stir the double cream into the cooled soup, together with some freshly ground white pepper. Cover the bowl and place the soup in the refrigerator for at least 3 hours, to chill it thoroughly.

To make the croûtons, preheat the oven to 220°C (425°F or Mark 7). Spread each slice of bread very thinly with the margarine and cut the slices into dice. Put the dice on a baking sheet and cook them in the oven for 15 to 20 minutes, until they are golden, turning them frequently during this time, to ensure that they brown evenly. Allow the croûtons to cool on the baking sheet, then transfer them to an airtight container to take to the picnic. Put the remaining chopped chervil into a small plastic bag.

Transport the soup to the picnic in a chilled vacuum flask. To serve it, shake the flask to blend the soup evenly, then pour the soup into a tureen. Sprinkle the chervil over the surface of the soup and serve the croûtons separately, in a small bowl.

Chilled Melon and Cucumber Soup

Serves 6
Working time: about 20 minutes
Total time: about 4 hours (includes chilling)

Calories **100**
Protein **10g**
Cholesterol **10mg**
Total fat **3g**
Saturated fat **1g**
Sodium **60mg**

Metric	Ingredient	Imperial
600 g	ripe Ogen melon, seeded, flesh cut into cubes	1¼ lb
600 g	cucumbers, peeled, seeded and cut into cubes	1¼ lb
½ tsp	salt	½ tsp
30 g	chopped fresh chervil	1 oz
60 cl	unsalted chicken stock (recipe, page 139)	1 pint
2 tbsp	double cream	2 tbsp
	white pepper	
3	slices white bread (about 90 g/3 oz), crusts removed	3
15 g	polyunsaturated margarine	½ oz

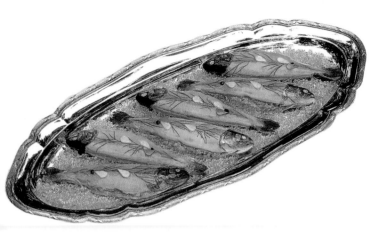

Trout in Aspic

Serves 6
Working time: about 1 hour and 30 minutes
Total time: about 7 hours and 15 minutes
(includes chilling)

Calories **250**	6	pink-fleshed trout (about 250 g/8 oz each), gutted and fins removed	6
Protein **35g**			
Cholesterol **120mg**	30 g	polyunsaturated margarine	1 oz
Total fat **11g**	90 g	spring onions, trimmed and chopped	3 oz
Saturated fat **2g**	5 cm	piece fresh ginger root, peeled and grated	2 inch
Sodium **305mg**			
	175 g	white crab meat, picked over	6 oz
	1 tsp	finely grated fresh horseradish, or 2 tsp prepared horseradish	1 tsp
	½ tsp	salt	½ tsp
		freshly ground black pepper	
	1	lemon, strained juice only	1
	90 cl	unsalted vegetable stock (recipe, page 139)	1½ pints
	45 g	powdered gelatine	1½ oz
	2	eggs, whites and washed shells only	2
	1 tbsp	red wine vinegar	1 tbsp
		fresh dill sprigs, for garnish	
		petals cut from thinly sliced mooli and blanched lemon rind, for garnish	
		small pieces of olive, for garnish	

Rinse the trout under cold running water, then pat them dry on paper towels. Using a small, sharp knife, bone each trout in turn. Lengthen the slit in the belly so that it extends the full length of the fish, from head to tail. Put the trout on the work surface on its back, to expose the inside. Use the tip of the knife to free the rib bones, one at a time, then run the knife down both sides of the spine, underneath the ribs, to free the flesh from the backbone. Using a pair of scissors, sever the backbone at the head and tail ends of the trout. Ease out the spine and its attached ribs, and use a pair of tweezers to remove any small bones that remain. Bone the remaining trout in the same way.

Preheat the oven to 220°C (425°F or Mark 7).

To make the stuffing, melt the margarine in a small, heavy frying pan over medium heat. Add the spring onions and cook them gently for about 5 minutes, until they are soft. Stir in the ginger and cook for a further minute. Remove the pan from the heat and allow the contents to cool for 10 minutes, then add the crab meat, horseradish, a little of the salt and some black pepper, and mix the stuffing together well. Fill the body cavity of each trout with some of the crab mixture, then reshape the fish neatly.

Lay a large sheet of foil on a baking sheet and grease the foil with a little polyunsaturated margarine. Place the trout on the foil in a single layer, and sprinkle them with the lemon juice and the remaining salt. Fold in the sides of the foil to enclose the fish but do not seal the parcel completely. Cook the trout in the oven for 15 to 20 minutes, until the flesh feels firm and is opaque. Remove them from the oven and open the foil a little to allow the steam to escape. Set the trout aside to cool for 1 hour at room temperature, then refrigerate them for 3 hours, until they are completely cold.

Rinse a large saucepan and fill it with cold water. Put a wire whisk, a large metal sieve and a large square of muslin into the saucepan. Bring the water to the boil. Remove the whisk, sieve and muslin from the pan; pour the boiling water into a large bowl to scald it, then pour the water away. Place the sieve over the bowl and line the sieve with the muslin.

Pour the stock into the pan and add the gelatine, egg whites and shells, and vinegar. With the scalded whisk, whisk the stock over medium heat until the egg whites form a thick foam on the surface. Stop whisking, then bring the mixture to the boil so that the foam rises to the top of the pan — do not allow it to boil over. Remove the pan from the heat and allow the foam to settle back down. Repeat this process twice more, then allow the mixture to stand for 5 minutes.

Very gently and carefully pour the aspic through the lined sieve into the bowl, without allowing the foam floating on top of the liquid to break up. Leave it to drain thoroughly, then let the aspic cool. Refrigerate it until it begins to thicken — 20 to 30 minutes.

Carefully remove the skin from one side of each trout, then place the trout, skinned side up, on a wire rack set over a large tray. Spoon a little of the partially set aspic over each trout, to coat them evenly. Pour the excess aspic that has drained into the tray back into the bowl. Refrigerate the trout for 15 minutes, to set the aspic firmly. Meanwhile, keep the bowl of aspic at room temperature, to prevent it from setting.

Remove the trout from the refrigerator. Dip the sprigs of dill, the mooli and lemon rind petals and the pieces of olive in aspic and use them to garnish the fish decoratively. Return the trout to the refrigerator for 10 minutes, to allow the garnish to set firmly in place, then coat them with more liquid aspic, again pouring the excess from the tray back into the bowl. Refrigerate the trout and the bowl of aspic until both are set firmly — about 1 hour. Cover the trout with ▶

plastic film and keep them refrigerated until you are ready to pack the picnic.

Carefully remove the trout from the wire rack and arrange them on a large serving platter. Cover them loosely with greaseproof paper. Chop the remaining set aspic and place it in a rigid container. Pack the chopped aspic into a cool box to go to the picnic.

To serve the dish, remove the greaseproof paper and arrange the chopped aspic round the trout.

Sweet Pepper Rice Ring

Serves 6
Working time: about 30 minutes
Total time: about 1 hour

Calories **125**		
Protein **3g**		
Cholesterol **0mg**		
Total fat **3g**		
Saturated fat **1g**		
Sodium **135mg**		

½ tsp	salt	½ tsp
150 g	long-grain rice	5 oz
1	small sweet red pepper	1
1	small sweet green pepper	1
1	small sweet yellow pepper	1
1 tbsp	virgin olive oil	1 tbsp
1 tbsp	white wine vinegar	1 tbsp
1	garlic clove, crushed	1
4 tbsp	finely chopped parsley	4 tbsp
	freshly ground black pepper	
	red, green and yellow pepper rings, for garnish	

Bring a saucepan of water to the boil with ¼ teaspoon of the salt. Add the rice, stir it once, then cover the pan and reduce the heat to low. Simmer the rice for 20 minutes, until it is cooked but still slightly firm. Drain it thoroughly and set it aside to cool.

Meanwhile, skin the peppers following the technique on page 138, then seed and derib them, retaining their juice. Cut the peppers into small dice.

Put the oil, vinegar, garlic and parsley into a large bowl, and add the remaining salt and some pepper. Mix the ingredients well. Add the diced peppers to the dressing, with 1 tablespoon of their juice, then add the rice and mix everything together thoroughly.

Fill a 1.25 litre (2 pint) ring mould with the rice salad, pressing the mixture down firmly. Cover the mould with plastic film and refrigerate it until you are ready to pack the picnic. Put the pepper rings for garnish into a plastic bag and chill them too.

To serve, turn the rice salad out on to a serving plate and arrange the pepper rings in the centre.

Salad of Lettuce and Nasturtium Flowers

Serves 6
Working (and total) time: about 20 minutes

Calories **25**		
Protein **1g**		
Cholesterol **10mg**		
Total fat **2g**		
Saturated fat **1g**		
Sodium **75mg**		

1	small cos lettuce, or two little gem lettuces, leaves washed and dried	1
1	red lollo lettuce, leaves washed and dried	1
12	nasturtium flowers	12
	Mustard-lemon dressing	
4 tbsp	soured cream	4 tbsp
2 tbsp	fresh lemon juice	2 tbsp
2 tsp	Dijon mustard	2 tsp
¼ tsp	salt	¼ tsp
	freshly ground black pepper	
2 tbsp	finely cut chives	2 tbsp

Tear or cut the lettuce leaves into pieces and put them into a lidded plastic container. Place the nasturtium flowers in a separate rigid container. Refrigerate both until you are ready to go to the picnic.

To make the dressing, put all the ingredients into a screw-top jar and shake them together vigorously. Chill the dressing until it is required, then pack it inside a cool box to take to the picnic.

At the picnic, shake the dressing again, then pour it into the bottom of a serving bowl. Place the salad leaves in the bowl and arrange the flowers on top. Just before serving, toss the salad with the dressing.

Passion Fruit and Raspberry Roulade

Serves 6
Working time: about 40 minutes
Total time: about 1 hour and 25 minutes

Calories **225**
Protein **7g**
Cholesterol **80mg**
Total fat **8g**
Saturated fat **2g**
Sodium **155mg**

4	passion fruits	4
125 g	thick Greek yogurt	4 oz
3 tsp	powdered gelatine	3 tsp
1	egg white	1
30 g	caster sugar	1 oz
	icing sugar, for dredging	
250 g	fresh raspberries	8 oz
Hazelnut sponge		
90 g	shelled hazelnuts, roasted and finely ground	3 oz
45 g	potato flour	1½ oz
2	eggs	2
90 g	caster sugar	3 oz
2	egg whites	2

Preheat the oven to 190°C (375°F or Mark 5). Grease a 32 by 22 cm (13 by 9 inch) Swiss roll tin, line the tin with non-stick parchment paper and grease the paper.

To make the sponge, put the hazelnuts and potato flour in a small bowl and mix them together well. Put the whole eggs and 60 g (2 oz) of the caster sugar in a large bowl, then place the bowl over a saucepan of gently simmering water, taking care that the bottom of the bowl does not touch the water. Using a hand-held electric mixer, whisk the eggs and sugar until the mixture becomes thick and pale. Remove the bowl from the heat and continue whisking until the mixture is cool and falls from the whisk in a thick ribbon trail. In a small bowl, whisk the egg whites until they are stiff, then gradually whisk into them the remaining caster sugar, until the meringue is stiff and shiny. Carefully fold the hazelnuts and flour into the whole egg mixture, then fold in the egg whites.

Pour the mixture into the prepared tin and spread it evenly. Gently tap the tin on the work surface to level the top. Bake the sponge for 15 to 20 minutes, until it is well risen, lightly browned and springy to the touch. Remove the tin from the oven and place it on a wire rack. Cover the sponge loosely with foil and leave it to cool in the tin — about 45 minutes.

Meanwhile, make the filling. Cut the passion fruits in half and spoon out their centres into a small nylon sieve set over a bowl. Press the seeds with the back of the spoon to extract the juice. Stir the Greek yogurt into the passion fruit juice until the mixture is smooth. Put 2 tablespoons of cold water in a second small bowl;

sprinkle the gelatine evenly over the surface, and set it aside. In another bowl, whisk the egg white until it will hold stiff peaks, then gradually whisk in the caster sugar until the mixture is stiff and shiny.

Set the bowl of gelatine over a saucepan of gently simmering water and stir until the gelatine has dissolved. Quickly whisk the gelatine solution into the passion fruit mixture, then gradually fold the mixture into the whisked egg white. Refrigerate the mixture until it is on the point of setting — about 10 minutes.

Lay a large sheet of non-stick parchment paper on the work surface and dredge it heavily with icing sugar. Invert the cooled sponge rectangle on to the icing sugar and remove the lining paper. Sprinkle the fresh raspberries evenly over the rectangle, then spread the passion fruit mixture evenly over the raspberries. Starting from one of the short sides, roll up the base and filling: lift one end of the underlying paper to start off the roulade, and nudge it along by gradually lifting the rest of the paper.

Wrap the roulade loosely in greaseproof paper and place it in a rigid container to go to the picnic. Chill it until required, and transport it to the picnic in a cool box. At the picnic, transfer the roulade to a long dish; cut it into slices for serving.

SUGGESTED ACCOMPANIMENT: *a bowl of fresh raspberries.*

EDITOR'S NOTE: *To roast hazelnuts, place them on a baking sheet in a preheated 180°C (350°F or Mark 4) oven for 10 minutes, stirring them from time to time to ensure that they brown evenly. Allow the nuts to cool before grinding them.*

CARIBBEAN FISH BARBECUE

Barbecued Squid with Hot Paprika Sauce
Sea Bass Cooked with Saffron, Thyme
and Lemon
Shark, Onion and Pepper Brochettes
Two-Potato Salad
Green Salad with Palm Hearts and Mange-Tout
Exotic Fruit Salad

Begin the preparation for this seafood barbecue 24 hours in advance by placing the shark cubes in their marinade. You may also, if you wish, prepare the hot paprika sauce and parboil the baby onions. Complete the preparation on the day of the barbecue; do not dress the salads until you are about to serve them. Have everything ready before you start to cook.

About 20 minutes before you wish to begin eating, place the sea bass on the barbecue rack. Allow it to cook for 10 minutes, then add the squid and mushroom skewers to the rack. They will need only 10 minutes' cooking; transfer them to a plate when they are done and serve them as a starter with the hot paprika sauce. Meanwhile, turn the sea bass over for its final 20 minutes' cooking, and add the shark brochettes to the rack half way through this time.

Accompany the dishes with jugs of a Caribbean-style beverage, such as the mixture of fresh orange and pineapple juice illustrated here. Spike it, if you like, with a little Jamaican rum, and serve it in hollowed-out baby pineapple shells to lend a stylish note.

A large sea bass flavoured with saffron, lemon and thyme is flanked by platters of shark brochettes and of squid and mushrooms with a hot paprika sauce. This seafood barbecue is accompanied by a yogurt-dressed salad of sweet and new potatoes, and a crisp green salad. A bowl of ripe tropical fruits steeped in passion fruit juice completes the meal.

Barbecued Squid with Hot Paprika Sauce

Serves 12
Working (and total) time: about 1 hour

Calories **75**	750 g	squid, cleaned and skinned, tentacles reserved	1 ½ lb
Protein **9g**			
Cholesterol **130mg**	48	small button mushrooms, wiped	48
Total fat **3g**		**Hot paprika sauce**	
Saturated fat **1g**			
Sodium **95mg**	2 tbsp	virgin olive oil	2 tbsp
	1	garlic clove, crushed	1

500 g	ripe tomatoes, skinned, seeded (page 138) and chopped	1 lb
2 tsp	red wine vinegar	2 tsp
2 tsp	paprika	2 tsp
1 tsp	Tabasco sauce	1 tsp
175 g	canned red pimentos, roughly chopped	6 oz

First make the sauce. In a heavy frying pan, heat the oil over medium heat. Add the garlic and tomatoes and cook them, stirring constantly, for 10 minutes. Strain off and discard 30 cl (½ pint) of the juice. Add the vinegar to the pan and simmer the mixture over low heat for a further 3 minutes. Pour the mixture into a food processor or blender, add the remaining ingredients, and process until smooth. Transfer the sauce to a bowl and set it aside.

Cut each squid pouch into three or four pieces and the tentacles into groups of four. Thread the squid and mushrooms on to skewers. Place the skewers flat on the rack of the barbecue, spreading out the squid tentacles. Cook the skewers for 5 minutes on each side, until golden-brown. Remove the squid and mushrooms from their skewers and mix them on a platter. Serve the bowl of sauce separately.

Shark, Onion and Pepper Brochettes

Serves 12
Working time: about 45 minutes
Total time: about 25 hours (includes marinating)

Calories **120**
Protein **8g**
Cholesterol **25mg**
Total fat **8g**
Saturated fat **2g**
Sodium **85mg**

2 tbsp	virgin olive oil	2 tbsp
8 cl	fresh lime juice	3 fl oz
1 tbsp	gin	1 tbsp
¼ tsp	salt	¼ tsp
	freshly ground black pepper	
750 g	shark fillet, skinned and cut into 3 cm (1 ¼ inch) cubes	1 ½ lb
200 g	baby onions, simmered in boiling water for 8 to 10 minutes, until tender	7 oz
2	sweet orange peppers, seeded, deribbed and cut into 3 cm (1 ¼ inch) pieces	2
2	sweet yellow peppers, seeded, deribbed and cut into 3 cm (1 ¼ inch) pieces	2
	bamboo leaves, for garnish (optional)	

First prepare a marinade for the cubed shark fillet. In a large, shallow, non-reactive dish, combine 1 tablespoon of the olive oil with the lime juice, gin, salt and some black pepper. Add the shark cubes to the dish, and turn them over thoroughly in the marinade, to coat all the surfaces. Arrange the cubes in a single layer, cover the dish and place it in the refrigerator for at least 24 hours. Turn the cubes over from time to time while they are marinating.

Divide the shark cubes, baby onions and pieces of orange and yellow pepper into 12 equal portions. Thread each portion on to a long metal skewer, then brush the filled skewers with the remaining olive oil.

Place the skewers on the barbecue rack over medium-hot coals and cook them for about 10 minutes, turning them over half way through cooking. Pile the skewers on to a serving platter, lined with a few bamboo leaves, if you are using them.

Sea Bass Cooked with Saffron, Thyme and Lemon

Serves 12
Working time: about 30 minutes
Total time: about 1 hour and 10 minutes

Calories **150**
Protein **27g**
Cholesterol **115mg**
Total fat **3g**
Saturated fat **trace**
Sodium **155mg**

2.5 kg	sea bass, gutted and scaled	5 lb
1 tsp	virgin olive oil	1 tsp
½ tsp	powdered saffron	½ tsp
½ tsp	salt	½ tsp
	freshly ground black pepper	
1	lemon, sliced	1
1	large bunch thyme, stalks trimmed	1
	tied bundles of chives, for garnish	
	lemon slices and lime wedges, for garnish	

Rinse the fish under cold running water and pat it dry with paper towels. Make four 5 mm (¼ inch) deep slashes in the flesh on each side of the fish. Using a small pastry brush, oil each slash with a little of the olive oil and paint in some saffron powder.

Place the fish on an oiled fish basket and season the stomach cavity with the salt and some freshly ground black pepper. Place the lemon slices and the bunch of thyme in the stomach cavity, arranging them so that the natural stomach shape is retained.

Close the fish basket and place it on the barbecue rack. Cook the sea bass over medium-hot coals for 20 minutes on each side, or until it is firm to the touch. Transfer the cooked fish to a large platter, and serve it garnished with the bundles of chives, the lemon slices and the lime wedges.

Green Salad with Palm Hearts and Mange-Tout

Serves 12
Working (and total) time: about 30 minutes

Calories **45**		
Protein **2g**	4	little gem or other small round lettuces, cut in half, leaves washed and dried	4
Cholesterol **0mg**	650 g	canned palm hearts, rinsed well, each cut crosswise into four equal pieces	22 oz
Total fat **3g**		
Saturated fat **trace**	175 g	watercress sprigs, trimmed, washed and dried	6 oz
Sodium **20mg**	2	cucumbers, halved lengthwise, seeded and cut into 5 cm (2 inch) long sticks	2
	600 g	mange-tout, strings removed, blanched, refreshed under cold running water	1 ¼ lb

Lemon vinaigrette		
2 tbsp	safflower oil	2 tbsp
2 tbsp	fresh lemon juice	2 tbsp
	freshly ground black pepper	

First prepare the lemon vinaigrette. In a small bowl, mix the oil and lemon juice using a fork, and season the dressing with plenty of black pepper.

Pile all the ingredients for the salad into a large bowl. Just before serving, pour on the lemon dressing and toss the salad thoroughly.

Two-Potato Salad

Serves 12
Working time: about 30 minutes
Total time: about 1 hour and 15 minutes

Calories **80**	500 g	sweet potatoes, scrubbed	1 lb
Protein **2g**	500 g	new potatoes, scrubbed, halved if large	1 lb
Cholesterol **0mg**	250 g	spring onions, trimmed and cut diagonally into thirds	8 oz
Total fat **trace**		
Saturated fat **trace**	2 tsp	Dijon mustard	2 tsp
Sodium **35mg**	15 cl	plain low-fat yogurt	¼ pint
		white pepper	
	2 tbsp	capers, rinsed well, dried and roughly chopped	2 tbsp

Place the sweet potatoes and new potatoes into separate heavy-bottomed saucepans and pour in sufficient cold water to cover the potatoes in each pan by 2.5 cm (1 inch). Bring both pans to the boil, then reduce the heat and simmer the vegetables until they are tender — 15 to 20 minutes for the new potatoes, and 25 to 30 minutes for the sweet potatoes.

Drain the potatoes and set them aside, on separate plates, until they are cool enough to handle. Peel the sweet potatoes and cut them into slices. Arrange the slices in a serving dish with the new potatoes and the spring onion pieces.

In a small bowl, stir the Dijon mustard into the yogurt and season with some white pepper. Pour this dressing over the potatoes and onions, and sprinkle the capers over the top of the salad.

Exotic Fruit Salad

Serves 12
Working (and total) time: about 40 minutes

Calories **115**
Protein **3g**
Cholesterol **0mg**
Total fat **2g**
Saturated fat **trace**
Sodium **60mg**

6	ripe passion fruits	6
2	small green-fleshed melons, halved and seeded, flesh scooped into balls with a melon-baller	2
1	pink-fleshed melon, halved and seeded, flesh scooped into balls with a melon-baller	1
1	pineapple, peeled and cored, flesh cut into chunks	1
3	guavas, halved lengthwise, seeded, each half sliced crosswise	3
2	pink grapefruits, peeled and segmented	2
3	papayas, peeled and seeded, flesh cut into chunks	3
2	large mangoes, peeled, flesh cut lengthwise into slices, stones discarded	2

Cut the passion fruits in half crosswise. Using a teaspoon, scoop out the seeds and pulp from each passion fruit into a fine nylon sieve set over a bowl. Using the back of the spoon, press all the juice through the sieve into the bowl; discard the seeds and fibrous pulp remaining in the sieve.

Place all the prepared fruits in a large serving bowl and pour the passion fruit juice over them. Gently mix and turn the fruits in the bowl, to ensure that they are all coated with juice. Store the fruit salad in the refrigerator until you are ready to serve it.

EDITOR'S NOTE: *The skin of a ripe passion fruit is very dark in colour and has a wrinkled, shrivelled appearance. Avoid any fruits that have paler, plumper-looking skins; the flesh will taste bitter and acidic.*

MIDDLE EASTERN PICNIC

*Coriander Pork Skewers
Kibbeh with Yogurt Mint Sauce
Felafel with Red Pepper Relish
Carrots Cooked with Honey and Spices
Tabbouleh
Fruit and Nut Triangles
Turkish Delight*

A *mezze* — a selection of Middle Eastern snacks and hors-d'oeuvre — provides a novel theme for a picnic. Because all the dishes in this *mezze* are served cold, they can easily be prepared ahead of time and stored in the refrigerator until you are ready to leave. The Turkish delight is best made the day before, to ensure that it has sufficient time to set firmly. Most of the items will benefit from being transported to the picnic site in a cool box, especially the kibbeh (balls of couscous and minced lamb) and its sauce, the coriander pork skewers and the Turkish delight.

To complete your Middle Eastern picnic, you may like to accompany the savoury dishes with some pitta bread, or with one of the many other types of Middle Eastern bread — such as those flavoured with olives, cheese, onions and herbs — that can be bought in Greek and Turkish bakeries and delicatessens. A thermos flask of iced mint tea is the ideal beverage to accompany these dishes.

Tender pork skewers, spicy lamb and couscous balls, and felafel diamonds with a red pepper relish provide the focal points to this mezze. Tabbouleh — a fresh salad of burghul, mint and parsley — and carrots cooked with honey and spices accompany them. Triangles of pastry topped with fruit and nuts, and cubes of Turkish delight, complete the meal.

Coriander Pork Skewers

Serves 6
Working time: about 25 minutes
Total time: about 1 hour and 30 minutes
(includes marinating)

Calories **185**
Protein **19g**
Cholesterol **45mg**
Total fat **10g**
Saturated fat **3g**
Sodium **120mg**

3	pieces pork fillet (about 350 g/12 oz), each about 15 cm (6 inches) long, trimmed of fat	3
1	garlic clove, crushed	1
2 tsp	coriander seeds, crushed	2 tsp
¼ tsp	ground allspice	¼ tsp
¼ tsp	paprika	¼ tsp
2 tbsp	safflower oil	2 tbsp
8 cl	dry red wine	3 fl oz
¼ tsp	salt	¼ tsp
1 tbsp	light brown sugar	1 tbsp

Cut each piece of meat lengthwise into four equal strips. Place the strips of meat in a large, shallow container and add the garlic, coriander, allspice, paprika and oil. Mix the ingredients together well, then cover the container and leave the meat to marinate in a cool place for at least 1 hour, or for up to 24 hours.

Thread each strip of marinated pork on to a fine wooden skewer and lay the skewers in a large, heavy, non-stick frying pan or in a heavy-bottomed roasting pan. Using a plastic spatula, scrape up any marinade remaining in the shallow container and spread it on top of the pork skewers.

Cook the skewers over medium heat for about 5 minutes, or until they are lightly browned, turning them once. In a small bowl, whisk together the wine, salt and sugar. Add this mixture to the pan, cover it, and simmer the pork skewers in the juices for 10 minutes. Transfer the skewers to a plate and continue to cook the pan juices over high heat until they have reduced to a syrupy glaze — 3 to 4 minutes. Dribble the glaze over the skewers and set them aside to cool.

To transport the skewers to the picnic site, wrap them in foil or arrange them in a rigid container. Pack the skewers inside a cool box.

Kibbeh with Yogurt-Mint Sauce

Serves 6
Working time: about 25 minutes
Total time: about 1 hour and 25 minutes
(includes soaking)

Calories **155**
Protein **13g**
Cholesterol **30mg**
Total fat **6g**
Saturated fat **2g**
Sodium **115mg**

125 g	couscous	4 oz
¼ tbsp	safflower oil	¼ tbsp
1	small onion, very finely chopped	1
1	garlic clove, crushed	1
¼ tsp	ground cinnamon	½ tsp
1 tsp	ground cumin	1 tsp
200 g	lean lamb, finely minced	7 oz
¼ tsp	salt	¼ tsp
	freshly ground black pepper	
	lemon slices, halved, for garnish	
	flat-leaf parsley sprig, for garnish	
Yogurt-mint sauce		
15 cl	plain low-fat yogurt	¼ pint
1½ tbsp	chopped mint leaves, plus two mint leaves, cut into strips, for garnish	1½ tbsp
¼ tsp	caraway seeds	¼ tsp
¼	cucumber, peeled and grated	¼
	freshly ground black pepper	

Put the couscous in a heatproof bowl and pour on 15 cl (¼ pint) of boiling water. Let the couscous soak for 15 minutes, until all the liquid has been absorbed; stir occasionally, to prevent lumps from forming.

Heat the oil in a small, heavy frying pan. Add the onion, garlic, cinnamon and cumin, and fry the mixture gently for 2 minutes, stirring frequently. Stir the mixture into the couscous, then stir in the lamb, the salt and some pepper. Mix the ingredients together thoroughly.

Preheat the oven to 190°C (375°F or Mark 5) and lightly grease a baking sheet. Divide the meat mixture into 12 equal portions. Take one portion and squeeze it firmly in your hand, to compact it, then roll it into a ball between your palms; neaten the shape by rolling the ball on a wooden board. Shape the remaining mixture into balls in the same way, then place all 12 on the prepared baking sheet.

Bake the kibbeh for 45 minutes, until they are a light golden colour. Transfer them to a plate to cool, then chill them until required.

For the yogurt-mint sauce, combine the yogurt, chopped mint, caraway seeds and cucumber in a bowl and add a little black pepper. Chill the sauce until you are ready to leave for the picnic.

Pack the kibbeh and the yogurt sauce, in separate rigid containers, inside a cool box. Place the garnishes — the lemon slices, the parsley sprig and the mint strips — into small plastic bags, and put them into the cool box too. At the picnic, arrange the kibbeh in a serving dish and garnish them with the lemon slices and parsley sprig. Transfer the yogurt sauce to a small bowl and scatter the mint strips over the surface.

them with at least twice their volume of fresh water. Bring the liquid to the boil, reduce the heat to maintain a strong simmer, and cook the peas until they are tender — about 1 hour.

Drain the peas and put them in a food processor with the onion and garlic. Process for about 1 minute, until the mixture is smooth. Turn the mixture into a bowl and add the cumin, garam masala and chili powder, 45 g (1½ oz) of the breadcrumbs, the parsley, salt, some pepper and ½ tablespoon of the beaten egg. Mix all the ingredients together thoroughly.

Preheat the oven to 190°C (375°F or Mark 5). Clean the food processor, and lightly oil a non-stick baking pan. Gather the chick-pea mixture into a ball and, working on a damp board, shape it into a long roll. Cut the roll into six equal portions, then use a metal spatula to form each portion into a diamond shape on the board. Slide the spatula under one of the diamonds, lift it off the board, brush the top and sides with beaten egg and cover them with breadcrumbs, pressing the crumbs on gently. Turn the diamond over and coat the second side with beaten egg and breadcrumbs. Coat the remaining diamonds in the same way, and place all six in the baking pan.

Bake the felafel for 15 minutes, then turn them over and bake them for a further 15 minutes. Leave them to cool. Cover the felafel and chill them until required.

For the relish, heat the oil in a small, heavy frying pan and cook the red pepper, onion and garlic over low heat for 1 minute. Add the remaining ingredients, and 5 tablespoons of water, then cover the pan and simmer the mixture gently for 10 minutes. Remove the lid and simmer for a further 5 minutes, then pour the contents into the cleaned food processor and process briefly, until the ingredients are just combined. Allow the relish to cool, then chill it until required.

When you are ready to go to the picnic, pack the felafel into a rigid container and spoon the relish into a separate container with a tight-fitting lid. Put the fig leaves in a plastic bag, if you are using them. Carry all the items in a cool box.

To serve the dish at the picnic site, spread the fig leaves on a serving plate and place the felafel on top. Transfer the relish to a serving bowl.

Felafel with Red Pepper Relish

Serves 6
Working time: about 40 minutes
Total time: about 2 hours and 50 minutes (includes soaking)

Calories **190**
Protein **19g**
Cholesterol **20mg**
Total fat **7g**
Saturated fat **1g**
Sodium **190mg**

75 g	dried chick-peas, picked over	2½ oz
30 g	onion, coarsely chopped	1 oz
1	garlic clove, coarsely chopped	1
¼ tsp	ground cumin	¼ tsp
½ tsp	garam masala	½ tsp
¼ tsp	chili powder	¼ tsp
75 g	fresh granary breadcrumbs	2½ oz
1 tbsp	chopped parsley	1 tbsp
¼ tsp	salt	¼ tsp
	freshly ground black pepper	
1½ tbsp	beaten egg	1½ tbsp
	fig leaves, for garnish (optional)	
	Red pepper relish	
1 tsp	safflower oil	1 tsp
½	sweet red pepper, seeded, deribbed and finely chopped	½
1	small onion, finely chopped	1
1	garlic clove, crushed	1
2 tbsp	malt vinegar	2 tbsp
½ tsp	dry mustard	½ tsp
2 tsp	sugar	2 tsp
⅛ tsp	Tabasco sauce	⅛ tsp

Rinse the chick-peas under cold running water, then put them in a large, heavy-bottomed saucepan and pour in enough cold water to cover them by about 7.5 cm (3 inches). Discard any that float to the surface. Cover the pan, leaving the lid ajar, and slowly bring the liquid to the boil over medium-low heat. Boil the chick-peas for 2 minutes, then turn off the heat and soak them for at least 1 hour. (Alternatively, soak the peas overnight in cold water.)

Drain the peas; return them to the pan and cover

Carrots Cooked with Honey and Spices

Serves 6
Working time: about 5 minutes
Total time: about 15 minutes

Calories **35**
Protein **1g**
Cholesterol **0mg**
Total fat **0g**
Saturated fat **0g**
Sodium **210mg**

500 g	carrots, sliced diagonally	1 lb
1	small onion, finely chopped	1
2 tbsp	clear honey	2 tbsp
2 tbsp	wine vinegar	2 tbsp
1 tsp	ground cumin	1 tsp
½ tsp	ground cinnamon	½ tsp
½ tsp	salt	½ tsp
2 tbsp	chopped parsley	2 tbsp

Place the carrots, onion, honey, wine vinegar, cumin, cinnamon and salt in a heavy-bottomed saucepan, and add 15 cl (¼ pint) of water. Set the pan over high heat and bring the liquid to the boil. Reduce the heat a little, and cook the carrots fairly rapidly, uncovered, for about 10 minutes, until most of the liquid has evaporated but the carrots are still slightly crunchy. Set the mixture aside to cool.

Transfer the carrots to a lidded plastic container to take to the picnic, then chill them in the refrigerator until you are ready to leave. Place the chopped parsley in a small plastic bag.

At the picnic, turn the carrots into a serving bowl and sprinkle on the chopped parsley.

Tabbouleh

Serves 6
Working time: about 30 minutes
Total time: about 1 hour (includes soaking)

Calories **75**
Protein **3g**
Cholesterol **0mg**
Total fat **3g**
Saturated fat **1g**
Sodium **10mg**

90 g	burghul	3 oz
20 g	mint leaves, finely chopped	¾ oz
60 g	parsley, finely chopped	2 oz
1	onion, finely chopped	1
3 tbsp	fresh lemon juice	3 tbsp
1 tbsp	virgin olive oil	1 tbsp
	tomato wedges, for garnish	

Put the burghul in a bowl and add sufficient boiling water to cover it. Leave the burghul to soak for 30 minutes, topping up the water as necessary to keep the grains covered. Tip the burghul into a nylon sieve and let it drain thoroughly; press it down with the back of a spoon to force out as much moisture as possible.

Turn the drained burghul into a mixing bowl and add the mint, parsley, onion, lemon juice and oil. Stir all the ingredients together thoroughly. Turn the tabbouleh into a lidded plastic container to take to the picnic, and place it in the refrigerator until required. Chill the tomato wedges in a separate container.

At the picnic, transfer the tabbouleh to a serving bowl and garnish it with the tomato wedges.

Fruit and Nut Triangles

Serves 6
Working time: about 25 minutes
Total time: about 45 minutes

Calories **205**
Protein **4g**
Cholesterol **0mg**
Total fat **12g**
Saturated fat **5g**
Sodium **100mg**

90 g	plain flour	3 oz
1 tbsp	caster sugar	1 tbsp
60 g	polyunsaturated margarine	2 oz
15 g	shelled walnuts, chopped	½ oz
15 g	pine-nuts, chopped	½ oz
15 g	shelled pistachio nuts, chopped	½ oz
20 g	semolina	¾ oz
2 tbsp	clear honey	2 tbsp
60 g	sultanas	2 oz

30 g	stoned dried dates, chopped	1 oz
30 g	dried apricots, chopped	1 oz
1 tsp	rose-water	1 tsp
1	shelled walnut half, for decoration	1

Preheat the oven to 200°C (400°F or Mark 6). Lightly grease and flour a 20 cm (8 inch) diameter loose-bottomed sandwich tin.

Sift the flour and sugar into a large bowl, and rub in the margarine with your fingertips until the mixture resembles breadcrumbs. Using a round-bladed knife, mix 1½ teaspoons of iced water into the dry ingredients to form a soft dough. Gather the dough into a ball and knead it briefly on a lightly floured work surface, to smooth it. Alternatively, you can prepare the dough in a food processor.

Press the dough evenly into the base of the prepared sandwich tin, and prick it all over with a fork. Spread out all the chopped nuts on a baking sheet. Cook the nuts and the pastry base in the oven for 10 minutes, stirring the nuts occasionally. Remove the nuts and pastry case from the oven, but leave the oven switched on. Run a sharp knife round the edge of the pastry base, to loosen it.

While the pastry and nuts are cooking, prepare the topping. Place the semolina, honey, sultanas, dates and apricots in a small, heavy-bottomed saucepan with 15 cl (¼ pint) of water. Stir the ingredients together and bring them just to the boil. Reduce the heat and simmer the mixture for about 8 minutes, or until it has formed a thick purée. Remove the pan from the heat and stir in the rose-water and the roasted nuts. Spread the fruit and nut filling over the pastry base in an even layer and return it to the oven for 20 minutes.

Allow the baked sweet pastry to cool in its tin, then cut it into 12 triangles. Cover the tin with plastic film and store the triangles in the refrigerator until you are ready to leave for the picnic. Transport the triangles in the tin and also take along a walnut half, for decoration. At the picnic, arrange the triangles on a round serving dish and place the walnut half in the centre.

Turkish Delight

Serves 6
Working time: about 20 minutes
Total time: about 3 hours and 35 minutes

Calories **70**
Protein **3g**
Cholesterol **0mg**
Total fat **3g**
Saturated fat **2g**
Sodium **5mg**

½ litre	unsweetened white grape juice	16 fl oz
15 g	shelled walnuts	½ oz
15 g	powdered gelatine	½ oz
½ tbsp	orange-flower water	½ tbsp
½ tsp	pure vanilla extract	½ tsp
	walnut oil, for brushing	
15 g	desiccated coconut	½ oz

Preheat the oven to 180°C (350°F or Mark 4).

Pour the unsweetened grape juice into a wide, heavy-bottomed saucepan and boil it gently until it has reduced to ¼ litre (8 fl oz). Transfer the grape juice to a bowl and set it aside.

Spread out the walnuts on a baking sheet and roast them in the oven for 15 minutes, stirring them occasionally during this time. When they are cool enough to handle, chop them roughly.

Sprinkle the gelatine over 5 tablespoons of cold water in a small, heatproof bowl. Leave the gelatine for 2 minutes, to allow the granules to soften and swell, then set the bowl over a pan of gently simmering water and stir until the gelatine has completely dissolved — about 3 minutes. Stir the gelatine solution, the orange-flower water and the vanilla extract into the reduced grape juice. Chill the mixture until it is on the point of setting — about 15 minutes.

Brush a 10 by 10 by 2.5 cm (4 by 4 by 1 inch) square tin or rigid plastic container with a little walnut oil. Stir the chopped walnuts into the partially set grape jelly, then turn the mixture into the prepared tin. Chill the grape jelly until it has set — at least 3 hours, or preferably overnight.

Unmould the set jelly on to a wooden board and cut it into 12 equal squares. Dip the squares in the desiccated coconut, pressing it on gently to ensure that each square is evenly coated. Store the squares in the refrigerator, packed in a rigid container, until you are ready to leave for the picnic. Carry the container to the picnic site in a cool box.

AMERICAN BARBECUE

Toasted Onion Dip
Chicken Drumsticks in Barbecue Sauce
Citrus-Marinated Rump Steak
Fruited Cabbage Salad
Garlic Potato Fans and Grilled Corn-on-the Cob
Iced Peach Yogurt with Hot Blueberry Compote

The iced yogurt dessert for this barbecue can be prepared a day or two in advance and stored in the freezer. The rump steak, too, can begin its marination the day before. Both the toasted onion dip and the fruited cabbage salad will benefit from thorough chilling, so make those ahead of time if you can. The hot foil parcels — of corn, of garlic potatoes and of fruit compote — can all be assembled together and placed ready for cooking at the appropriate time.

About 1½ hours before you plan to eat, place the potatoes on the barbecue rack, and add the corn parcels after 40 minutes. Set the vegetables aside once they are cooked — they will remain hot in their foil wrappings. Next, begin to barbecue the chicken drumsticks; after 10 minutes, move them to the edges of the rack for the remainder of their cooking time and cook the steaks in the centre, over the hottest coals. When the chicken and the steaks are cooked, the vegetables may be reheated briefly.

Shortly before you wish to serve the dessert, place the parcels of fruit on the rack to cook in the residual heat of the barbecue.

A smooth onion dip with crudités is served as a prelude to this American-inspired barbecue. The main course of chicken drumsticks and citrus-marinated steak is accompanied by a colourful salad of fruits and crisp shredded cabbage in a light yogurt dressing. Garlic potatoes and juicy corn-on-the-cob round out the meal, which concludes with bubbling-hot parcels of fruit compote topped with iced peach yogurt.

Toasted Onion Dip

Serves 12
Working time: about 30 minutes
Total time: about 2 hours and 30 minutes
(includes chilling)

Calories **45**			
Protein **5g**	3	large Spanish onions, two	3
		coarsely chopped	
Cholesterol **trace**	175 g	low-fat ricotta cheese	6 oz
Total fat **2g**	175 g	low-fat soft cheese	6 oz
Saturated fat **trace**	6 tbsp	finely cut chives	6 tbsp
Sodium **30mg**		freshly ground black pepper	

Preheat the oven to 190°C (375°F or Mark 5) and line a baking sheet with foil.

Put the coarsely chopped Spanish onions in a heavy-bottomed saucepan and cover them with cold water. Bring the water to the boil, cover the pan and simmer the onions gently for 30 to 40 minutes, until they are very soft and tender.

Meanwhile, cut the remaining onion into 5 mm (¼ inch) thick slices and spread them out on the baking sheet. Toast the onion slices in the oven for about 20 minutes, turning them so that they brown evenly and removing them as they brown; do not let the onions burn. Alternatively, toast the onion slices under a preheated medium-hot grill, again watching carefully to avoid burning them. Set them aside.

When the chopped onions are cooked, drain them well and allow them to cool. Transfer them to a food processor and process them to a smooth purée. Add the low-fat cheeses and process briefly to combine the ingredients. Turn the dip into a bowl.

Crumble the toasted onion slices. Reserve 1 tablespoon for garnish, and add the remainder to the bowl, with the chives and some black pepper. Gently fold them into the dip. Cover the bowl and chill the dip for at least 1 hour. Just before serving, sprinkle the dip with the reserved toasted onion.

SUGGESTED ACCOMPANIMENT: *a selection of crunchy fresh vegetables, for dipping.*

Chicken Drumsticks in Barbecue Sauce

Serves 12
Working time: about 30 minutes
Total time: about 2 hours and 30 minutes

Calories **130**
Protein **16g**
Cholesterol **75mg**
Total fat **5g**
Saturated fat **2g**
Sodium **95mg**

1	onion, chopped	1
1	stick celery, trimmed and diced	1
1	garlic clove, crushed	1
850 g	canned tomatoes, chopped	1¾ lb
45 g	muscovado sugar	1½ oz
1 tbsp	Worcester sauce	1 tbsp
1 tsp	hot paprika	1 tsp
	freshly ground black pepper	
12	chicken drumsticks (about 140 g/ 4½ oz each)	12

To make the barbecue sauce, put all the ingredients except the drumsticks in a heavy-bottomed saucepan. Cover the pan and simmer the ingredients gently for 1 hour, or until the vegetables are very tender. Remove the pan from the heat. When the mixture has cooled, purée it in a food processor. Press the purée through a sieve into a clean pan, discarding the solids which remain in the sieve. Cook the sauce, uncovered, at a hard simmer, stirring it occasionally, until it is thick and the quantity has reduced by half — about 30 minutes.

Brush the chicken drumsticks with some of the sauce and arrange them on a lightly oiled rack over hot coals. Cook the drumsticks for 10 minutes, turning them frequently and basting them with more of the sauce each time they are turned. Move the drumsticks to the outer edges of the rack and continue to cook them for another 10 to 15 minutes, again turning them frequently and basting them with the sauce.

Insert a skewer into the thickest part of the flesh of one of the drumsticks; if the juices run clear, the drumsticks are ready. Pile the cooked drumsticks on to a serving plate. Transfer the remaining barbecue sauce to a bowl and serve it with the drumsticks.

SUGGESTED ACCOMPANIMENT: *spring onions.*

Citrus-Marinated Rump Steak

Serves 12
Working time: about 25 minutes
Total time: about 5 hours and 30 minutes
(includes marinating)

Calories **170**
Protein **24g**
Cholesterol **50mg**
Total fat **8g**
Saturated fat **3g**
Sodium **40mg**

3 tbsp	fresh orange juice	3 tbsp
2 tbsp	fresh lime juice	2 tbsp
1 tsp	fresh lemon juice	1 tsp
2 tbsp	virgin olive oil	2 tbsp
1 or 2	garlic cloves, finely chopped	1 or 2
1 tbsp	dried green peppercorns, coarsely crushed	1 tbsp
1 tbsp	fresh thyme leaves, or 1 tsp dried thyme	1 tbsp
1 kg	rump steak, 2.5 to 4 cm (1 to 1½ inches) thick, trimmed of all fat and cut into two equal pieces	2 lb

In a shallow, non-reactive dish that is just large enough to hold the steaks comfortably, mix together the citrus juices, olive oil, garlic, peppercorns and thyme leaves. Put the steaks into the dish and turn them over to coat both sides with the marinade. Cover the dish closely and leave the meat to marinate in the refrigerator for at least 4 hours, or overnight.

Remove the meat from the refrigerator about 1 hour before you wish to cook it. Reserving the marinade, lay the steaks on the rack over hot coals, and cook for 4 to 5 minutes on each side for medium-rare meat; increase the cooking time to 6 to 7 minutes on each side for medium to well-done meat. Baste the steaks with the marinade when you turn them.

Transfer the cooked steaks to a carving board and allow them to rest for 5 minutes. To serve, slice each steak into six portions.

Fruited Cabbage Salad

Serves 12
Working time: about 25 minutes
Total time: about 1 hour

Calories **105**
Protein **4g**
Cholesterol **trace**
Total fat **3g**
Saturated fat **1g**
Sodium **45mg**

350 g	trimmed red cabbage, finely shredded	12 oz
350 g	trimmed white cabbage, finely shredded	12 oz
250 g	trimmed Chinese cabbage, finely shredded	8 oz
1	red onion, cut into fine slivers	1
250 g	seedless green grapes, halved if large	8 oz
2	dessert apples, cored, diced and sprinkled with a little fresh lemon juice	2
1 tbsp	caraway seeds	1 tbsp
Honey dressing		
8 cl	cider vinegar	3 fl oz
3 tbsp	Greek honey, or other clear honey	3 tbsp
1 tbsp	Dijon mustard	1 tbsp
2 tbsp	corn or safflower oil	2 tbsp
¼ litre	plain low-fat yogurt	8 fl oz
	freshly ground black pepper	

First make the dressing. In a small bowl, combine the vinegar, honey and mustard, and whisk them together. Gradually whisk in the corn oil, followed by the yogurt. Season the dressing with some black pepper.

In a large mixing bowl, combine the red, white and Chinese cabbages, the onion, grapes and apples. Pour the dressing over the salad, and sprinkle on the caraway seeds. Lift and toss the salad until the fruit and vegetables are evenly coated with the dressing.

Cover the bowl and chill the salad for at least 30 minutes before serving it. Stir and toss the salad again before transferring it to a serving dish.

Garlic Potato Fans and Grilled Corn-on-the-Cob

Serves 12
Working time: about 30 minutes
Total time: about 2 hours and 30 minutes

Calories **385**
Protein **9g**
Cholesterol **0mg**
Total fat **8g**
Saturated fat **1g**
Sodium **15mg**

1	large garlic clove, lightly crushed	1
4 tbsp	corn or safflower oil	4 tbsp
12	baking potatoes (about 250 g/8 oz each), scrubbed	12
12	ears sweetcorn in the husk	12

At least 1 hour before you begin to cook the potatoes, combine the garlic and oil in a cup. Set them aside to allow the garlic to infuse the oil.

Make crosswise cuts about 1 cm (½ inch) apart in the baking potatoes, cutting about two thirds of the way through. Place each potato on a double-thickness square of foil that is large enough to wrap round it. Brush the garlic-flavoured oil over the potatoes so that it can seep down into the cuts. Wrap the foil square securely round the potatoes.

Place the foil parcels on the barbecue rack, over hot coals. Roast the potatoes for about 1 hour, turning them occasionally so that they cook evenly.

To prepare the corn-on-the-cob, fold back the husks on each ear and remove the silk. Fold the husks back up round the corn, then wrap each ear securely in a double thickness of foil. Place the foil-wrapped corn on the barbecue rack and cook it for 15 to 20 minutes, turning it occasionally so that it cooks evenly.

To serve, remove the foil from the corn cobs, then very carefully peel back and trim off one side of the husks: the corn inside will be extremely hot. Open out the foil round the potatoes and pinch their sides to open up the cuts. Pile the vegetables on platters.

Iced Peach Yogurt with Hot Blueberry Compote

Serves 12
Working time: about 1 hour and 15 minutes
Total time: about 5 hours (includes freezing)

Calories **165**	90 cl	plain low-fat yogurt	1 ½ pints
Protein **5g**	750 g	ripe peaches, peeled and stoned	1 ½ lb
Cholesterol **trace**	150 g	caster sugar	5 oz
Total fat **1g**	1	orange, juice only	1
Saturated fat **trace**	2	egg whites	2
Sodium **70mg**	**Hot blueberry compote**		
	850 g	fresh or thawed frozen blueberries or blackberries	1 ¾ lb
	3 tbsp	cornflour	3 tbsp
	12.5 cl	fresh orange juice	4 fl oz
	1 tsp	finely grated orange rind	1 tsp
	½ tsp	freshly grated nutmeg	½ tsp
	2 tbsp	Kirsch	2 tbsp

Line a large nylon sieve with a double thickness of paper towels and set it over a bowl. Pour the yogurt into the sieve and leave it to drain for 1½ hours.

Meanwhile, purée the peaches in a food processor: there will be about 60 cl (1 pint) of purée. Pour the peach purée into a bowl, and add 100 g (3½ oz) of the sugar and the orange juice. Stir the mixture until the sugar has dissolved. Add the drained yogurt to the purée, scraping it carefully off the paper towels, and stir it in. Whisk the egg whites until they are foamy. Gradually whisk in the remaining sugar, and continue whisking until the egg whites are stiff. Lightly fold the egg whites into the peach purée.

Pour the mixture into a metal tray, cover the tray with foil and put it in the freezer. When the mixture has set round the edges — after 30 to 40 minutes — turn it into a food processor and process it briefly to break down the frozen parts. Return the mixture to the metal tray, cover it as before and replace it in the freezer. Process the mixture for a second time when it has again set round the edges, then return it to the freezer until it is completely frozen — 2 to 3 hours.

Alternatively, pour the mixture into the container of an electric ice cream maker and insert the paddle. Cover the ice cream and freeze it until the paddle stops turning, then remove the paddle and leave the ice cream to "ripen" in the freezer for a further hour.

Remove the iced yogurt from the freezer and place it in the refrigerator 30 minutes before you plan to serve it, or 1 hour before serving if it has been stored in the freezer for a day or two.

To make the compote, put the blueberries in a bowl and toss them with the cornflour. Add the remaining ingredients and toss them with the blueberries until they are evenly mixed.

Cut out twelve 25 by 12 cm (10 by 5 inch) strips of foil and fold each one in half crosswise into a 12 cm (5 inch) square. Cut out 12 squares of non-stick parchment paper slightly smaller than the foil squares. Place a parchment paper square on each foil square. Press one pair of squares, with the foil underneath, into a dessert bowl to mould it, then spoon in a portion of the blueberry mixture. Wrap the paper and foil round the fruit, sealing the parcel well. Prepare 11 more parcels in the same way.

After the main course has been cooked, place the parcels of fruit mixture on the barbecue rack and cook them for 10 to 15 minutes, depending on the heat left in the coals. Shake each parcel half way through the cooking time to redistribute the contents. To check that the compote is ready, open up a parcel: the juices should be thickened and the berries piping hot.

To serve, open up the parcels and top the cooked compote with scoops of the iced peach yogurt. Serve the desserts in their parcels.

EDITOR'S NOTE: *To make peaches easier to peel, first immerse the fruit in boiling water for 2 minutes, to loosen the skins.*

4 A hollowed-out squash shell provides the perfect serving vessel for this creamy salad of chicken, baby sweetcorn and spaghetti squash (recipe, opposite).

An Indoor Aid to Outdoor Meals

The marriage of modern technology with the most ancient traditions of cookery is nowhere more surprising than in the contribution of the microwave oven to outdoor eating. In fact, the well-known advantages of microwave cookery prove particularly useful to anyone preparing meals to eat alfresco.

Bright, festive foods are ideal for picnics. Cooked in a microwave oven, vegetables retain their original, vivid colours. The three-pepper flan on page 131 brings a touch of Mediterranean brilliance to the most overcast of picnics. Moreover, because it saves you time in the kitchen, the microwave oven frees you to enjoy the sun. Even apparently time-consuming composite dishes become short work with a microwave oven. For the elegant chicken salad on the right, for instance, a whole spaghetti squash cooks in just 10 to 12 minutes, while the strips of chicken breast require only 3 minutes' cooking time.

Another salad — the Atlantic kedgeree on page 136 — highlights the microwave oven's renowned capacity to produce moist, tender fish. And because microwave cookery destroys very few vitamins and minerals, you can be assured of a nutritious meal for healthy outdoor eating. Even at a barbecue — where old-fashioned cookery justly takes centre stage — the microwave oven plays an invaluable supporting role. Before the charcoal briquettes are fully alight, you can make the sauces and relishes *(pages 132 and 133)*.

A few simple techniques help ensure perfect results. If covering a dish with plastic film, turn back one corner in order to prevent the build-up of steam. Use film that is plasticizer-free so that potentially harmful substances do not leach out into the hot food.

The recipes in this chapter include instructions for turning the food as it cooks; if your microwave oven has a turntable, these instructions may be ignored. Soups and sauces require occasional stirring to ensure even cooking. And remember that microwaved food is not necessarily done when the oven turns off. Many recipes call for additional ''standing time'' of up to half the total cooking time.

These microwave recipes have been tested in 650-watt and 700-watt ovens. Most of the dishes are cooked on ''high'', or 100 per cent power; the term ''medium'' refers to 50 per cent power.

Golden Chicken Salad in a Vegetable Squash

Serves 4
Working time: about 35 minutes
Total time: about 2 hours and 35 minutes (includes cooling)

Calories **205**
Protein **26g**
Cholesterol **65mg**
Total fat **6g**
Saturated fat **3g**
Sodium **440mg**

4 tbsp	sweet white wine	4 tbsp
2.5 cm	piece fresh ginger root, sliced	1 inch
1/8 tsp	powdered saffron	1/8 tsp
350 g	skinned and boned chicken breasts, cut into 4 by 1 cm (1 1/2 by 1/2 inch) strips	12 oz
125 g	baby sweetcorn, trimmed if necessary	4 oz
2	small spaghetti squashes (about 750 g/1 1/2 lb each)	2
45 g	thick Greek yogurt	1 1/2 oz
2 tbsp	soured cream	2 tbsp
1/4 tsp	freshly grated nutmeg	1/4 tsp
1/8 tsp	salt	1/8 tsp
1/8 tsp	white pepper	1/8 tsp
1 1/2 tsp	yellow mustard seeds	1 1/2 tsp

Place the wine, ginger and saffron in a dish, and stir to distribute the saffron. Add the chicken and stir to coat all the strips in the wine mixture. Cover the dish with plastic film, pulled back at one edge, and cook the chicken on high for 2 1/2 to 3 minutes, until all the strips are cooked; stir twice during the cooking time. Leave the chicken to cool in the liquid — about 2 hours.

Meanwhile, place the baby sweetcorn in a dish with 3 tablespoons of cold water. Cover the dish as before, and cook the sweetcorn on high for 3 minutes, stirring half way through cooking. Leave the sweetcorn to rest for 2 minutes, then uncover and drain it.

Wash the squashes and pierce each one in three or four places with a thin skewer. Place both squashes in the microwave oven on a double layer of paper towels. Cook them on high for 16 minutes, or until they are slightly soft to the touch and aromatic, rearranging them two or three times during cooking. Leave the squashes to rest for 5 minutes.

Remove the chicken strips from their cooking liquid, and set them aside. Cook the liquid, uncovered, on high until it has reduced to 1 tablespoon — 3 to 4 minutes; watch carefully while you do this, to avoid boiling the liquid dry. Strain the reduced liquid into a bowl, discarding the ginger. Allow the liquid to cool for 1 minute, then stir in the Greek yogurt, soured cream, nutmeg, salt and pepper.

Place the mustard seeds in a narrow, deep dish, ▶

and cook them on high for 2 minutes, or until they start to pop and release their aroma. Reserve about a quarter of the seeds for garnish, and place these in a small screw-top jar to take to the picnic. Lightly crush the remainder using a mortar and pestle, and stir them into the yogurt dressing.

Halve each squash lengthwise. Use a fork to scrape out the seeds and fibre from the middle of each squash portion. Fork out the strands, and pile them into a large mixing bowl; reserve the squash shells.

Gently mix the chicken and sweetcorn with the squash strands. Pour in the dressing, and continue to mix until all the ingredients are thoroughly combined.

Pile the mixture lightly into the four squash shells, and cover them with plastic film. Chill the shells until required. Transport them to the picnic site in a cool box, inside rigid plastic containers packed with paper towels. Sprinkle over the reserved yellow mustard seeds when you unwrap the squash, and add a little extra grated nutmeg if you like.

Chilled Beetroot Soup

Serves 6
Working time: about 25 minutes
Total time: about 3 hours and 25 minutes (includes chilling)

Calories **60**			
Protein **2g**	125 g	tomatoes, quartered	4 oz
Cholesterol **5mg**	350 g	raw beetroots, peeled and grated	12 oz
Total fat **1g**	1	carrot, grated	1
Saturated fat **trace**	1	onion, grated	1
Sodium **205mg**	1	small potato, peeled and grated	1
	2	bay leaves	2
	90 cl	unsalted vegetable stock (recipe, page 139)	1½ pints
	175 g	thick Greek yogurt	6 oz
	½ tsp	salt	½ tsp
		freshly ground black pepper	

Put the tomatoes in a bowl with 3 tablespoons of cold water. Cover the bowl with plastic film, pulled back at one edge, and cook the tomatoes on high for 3 to 4 minutes, until they are pulpy. Sieve the tomato pulp.

Place the beetroot, carrot, onion and potato in a large bowl. Stir in the sieved tomatoes, the bay leaves and half of the stock. Cover the bowl as before, and cook the soup on high for 25 to 30 minutes, until the vegetables are tender; stir the mixture twice during the cooking time. Remove the bay leaves from the soup, then stir in the remaining stock and leave the soup to cool — 30 to 45 minutes.

Ladle a little of the cooled soup into a bowl and stir in the yogurt. When the mixture is smooth, add it to the soup and stir to mix it in evenly. Add the salt and some pepper. Chill the soup for 2 hours, then transfer it to chilled vacuum flasks to take to the picnic.

Three-Pepper Flan

Serves 6
Working (and total) time: about 1 hour

Calories **220**
Protein **8g**
Cholesterol **75mg**
Total fat **12g**
Saturated fat **3g**
Sodium **185mg**

60 g	polyunsaturated margarine	2 oz
1 tbsp	smooth peanut butter	1 tbsp
175 g	wholemeal flour	6 oz
1	small sweet red pepper, seeded, deribbed and cut into thin rings	1
1	small sweet green pepper, seeded, deribbed and cut into thin rings	1
1	small sweet yellow pepper, seeded, deribbed and cut into thin rings	1
2	eggs	2
¼ litre	skimmed milk	8 fl oz
¼ tsp	salt	¼ tsp
	freshly ground black pepper	
1 tbsp	chopped fresh coriander	1 tbsp

Using your fingertips, lightly rub the margarine and peanut butter into the wholemeal flour until the mixture resembles fine breadcrumbs. Make a well in the centre of the dry ingredients. Using a round-bladed knife, mix in 8 to 10 teaspoons of iced water to form a soft but not sticky dough.

Gather the dough into a firm ball, and knead it briefly on a lightly floured surface until it is smooth. Roll out the dough into a circle large enough to line a 20 cm (8 inch) flan dish. Taking care not to stretch the dough, line the dish, then chill it for 20 minutes.

Lay a piece of paper towel over the flan case, pressing it lightly on to the base. Microwave the flan case on high for 3½ minutes, or until the pastry has lost its wet, glossy appearance and looks dry; give the flan case a half turn after 2 minutes. Remove the paper towel and leave the pastry to cool.

Place the pepper rings in a bowl, and sprinkle 1 tablespoon of cold water over them. Cover the bowl with plastic film, leaving one edge open to let steam escape. Cook the pepper rings on high for 2 minutes, or until they are soft. Allow them to stand for 5 minutes, then arrange them evenly in the pastry case.

Beat the eggs and milk together with the salt and a generous grinding of black pepper. Stir in the chopped coriander, and pour the mixture over the peppers in the flan case. Cook the flan on medium for 15 minutes, giving it a quarter turn every 2 minutes. If the filling is not quite set at the end of this time, cook the flan, in short bursts of power, for a further 15 to 30 seconds.

Let the flan cool completely, in its dish, before covering it with foil or plastic film to take on a picnic.

Five Colourful Accompaniments

These quick-to-prepare sauces and relishes make a wholesome range of accompaniments to the picnic and barbecue recipes in this volume. They all keep well and may be made in advance. Store them in the refrigerator, either in a covered bowl or in a screw-top jar for taking on a picnic, for up to three days. If you wish to freeze any, allow them to cool fully and then transfer them to plastic containers. Once thawed, they should be stirred thoroughly before serving.

Nutritionally, these relishes are greatly superior to their shop-bought equivalents. A tablespoon of one of them will provide between 20 and 30 calories, or 15 calories in the case of the Mexican chili relish. The green garlic sauce contains about 5 mg of cholesterol per tablespoon; the other four have negligible amounts. A portion of any one of these relishes contains only a trace of saturated fat and little sodium.

Mexican Chili Relish

Makes 45 cl (¾ pint)
Working time: about 25 minutes
Total time: about 1 hour (includes cooling)

175 g	frozen sweetcorn kernels	6 oz
2	sticks celery, finely chopped	2
1	small onion, finely chopped	1
2	small green chili peppers, seeded and finely chopped (caution, page 63)	2
15 g	caster sugar	½ oz
8 cl	white wine vinegar	3 fl oz
1	sweet green pepper, seeded, deribbed and finely diced	1
1	sweet red pepper, seeded, deribbed and finely diced	1
1 tsp	fennel seeds, crushed	1 tsp
1 tbsp	mustard seeds, crushed	1 tbsp
1 tsp	cornflour	1 tsp

Place the sweetcorn in a small bowl with 1 tablespoon of water. Cover the bowl with plastic film, pulled back at one edge, and microwave it on high for 1 minute. Drain the sweetcorn and refresh it under cold water.

Place the celery, onion, chili peppers, sugar and vinegar in a bowl, and cook them on high for 4 minutes, stirring twice. Add the sweetcorn, diced sweet peppers, and crushed fennel and mustard seeds, and stir to mix all the ingredients together. Cover the bowl with plastic film, pulling back one edge as before. Cook the mixture on high for 2 minutes, or until it is hot, stirring once. Blend the cornflour to a smooth paste with 2 tablespoons of cold water, and stir it into the hot mixture. Cook the relish on high for a further 2 minutes, or until it has thickened, stirring it twice. Transfer the chili relish to a serving bowl and leave it to cool.

Goes well with all steaks, hamburgers and sausages.

Green Garlic Sauce

Makes 30 cl (½ pint)
Working (and total) time: about 20 minutes

½ tbsp	unsalted butter	½ tbsp
4	shallots, roughly chopped	4
3	garlic cloves, roughly chopped	3
30 g	gherkins, rinsed and sliced	1 oz
15 g	capers, rinsed	½ oz
20 cl	medium-dry white wine	7 fl oz
1 tsp	caster sugar	1 tsp
20 g	parsley	¾ oz
2 or 3	tarragon sprigs	2 or 3

Place the butter in a dish and microwave it on high for 30 seconds, to melt it. Add the chopped shallots and garlic, and stir them into the melted butter. Cook them on high for 2 minutes, or until the shallots are soft; stir once during this time. Mix in the gherkins, capers, wine and sugar, and cover the dish with plastic film, pulled back at one edge. Cook on high for 2 minutes, stirring once.

Transfer the cooked ingredients to a food processor or blender. Add the parsley and tarragon, then blend the mixture until it is almost smooth. Transfer the sauce to a serving bowl, and reheat it on high for 1 minute. Alternatively, you can leave the sauce to cool completely and serve it cold.

Goes well with lamb and white fish, or can be used to dress pasta.

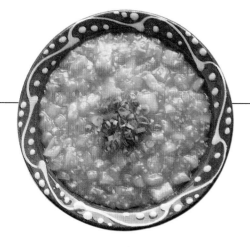

Sweet-and-Sour Sauce

Makes 60 cl (1 pint)
Working time: about 20 minutes
Total time: about 30 minutes

1 tsp	sesame oil	1 tsp
1	bunch spring onions, white parts chopped, a few green tops sliced, for garnish	1
2.5 cm	piece fresh ginger root, finely chopped	1 inch
1	sweet yellow pepper, seeded, deribbed and diced	1
2 tbsp	low-sodium soy sauce or shoyu	2 tbsp
1 tbsp	white wine vinegar	1 tbsp
3 tbsp	medium-dry sherry	3 tbsp
1	small fresh pineapple (about 1.25 kg/2 ¾ lb), peeled, cored and cut into 1 cm (½ inch) dice	1
1 tbsp	sesame seeds	1 tbsp
1 tbsp	cornflour	1 tbsp

In a large bowl, mix the sesame oil and the white parts of the spring onions. Cook them on high for 2 minutes, stirring once. Stir in the ginger root, yellow pepper, soy sauce, wine vinegar and sherry. Add 8 cl (3 fl oz) of water, stir, and cover the bowl with plastic film, leaving one edge open to allow steam to escape. Microwave the sauce on high for 1 minute, until it is hot.

Stir in the pineapple and sesame seeds. Blend the cornflour to a smooth paste with 2 tablespoons of cold water, and stir it into the sauce. Cover the bowl as before, and cook the sauce on high for 5 minutes, or until it has thickened, stirring it several times during cooking. Put the sauce in a serving bowl and serve it, hot or cold, garnished with a few slices of green spring onion tops.

Goes well with chicken and pork dishes.

Barbecue Sauce

Makes 45 cl (¾ pint)
Working (and total) time: about 20 minutes

1	large red onion, chopped	1
1	rasher green back bacon, trimmed of all fat and roughly chopped	1
1 tsp	virgin olive oil	1 tsp
2	bay leaves	2
1 tbsp	red wine vinegar	1 tbsp
1 tbsp	molasses or muscovado sugar	1 tbsp
1 tsp	paprika	1 tsp
2 tbsp	tomato paste	2 tbsp
1 tbsp	grainy mustard	1 tbsp
2 tsp	Worcester sauce	2 tsp
20 cl	fresh orange juice	7 fl oz
½ tsp	very finely chopped orange rind, for garnish	½ tsp

Mix the onion, bacon, oil and bay leaves in a large bowl, and cook them on high for 3 minutes, stirring once. Add the vinegar, molasses, paprika, tomato paste, mustard, Worcester sauce and fresh orange juice. Stir all the ingredients together, and cover the bowl with plastic film, leaving one edge open to allow steam to escape. Cook the mixture on high for 2 minutes.

Remove the bay leaves, then transfer the contents of the bowl to a food processor or blender, and process until a smooth sauce is formed. Pour the sauce into a serving bowl, and reheat it on high for 1 minute. Alternatively, allow the sauce to cool and serve it cold. Before serving the sauce, sprinkle the finely chopped orange rind over the surface.

Goes well with all types of barbecued food.

Curried Mango Relish

Makes 60 cl (1 pint)
Working time: about 20 minutes
Total time: about 30 minutes

1	fresh green chili pepper, seeded and roughly chopped (caution, page 63)	1
2 tsp	safflower oil	2 tsp
2	garlic cloves, crushed	2
¼ tsp	ground turmeric	¼ tsp
1 tsp	ground coriander	1 tsp
1 tsp	ground cumin	1 tsp
2	ripe mangoes (about 600 g/1 ¼ lb each), peeled, flesh roughly chopped, stones discarded	2
2 tsp	white wine vinegar	2 tsp
15 cl	plain low-fat yogurt	¼ pint

In a large bowl, mix the chopped chili pepper with the oil, garlic, turmeric, coriander and cumin. Cook the mixture on high for 1 minute, stirring half way through. Stir in the chopped mangoes and the vinegar. Cover the bowl with plastic film, leaving one edge open to allow steam to escape. Cook on high for 3 minutes, stirring once. Mash the mixture with a potato masher until it is pulpy, then leave the pulp to cool for 5 minutes.

Stir three quarters of the yogurt into the relish, and chill it until required. Just before serving, turn the relish into a serving bowl and swirl the remaining yogurt over the top.

Goes well with cold chicken, barbecued fish and meat — particularly lamb.

Greek-Style Celery and Tomato Salad

Serves 4 as a main course or 6 as a side dish
Working time: about 25 minutes
Total time: about 2 hours (includes cooling)

Calories **150**
Protein **6g**
Cholesterol **30mg**
Total fat **11g**
Saturated fat **4g**
Sodium **410mg**

500 g	ripe tomatoes, quartered, plus six tomatoes, skinned (page 138) and quartered	1 lb
1 tbsp	tomato paste	1 tbsp
1	large head celery, trimmed, sliced diagonally into 2.5 cm (1 inch) pieces	1
1	garlic clove, crushed	1
1 tbsp	virgin olive oil	1 tbsp
3 tbsp	fresh lemon juice	3 tbsp
2	bay leaves	2
⅛ tsp	ground coriander	⅛ tsp
4	spring onions, trimmed and chopped	4
	freshly ground black pepper	
125 g	feta cheese, cut into 1 cm (½ inch) cubes	4 oz
4	black olives, stoned and cut into sixths lengthwise	4
2 tsp	chopped flat-leaf parsley, plus parsley sprig, for garnish	2 tsp
1 tsp	chopped fresh oregano	1 tsp

Place the unskinned tomato quarters in a bowl with 2 tablespoons of cold water. Cover the bowl with plastic film, pulled back at one edge, and cook the tomatoes on high for 6 minutes, or until they are pulpy; stir them once during this time. Sieve the tomato pulp, and stir the tomato paste into it.

Place the celery in a large bowl, and add the sieved tomatoes, garlic, oil, lemon juice, bay leaves and coriander. Stir to mix the ingredients, then cover the bowl as before. Cook on high for 8 minutes, stirring once. Stir in the spring onions and skinned tomato quarters, and cook on high for a further 2 minutes, or until the celery is tender but still crisp. Add some black pepper and let the mixture cool — 1½ to 2 hours.

Remove the bay leaves and transfer the celery and tomato salad to a rigid plastic container to take to the picnic site. Pack the feta cheese, olive slices and chopped herbs separately.

At the picnic, arrange the salad in a serving dish, and scatter on the cheese, olive slices and chopped herbs. Garnish the salad with the parsley sprig.

SUGGESTED ACCOMPANIMENT: *crusty brown rolls.*

Mushroom and Parsley Pâté

Serves 6
Working time: about 25 minutes
Total time: about 24 hours (includes chilling)

Calories **85**
Protein **4g**
Cholesterol **0mg**
Total fat **3g**
Saturated fat **1g**
Sodium **205mg**

1 tbsp	polyunsaturated margarine	1 tbsp
2	garlic cloves, crushed	2
1	large onion, finely chopped	1
625 g	flat mushrooms, wiped and roughly chopped	1 ¼ lb
20 g	flat-leaf parsley, chopped	¾ oz
	freshly ground black pepper	
1 tbsp	mango chutney, chopped	1 tbsp
2 tbsp	white wine vinegar	2 tbsp
¼ tsp	salt	¼ tsp
90 g	fresh wholemeal breadcrumbs	3 oz

Place the margarine in a large bowl and microwave it on high for 30 seconds, or until it has melted. Stir the garlic and onion thoroughly into the margarine, and cook them on high for 2 minutes.

Stir in the mushrooms, and cook the mixture on high for another 5 minutes. Add half the chopped parsley and some black pepper, mix them in, and cook on high for a further 5 minutes. Stir the chopped mango chutney, wine vinegar and salt into the mushroom mixture, making sure that all the ingredients are thoroughly combined. Cook on high for 5 minutes more, or until all the liquid has evaporated. Mix in the breadcrumbs and the remaining chopped parsley.

Spoon the pâté into a round dish measuring about 15 cm (6 inches) in diameter and 7.5 cm (3 inches) in depth. Press the mixture down lightly with the back of the spoon. Leave the pâté to cool, then cover the dish with a close-fitting lid or with plastic film, taped down securely, to go on a picnic. Chill the pâté for about 24 hours to allow the flavours to develop fully.

SUGGESTED ACCOMPANIMENT: *home-made Melba toast or crispbreads, carried in an airtight tin.*

Atlantic Kedgeree

Serves 6

Working time: about 45 minutes

Total time: about 2 hours and 30 minutes (includes cooling)

Calories **280**
Protein **23g**
Cholesterol **90mg**
Total fat **2g**
Saturated fat **trace**
Sodium **170mg**

500 g	mussels, scrubbed and debearded	1 lb
300 g	long-grain rice	10 oz
3	sticks celery, sliced	3
90 cl	unsalted vegetable stock (recipe, page 139)	1½ pints
150 g	French beans, trimmed, cut into 2.5 cm (1 inch) lengths	5 oz
350 g	cod fillets	12 oz
½	sweet orange pepper, seeded, deribbed and thinly sliced	½
½	sweet yellow pepper, seeded, deribbed and thinly sliced	½
175 g	peeled cooked prawns	6 oz
	freshly ground black pepper	
2 tbsp	fresh lemon juice (optional)	2 tbsp
1 tbsp	finely cut chives	1 tbsp
	samphire, for garnish (optional)	

Place the mussels in a large bowl. Sharply tap any that are open; if they remain open, discard them. Cover the bowl with plastic film, pulled back at one edge, and cook the mussels on high for 5 to 6 minutes, shaking the bowl or stirring the mussels after 3 minutes. Leave them to cool, then discard any that remained closed during cooking. Remove the mussels from their shells. Strain any cooking liquid through a muslin-lined sieve into a bowl, and set it aside.

Place the rice and celery in a large bowl. Bring the stock to the boil, then add it to the bowl with the reserved mussel-cooking liquid. Cover the bowl with plastic film as before, and cook the rice on high for 10 minutes. Quickly stir in the French beans. Set the rice aside to cool; any stock that was left at the end of the cooking time will be absorbed as the rice cools.

Put the cod on a plate, thinner pieces towards the centre, and cover with plastic film pulled back at one edge. Cook the cod on high for 3 to 4 minutes, until the flesh flakes easily. Flake the fish, discarding the skin and any bones. Set the flaked fish aside to cool.

Meanwhile, place the orange and yellow pepper strips in a bowl. Cover the bowl as before, and cook the strips on high for 1½ minutes, until tender. Pour away any juices, and leave the peppers to cool.

Toss together the French beans and rice, the flaked fish, peppers, mussels and prawns. Season the mixture with some freshly ground black pepper, and add the lemon juice, if you are using it.

Transfer the kedgeree to a rigid plastic container and cover it with a tight-fitting lid. Place the chives and samphire in plastic bags, and put all three in a cool box to take to the picnic. At the site, arrange the kedgeree on a serving platter, sprinkle on the chives and garnish the dish with the samphire.

Smoked Haddock Roulade

Serves 6
Working time: about 50 minutes
Total time: about 1 hour and 20 minutes

Calories **130**
Protein **12g**
Cholesterol **100mg**
Total fat **6g**
Saturated fat **2g**
Sodium **460mg**

175 g	smoked haddock fillet, skinned	6 oz
2	eggs	2
1	egg white	1
30 g	plain flour	1 oz
	freshly ground black pepper	
1 tbsp	freshly grated Parmesan cheese	1 tbsp
	Watercress filling	
20 g	polyunsaturated margarine	¾ oz
20 g	plain flour	¾ oz
15 cl	skimmed milk	¼ pint
100 g	watercress, finely chopped	3½ oz
1 tbsp	finely cut chives	1 tbsp

First make the sauce for the filling. Put the margarine, flour and milk in a 60 cl (1 pint) jug, and whisk the mixture until the flour is evenly dispersed in the milk. Cook the sauce on high for 3 minutes, or until it is thick and smooth, stirring it briskly every 30 seconds. Stir in the watercress and chives. Cover the surface of the sauce with a circle of damp greaseproof paper, to prevent a skin from forming. Set the sauce aside to cool to room temperature, then chill it until required.

Lay the fish fillet on a plate and cover it with plastic film, pulling back one edge to allow steam to escape. Cook the fish on high for 3 minutes, or until the flesh flakes easily; give the plate a quarter turn after 1½ minutes. Flake the fish and remove any bones, then lightly mash the flakes with a fork.

Line the base of a 25 by 18 cm (10 by 7 inch) baking dish with non-stick parchment paper. Put the eggs and egg white in a bowl, and stand the bowl over a saucepan of simmering water. Using an electric hand-held whisk, whisk the eggs until they are thick and creamy and have doubled in volume — about 15 minutes. Sift the flour over the egg mixture. Season the flaked haddock with some black pepper, and add it to the bowl. Using a metal tablespoon, carefully fold in the flour and fish. Turn the mixture into the prepared baking dish, spreading it in an even layer right into the corners of the dish. Cook the mixture on high for 4 minutes, or until it is just firm to the touch; give the dish a half turn after 2 minutes.

Sprinkle the Parmesan cheese over a sheet of greaseproof paper, and invert the cooked rectangle on to the paper. Peel off the parchment paper. Spread the watercress sauce evenly over the rectangle to within 4 cm (1½ inches) of the edges. Starting from one of the short sides, roll the base and filling into a cylinder: lift one end of the underlying greaseproof paper to start the roulade off, and nudge it along by gradually lifting the rest of the paper.

Wrap the roulade loosely in greaseproof paper, and set it aside to cool. Once cold, wrap the roulade carefully in a double thickness of foil or greaseproof paper, ready to go on a picnic, then chill it until required. To avoid crushing the roulade, place it in a rigid container, and carry this to the picnic site inside a cool box. Take with you a sharp knife and a board so that the roulade can be sliced for serving.

SUGGESTED ACCOMPANIMENT: *salad of radish and cucumber.*

Peeling and Seeding a Tomato

1 *SKINNING THE TOMATO. Core the tomato by cutting a conical plug from its stem end. Cut a shallow cross in the base. Immerse the tomato in boiling water for 10 to 30 seconds, then plunge it into cold water. When the tomato has cooled, peel the skin away from the cross in sections.*

2 *SEEDING THE TOMATO. Halve the skinned tomato. Gently squeeze one of the halves, forcing out its seeds and juice. Rotate the tomato 90 degrees and squeeze once more. Dislodge any seeds from the inner chambers. Repeat the process with the other half.*

Peeling Sweet Peppers

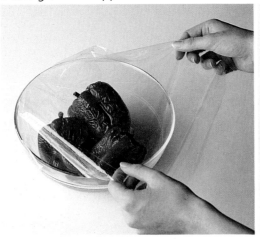

1 *LOOSENING THE SKIN. Place the peppers about 5 cm (2 inches) below a preheated grill. Turn the peppers as their sides become slightly scorched, until their skin has blistered on all sides. Transfer the peppers to a bowl and cover it with plastic film, or put them in a paper bag and fold it shut; the trapped steam will make the peppers limp and loosen their skins.*

2 *REMOVING THE SKIN. With a paring knife, peel off a pepper's skin in sections, from top to bottom. Repeat the process to skin the other peppers. The peppers may then be seeded and deribbed.*

Chicken Stock

Makes 2 to 3 litres (3½ to 5 pints)
Working time: about 20 minutes
Total time: about 3 hours

2 to 2.5 kg	uncooked chicken trimmings and bones (preferably wings, necks and backs), the bones cracked with a heavy knife	4 to 5 lb
2	carrots, scrubbed, sliced into 1 cm (½ inch) rounds	2
3	sticks celery, sliced into 2.5 cm (1 inch) lengths	3
2	large onions, cut in half, one half stuck with two cloves	2
2	fresh thyme sprigs, or ½ tsp dried thyme	2
1 or 2	bay leaves	1 or 2
10 to 15	parsley stems	10 to 15
5	black peppercorns	5

Put the trimmings and bones in a heavy stockpot and pour in enough water to cover them by 5 cm (2 inches). Slowly bring the liquid to the boil, skimming off the scum that rises to the surface. Boil for 10 minutes, skimming and adding a little cold water from time to time to help precipitate the scum.

Add the vegetables, herbs and peppercorns, and submerge them in the liquid. If necessary, add enough additional water to cover the vegetables and bones. Reduce the heat to low. Simmer the mixture for 2 to 3 hours, skimming once more during the process.

Strain the stock and allow it to stand until it is tepid, then refrigerate it overnight or freeze it long enough for the fat to congeal. Spoon off and discard the layer of fat.

Tightly covered and refrigerated, the stock may safely be kept for three to four days. Stored in small, tightly covered freezer containers and frozen, the stock may be kept for as long as six months.

EDITOR'S NOTE: *The chicken gizzard and heart may be added to the stock. Wings and necks — rich in gelatine — produce a particularly gelatinous stock, ideal for sauces and jellied dishes. The chicken liver should never be used.*

Vegetable Stock

Makes about 1½ litres (2½ pints)
Working time: about 25 minutes
Total time: about 1 hour and 30 minutes

3	sticks celery (with leaves), finely chopped	3
3	carrots, scrubbed, sliced into 3 mm (⅛ inch) rounds	3
3	large onions (about 750 g/ 1½ lb), coarsely chopped	3
2	large broccoli stems, coarsely chopped (optional)	2
1	medium turnip, peeled and cut into 1 cm (½ inch) cubes	1
5	garlic cloves, coarsely chopped	5
25 g	parsley (with stems), coarsely chopped	¾ oz
10	black peppercorns	10
2	fresh thyme sprigs, or 1 tsp dried thyme	2
2	bay leaves	2

Place the celery, carrots, onions, broccoli if you are using it, turnip, garlic, parsley and peppercorns in a heavy stockpot. Pour in water to cover them by 5 cm (2 inches). Slowly bring the liquid to the boil over medium heat, skimming off any scum that rises to the surface. When the liquid reaches the boil, add the thyme and bay leaves. Stir the stock once and reduce the heat to low; cover the pot, leaving the lid slightly ajar. Let the stock simmer undisturbed for 1 hour.

Strain the stock into a large bowl, pressing down lightly on the vegetables to extract all their liquid. Discard the vegetables. Allow the stock to stand until it is tepid, then refrigerate or freeze it.

Tightly covered and refrigerated, the stock may safely be kept for five to six days. Stored in small, tightly covered freezer containers and frozen, the stock may be kept for as long as six months.

Veal Stock

Makes about 3 litres (5 pints)
Working time: about 30 minutes
Total time: about 4 hours and 30 minutes

1.5 kg	veal breast or shin meat, cut into 7.5 cm (3 inch) pieces	3 lb
1.5 kg	veal bones (preferably knuckles), cracked	3 lb
2	onions, quartered	2
2	sticks celery, sliced	2
1	carrot, sliced	1
8	black peppercorns	8
3	unpeeled garlic cloves, crushed (optional)	3
1 tsp	fresh thyme, or ¼ tsp dried thyme	1 tsp
1	bay leaf	1

Half fill a large pot with water. Bring the water to the boil, add the veal meat and bones, and blanch them for 2 minutes to clean them. Drain the meat and bones in a colander, discarding the liquid, then rinse them under cold running water and return them to the pot.

Add the vegetables, peppercorns, and garlic, if you are using it. Pour in enough water to cover the contents by about 7.5 cm (3 inches), and bring the water to the boil over medium heat. Reduce the heat to maintain a simmer, and skim off any impurities. Add the thyme and bay leaf; simmer very gently for 4 hours, skimming occasionally.

Strain the stock into a large bowl; let the solids drain thoroughly before discarding them. Allow the stock to cool until it is tepid, then refrigerate it overnight or freeze it long enough for the fat to congeal. Spoon off and discard the layer of fat.

Tightly covered and refrigerated, the stock may safely be kept for three to four days. Stored in small, tightly covered freezer containers and frozen, the stock may be kept for as long as six months.

EDITOR'S NOTE: *Any combination of veal meat and bones may be used to make this stock; ideally, the meat and bones together should weigh about 3 kg (6 lb). Ask your butcher to crack the bones.*

Glossary

Acidulated water: a dilute solution of lemon juice in water, used to keep certain vegetables and fruits from discolouring after they are peeled.

Al dente: an Italian term meaning "to the tooth". It is used to describe the texture and taste of perfectly cooked pasta: chewy but with no flavour of flour.

Balsamic vinegar: a mild, intensely fragrant wine-based vinegar made in northern Italy; traditionally it is aged in wooden casks.

Baste: to help brown and flavour a food, and keep it from drying out, by brushing it with marinade, pan juices or other liquid during cooking.

Blanch: to plunge food into boiling water, which is then drained off as soon as it has returned to the boil. Blanching softens vegetables and fruits and can also mellow strong flavours.

Brown flour: wheat flour which contains about 85 per cent of the wheat grain; some of the bran and germ has been removed.

Brown sugars: ranging in colour from pale beige to dark brown, brown sugars are often prepared by purifying raw cane sugar to some degree. Alternatively, brown sugar is produced from fully refined white sugar mingled with molasses. Nutritionally, brown sugars have only a fractional advantage over white sugars but they are valued for their stronger flavour.

Calorie (or kilocalorie): a precise measure of the energy food supplies when it is broken down for use in the body.

Canelle knife: a kitchen utensil used to create small grooves in vegetables for decorative purposes.

Caul: a weblike fatty membrane that surrounds a pig's stomach. When wrapped round a lean minced-meat filling, it melts during cooking and moistens the meat.

Chili peppers: a variety of hot or mild red or green peppers. Fresh or dried, most chili peppers contain volatile oils that can irritate the skin and eyes; they must be handled with extreme care (caution, page 63).

Cholesterol: a waxlike substance manufactured in the human body and also found in foods of animal origin. Although a certain amount of cholesterol is necessary for proper body functioning, an excess can accumulate in the arteries, contributing to heart disease. See also Monounsaturated fats; Polyunsaturated fats; Saturated fats.

Coral: the edible roe of the scallop, lobster or crab.

Debeard: to remove the fibrous threads from a mussel. These tough threads, called the beard, are produced by the mussel to attach itself to stationary objects. See also Mussel.

Dietary fibre: a plant-cell material that passes undigested through the human body, but promotes healthy digestion of other food matter.

Fat: a basic component of many foods, comprising three types of fatty acid — saturated, monounsaturated and polyunsaturated — in varying proportions. See also Monounsaturated fats; Polyunsaturated fats; Saturated fats.

Fibre: see Dietary fibre.

Fillet: the most tender muscle in an animal's carcass, located inside the loin. Also a full-length section of a fish cut from the ribs and backbone. Can be used to describe the act of removing a fillet from a fish.

Five-spice powder: a pungent blend of ground Sichuan pepper, star anise, cassia, cloves and fennel seeds; available in Asian food shops.

Galangal: a brown rhizome with white flesh, similar in appearance and taste to ginger. In the West it is more commonly available in its powdered form, which is also known as Laos powder.

Garam masala: an aromatic mixture of ground spices used in Indian cookery. It usually contains coriander, cumin, cloves, ginger and cinnamon. It is available in Asian shops and some supermarkets.

Gelatine: a virtually tasteless protein, available in powdered form or in sheets. Dissolved gelatine is used to set chilled moulded dishes and desserts so that they retain their shape when unmoulded.

Ginger: the spicy, buff-coloured rhizome, or rootlike stem, of the ginger plant, used as a seasoning either in fresh form or dried and powdered. Dried ginger makes a poor substitute for fresh ginger root.

Julienne: the French term for food cut into thin strips.

Juniper berries: the berries of the juniper tree, used as the key flavouring in gin. They lend a resinous tang to marinades and sauces for game and other meats.

Kirsch (also called Kirschwasser): a clear cherry brandy distilled from small black cherries grown in Switzerland, Germany and the Alsace region of France; often used to macerate fruit desserts.

Lemon grass (citronella): a long, woody, lemon-flavoured stalk that is shaped like a spring onion. Lemon grass is available in Asian shops. To store, refrigerate in plastic film for up to two weeks; lemon grass may also be frozen for storage.

Mango: a fruit grown throughout the tropics, with sweet, succulent, yellow-orange flesh that is extremely rich in vitamin A. Like papaya, it may cause an allergic reaction in some individuals.

Marinade: a mixture of aromatic ingredients in which meat, vegetables or fruit are allowed to stand before cooking to enrich their flavour. Some marinades will tenderize meat.

Medallion: a round or oval-shaped slice of lean meat for grilling or frying.

Monounsaturated fats: one of the three types of fats found in foods. Monounsaturated fats are believed not to raise the level of cholesterol in the blood.

Mussel: a bivalve mollusc with a bluish-black shell found along Atlantic and Pacific coasts as well as in the Mediterranean. The mussel's sweet flesh varies from beige to orange-yellow in colour when cooked. See also Debeard.

Nam pla: a thin, brown, salty liquid made from fermented fish and used in South-East Asian cooking to bring out the flavours of a dish.

Noisettes: boned lamb from the best end of neck or loin, rolled, tied and cut into rounds for grilling or frying.

Non-reactive pan: a cooking vessel whose surface does not chemically react with food. Materials used include stainless steel, enamel, glass and some alloys. Untreated cast iron and aluminium may react with acids, producing discoloration or a peculiar taste.

Olive oil: any of various grades of oil extracted from olives. Extra virgin olive oil has a full, fruity flavour and the lowest acidity. Virgin olive oil is slightly higher in acidity and lighter in flavour. Pure olive oil, a processed blend of olive oils, has the highest acidity and the lightest taste.

Paprika: a slightly sweet, spicy powder produced by grinding dried red peppers. The best type of paprika is Hungarian. Available in various colours and strengths.

Parboil: to partially cook a food in liquid in order to prepare it for a second cooking method that would otherwise leave it underdone.

Parchment paper: a reusable paper that has been treated with silicone to produce a non-stick surface. It is used to line tins and baking sheets, and to wrap foods for baking.

Passion fruit: a juicy, fragrant, egg-shaped tropical fruit with wrinkled skin, yellow flesh and many small black seeds. The seeds are edible; the skin is not.

Pernod: an anise-flavoured spirit made in France.

Phyllo (also spelt "filo"): a paper-thin flour-and-water pastry popular in Greece and the Middle East. It can be made at home or bought, fresh or frozen, from delicatessens and some supermarkets.

Plantain: a starchy variety of banana that is normally cooked before it is eaten. Although the skin turns yellowish-brown and then black as the plantain ripens, the flesh remains creamy yellow or slightly pink.

Poach: to cook gently in simmering liquid. The temperature of the poaching liquid should be approximately 90°C (200°F), and its surface should merely tremble.

Polyunsaturated fats: one of the three types of fats found in foods. They exist in abundance in such vegetable oils as safflower, sunflower, corn and soya bean. They are also found in seafood. Certain highly polyunsaturated fatty acids called omega-3s occur exclusively in seafood and marine animals. Polyunsaturated fats are known to lower the level of cholesterol in the blood.

Prawn: a crustacean that lives in cold and warm waters in all parts of the world, called prawn or shrimp (or both) depending on local preference and size. There are hundreds of species, from the huge Asian striped tiger prawn and large Mediterranean prawn, to the medium-sized deep-water prawn of the North Atlantic and the tiny brown shrimp. Prawns and shrimps can be cooked in or out of the shell. They are moderately high in cholesterol but very low in fat.

Purée: to reduce food to a smooth, even, pulplike consistency by mashing it, passing it through a sieve, or processing it in a blender or food processor.

Recommended Daily Amount (RDA): the average daily amount of an essential nutrient recommended for healthy people by the U.K. Department of Health and Social Security.

Reduce: to boil down a liquid in order to concentrate its flavour or thicken its consistency.

Refresh: to rinse a briefly cooked vegetable under cold water to arrest its cooking and set its colour.

Rice-paper wrappers: brittle wrappers for small portions of food, made from rice flour and available from shops specializing in South-East Asian foods. They are softened by dipping them in hot water.

Rice wine: Chinese rice wine (shao-hsing) is brewed from rice and wine. Japanese rice wine (sake) has a different flavour but may be used as a substitute. If rice wine is not available, dry sherry may be used as an alternative.

Rind: the flavoured outermost layer of citrus-fruit peel; it should be cut or grated free of the white pith that lies beneath it.

Roe: refers primarily to fish eggs, but edible roe is also found in scallops, crabs and lobsters.

Roulade: a light sponge mixture baked in a shallow, rectangular tin, then turned out, spread with filling and rolled up.

Safflower oil: a vegetable oil that contains the highest amount of polyunsaturated fats.

Saffron: the dried, yellowish-red stigmas (or threads) of the saffron crocus, which yield a powerful yellow colour as well as a pungent flavour. Powdered saffron has less flavour than the threads.

Saturated fats: one of the three types of fats found in foods. They exist in abundance in animal products and coconut and palm oils; they raise the level of cholesterol in the blood. Because high blood cholesterol levels may cause heart disease, saturated fat consumption should be restricted to less than 15 per cent of the calories provided by the daily diet.

Sausage casing: natural casings, stronger than commercial casings, are the cleaned intestines of lamb, pig or ox. Usually sold preserved in brine or dry salt, they can be ordered from butchers or specialist suppliers and should be soaked before use. Lamb casings are generally used for thin sausages, pig or ox casings for thicker ones.

Sear: to brown meat by exposing it briefly to very high heat, sealing in natural juices.

Sesame paste: see Tahini.

Shallot: a refined cousin of the onion, with a subtle flavour and papery, red-brown skin.

Shoyu: see Soy sauce.

Sichuan pepper (also called Chinese pepper, Japanese pepper or anise pepper): a dried shrub berry with a tart, aromatic flavour that is less piquant than black pepper.

Simmer: to maintain a liquid at a temperature just below its boiling point so that the liquid's surface barely ripples.

Skimmed milk: milk from which almost all the fat has been removed.

Sodium: a nutrient essential to maintaining the proper balance of fluids in the body. In most diets, a major source of the element is table salt, which contains 40 per cent sodium. Excess sodium may contribute to high blood pressure, which increases the risk of heart disease. One teaspoon (5.5 g) of salt, with 2,132 milligrams of sodium, contains just over the maximum daily amount recommended by the World Health Organization.

Soy sauce: a savoury, salty brown liquid made from fermented soya beans and available in both light and dark versions. One tablespoon of ordinary soy sauce contains 1,030 milligrams of sodium; lower-sodium variations, such as naturally fermented shoyu, used in the recipes in this book, may contain half that amount.

Spaghetti squash: a yellow-skinned squash whose cooked flesh resembles strands of spaghetti.

Spatchcock: to split and flatten a bird, rendering it suitable for grilling or baking.

Stock: a savoury liquid prepared by simmering meat, bones, trimmings, aromatic vegetables, herbs and spices in water. Stock forms a base for sauces which is rich in flavour.

Sun-dried tomatoes: tomatoes that have been naturally dried in the sun, to concentrate their flavour and preserve them; some are then packed in oil with seasoning and herbs. Most sun-dried tomatoes are of Italian origin.

Tabasco sauce: a hot, unsweetened chili sauce.

Tahini (also called sesame paste): a nutty-tasting paste made from ground sesame seeds. Light tahini, made from raw sesame seeds, and dark tahini, made from roasted seeds, are both available from health food shops and delicatessens.

Tamarind concentrate: the brown, acidic-flavoured pulp from the seed pod of the tamarind tree, available from Oriental speciality shops.

Tarragon: a strong herb with a sweet anise taste. In combination with other herbs — especially rosemary, sage or thyme — it should be used sparingly, to avoid a clash of flavours. Because heat intensifies tarragon's flavour, cooked dishes require smaller amounts.

Tofu: a low-fat, high-protein curd made from soya beans. It looks like white cheese.

Tomato paste: a concentrated tomato purée, available in cans and tubes.

Total fat: an individual's daily intake of polyunsaturated, monounsaturated and saturated fats. Nutritionists recommend that total fat constitute no more than 35 per cent of the energy in the diet. The term as used in this book refers to the combined fats in a given dish or food.

Turmeric: a spice used as a colouring agent and occasionally as a substitute for saffron. It has a musty odour and a slightly bitter flavour.

Vanilla sugar: sugar flavoured by placing a whole vanilla pod in a closed container of sugar for about a week.

Virgin olive oil: see Olive oil.

Water bath (also called bain-marie): a large pan filled part way with hot water and placed in a preheated oven as a cooking vessel for foods in smaller containers. The combination of ambient hot water and air serves to cook the food slowly and evenly.

Wholemeal flour: wheat flour which contains the whole of the wheat grain with nothing added or taken away. It is nutritionally valuable as a source of dietary fibre and it is higher in B vitamins than white flour.

Worcester sauce: a hot sauce containing vinegar, molasses, chili peppers and tropical fruits and spices.

Yeast: a micro-organism which feeds on sugars and starches to produce carbon dioxide and thus leaven bread. Yeast can be bought either fresh or dried; fresh yeast will keep for up to six weeks in a refrigerator.

Yeast, easy-blend: a recently developed strain of yeast that reduces the amount of time necessary for rising.

Yogurt: a smooth-textured, semi-solid cultured milk product. Low-fat yogurt contains about 1 per cent fat. Greek yogurt, which is made from full-cream milk, has a 10 per cent fat content.

Index

Picture Credits

Cover: James Murphy. 4: top, James Murphy; bottom right, Martin Brigdale; bottom left, Chris Knaggs. 5: top right, David Johnson; top left, Andrew Williams; bottom: Martin Brigdale. 6: Jacqui Hurst. 10-12: John Elliott. 13: James Jackson. 14-16: David Johnson. 17: James Jackson. 18-21: John Elliott. 22: Chris Knaggs. 23: James Jackson. 24-25: Chris Knaggs. 26: John Elliott. 27: James Murphy. 28-29: Chris Knaggs. 30: James Murphy. 31: Chris Knaggs. 32: John Elliott, 33: James Murphy. 34: Chris Knaggs. 35: James Murphy. 36: John Elliott. 37: James Murphy. 38: John Elliott. 39: Andrew Whittuck. 40-41: John Elliott. 42: David Johnson. 43: John Elliott. 44: David Johnson. 46-47: Chris Knaggs. 48: John Elliott. 49: James Murphy. 50: David Johnson. 51: James Jackson. 52-54: Chris Knaggs. 55: David Johnson. 56: James Murphy. 57: David Johnson. 58-62: John Elliott. 63: top, Andrew Williams; bottom, Andrew Whittuck. 64: John Elliott. 65: James Jackson. 66: John Elliott. 67-69: Martin Brigdale. 70: Andrew Williams. 71: David Johnson. 72: John Elliott. 73: Andrew Williams. 74: Andrew Whittuck. 75: James Jackson. 76: Andrew Whittuck. 77: John Elliott. 78: David Johnson. 79: Andrew Whittuck. 80-82: Andrew Williams. 83-84: David Johnson. 85: Andrew Williams. 86: Martin Brigdale. 88-89: Andrew Whittuck. 90: John Elliott. 91: David Johnson. 92-93: Andrew Whittuck. 94: Andrew Williams. 95: James Jackson. 96: Andrew Wittuck. 97-98: John Elliott. 99-101: Andrew Williams. 102-103: John Elliott. 105: Andrew Williams. 106-111: James Murphy. 112-115: Martin Brigdale. 116-117: top left, Martin Brigdale; right, Andrew Williams. 118-121: Andrew Williams. 122-127: John Elliott. 128: David Johnson. 130: James Jackson. 131: David Johnson. 132-133: Martin Brigdale. 134-136: John Elliott. 137: David Johnson. 138: Taran Z. Photography.

Props: The editors wish to thank the following outlets and manufacturers; all are based in London. 18: plate, Hutschenreuther (U.K.) Ltd. 50: napkin, Next Interior. 65: napkin, Ewart Liddell. 71: pottery, Winchcombe Pottery, The Craftsmen Potters Shop. 90: plate, Hutschenreuther (U.K.) Ltd. 92: china, Line of Scandinavia. 94: china, Villeroy & Boch. 98: plate, Daphne Carnegy, The Craftsmen Potters Shop. 106-107: linen, Ewart Liddell; hamper, Fortnum & Mason; silver platter and cutlery, Mappin & Webb Silversmiths; china, Villeroy & Boch; glasses, Chinacraft Ltd. 135: plate, Tony Grant; casserole, Owen Thorpe, The Craftsmen Potters Shop. 137: plates, Villeroy & Boch.

Acknowledgements

The index for this book was prepared by Myra Clark, London. The editors also wish to thank the following: Paul van Biene, London; Maureen Burrows, London; Stuart Cullen, London; Jonathan Driver, London; Neil Fairbairn, Wivenhoe, Essex; Bridget Jones, Guildford, Surrey; James Knight of Mayfair, London; Lidgates of Holland Park, London; Perstorp Warerite Ltd., London; Sharp Electronics (U.K.) Ltd., London; Mhairi Sharpley, Chesham, Bucks.; Jane Stevenson, London; Toshiba (U.K.) Ltd., London.

Colour separations by Fotolitomec, S.N.C., Milan, Italy
Typesetting by G.Beard and Son Ltd, Brighton, Sussex, England
Printed and bound by Oriental Press, Dubai